FADING CORNERS & ABANDONED IMAGES

BROKEN STONES, FADED DREAMS

A jungle of shattered cement,
silent—along Irving Park Road,
in an abandoned lot.

Crab grass emerges from gravel,
pushing aside shards of glass
that shattered when bulldozers came.

A twisted mesh of iron wires
reaches towards the sky, trying to grab
those last tangles of faded dreams.

I don't know when it all went wrong.
I thought you would always be there,
at least on the inside.

Now I see that nothing is forever,
not even cement, not even steel bars,
or an immigrant's dream. Not even me.

FADING CORNERS & ABANDONED IMAGES

MICHAEL KLEEN

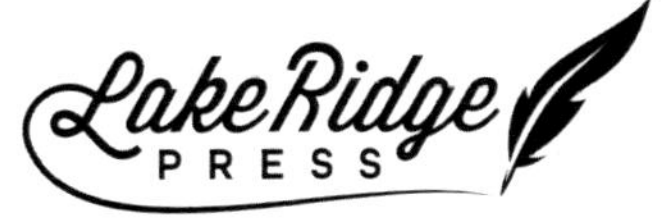

FADING CORNERS & ABANDONED IMAGES

First Edition

This book was printed in the United States by Lightning Source, Inc.

ISBN-13: 978-1-61876-026-5
Library of Congress Control Number: 2024907219

Published by

Lake Ridge Press
Stafford, Virginia

www.michaelkleen.com

www.flickr.com/photos/makleen/

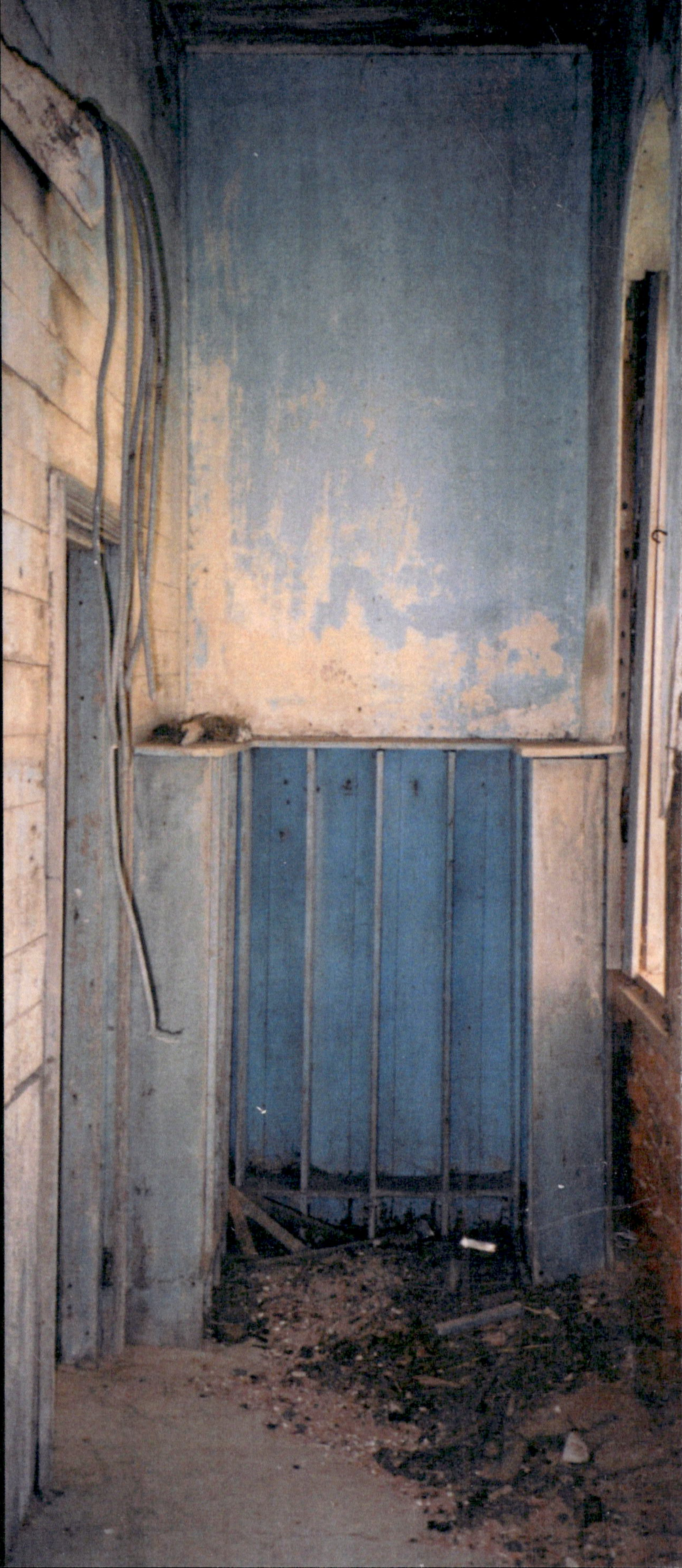

CONTENTS

"He knew what the wind was doing to them, where it was taking them, to all the secret places that were never so secret again in life."

RAY BRADBURY

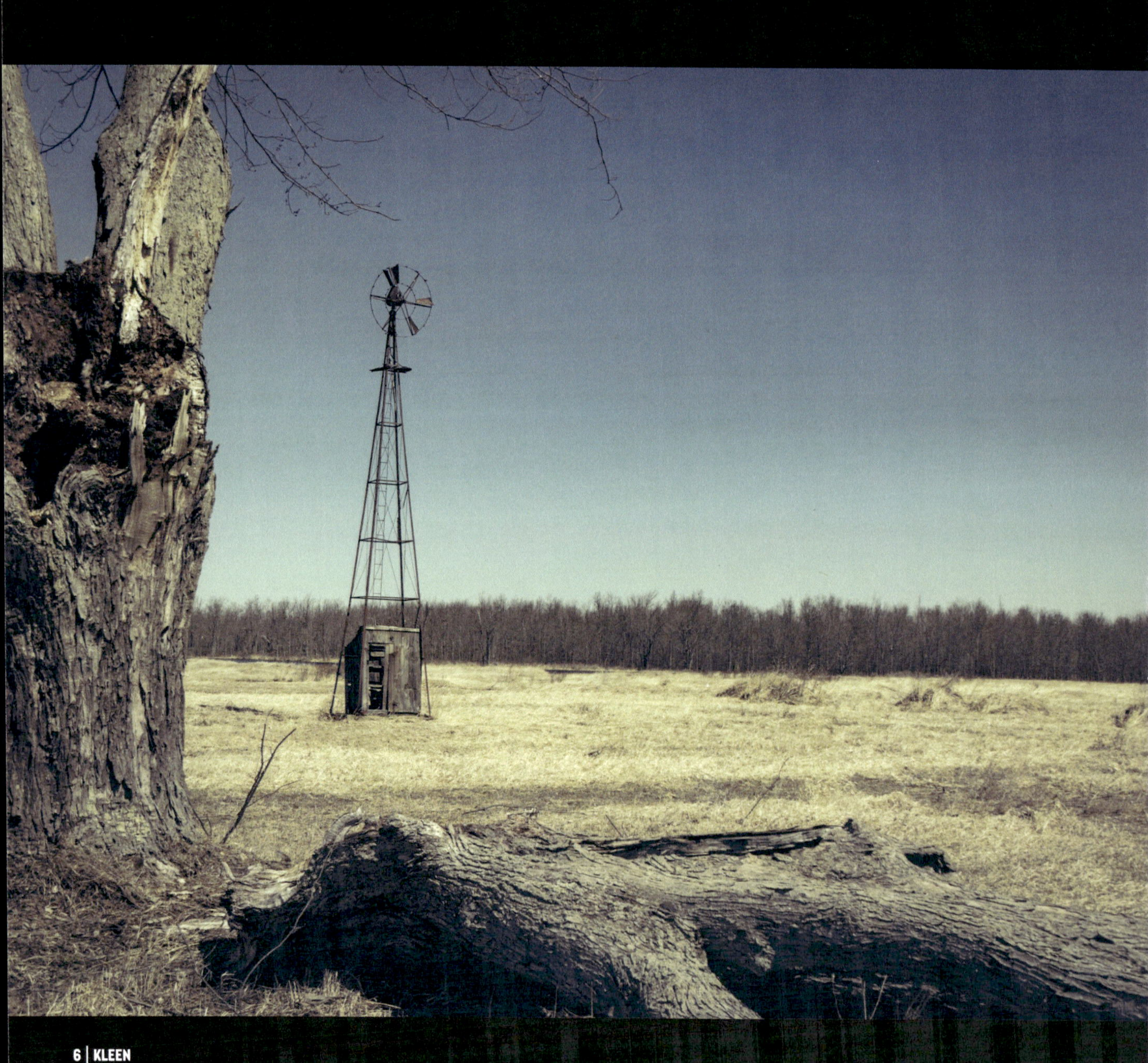

INTRODUCTION

Abandoned places have always fascinated me. A place is warm, comfortable, inviting, filled with life—until it's not. We move on and leave behind a cold shell, decaying, lifeless, and dark. Haunted by memories. Haunted by stories. By secrets buried in dust.

I was born in Chicago and grew up in the northwest suburbs. As a young man, I loved to explore. My dad and I traversed the suburban forest preserves, finding places and things long forgotten. What could possibly be discovered so close to bright city lights, you ask? You'd be surprised. Before the city, there were farms, and much was left behind when Cook County bought the land.

Stumbling across half-buried cement foundations, old wells, discarded bottles, porcelain jars, and more, you wonder who lived there and for how long? Did they ever think their homestead would be reclaimed by nature, their belongings dug up by curious passersby?

A few years ago, I learned something about how that must feel. Growing up, I spent many summers at the United Methodist Campground along the Des Plaines River, whether it was at summer camp, in the swimming pool, attending weekend fairs, or just riding bikes along the streets with my dad, stopping to take a break at the snack shop.

On a return visit to Illinois, I was feeling nostalgic and decided to check out the old campground. While it was never in pristine condition, it has deteriorated significantly. Flooding damaged the old wooden cabins, many of which are beyond repair, and the grand circular tabernacle is boarded up. Blue vinyl tarps hang in tatters over shattered windows, the roof threatening to collapse. The pool where I took swimming lessons is torn up, never to be filled with water and laughter again.

And then I found myself visiting my old elementary school, St. Mary's on Center Street. The gym where I attended Boy Scout meetings, went to school dances, and performed in recitals is now a homeless shelter. My wife and I persuaded a shelter volunteer to let us look around. While not quite abandoned, the empty hallways, classrooms, and library evoked the Portuguese feeling of *saudade*—a longing for something past. I could still imagine our class sitting in neat rows, the rush of kids in the hallway, the framed photos of graduating classes stretching back to the 1920s.

How long until no one is left to remember?

I don't claim to be an artist. I take photos to capture a moment in time, to preserve that piece of the past that stubbornly hangs on. Most of the places in this book will be gone soon. Some already are.

M. KLEEN
2024

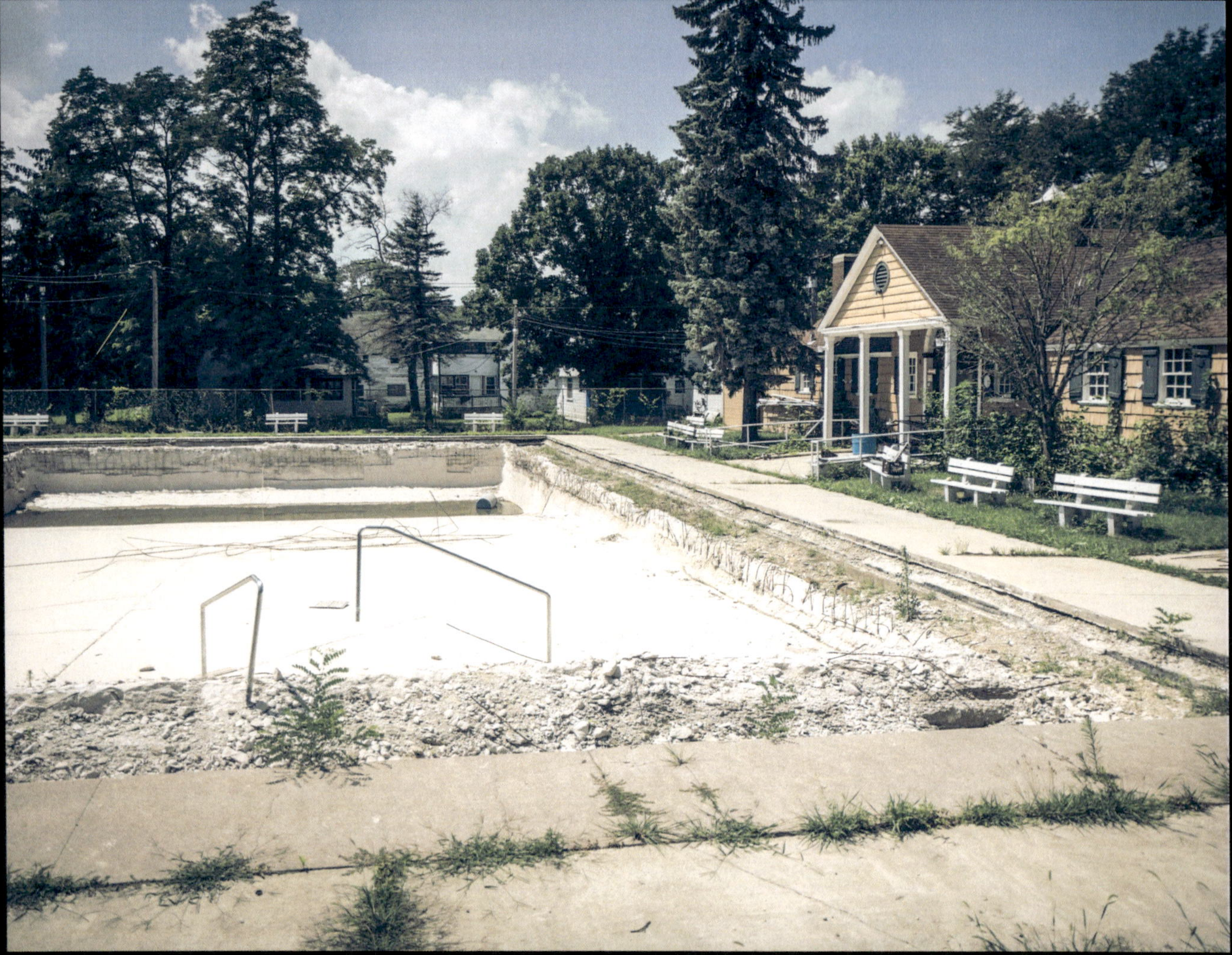

The Methodist Campground pool opened in 1928 after a group of men raised $30,000 for its construction by playing a piano and asking for donations. My family frequented this pool throughout the 1990s. After 90 years, it was demolished in 2018.

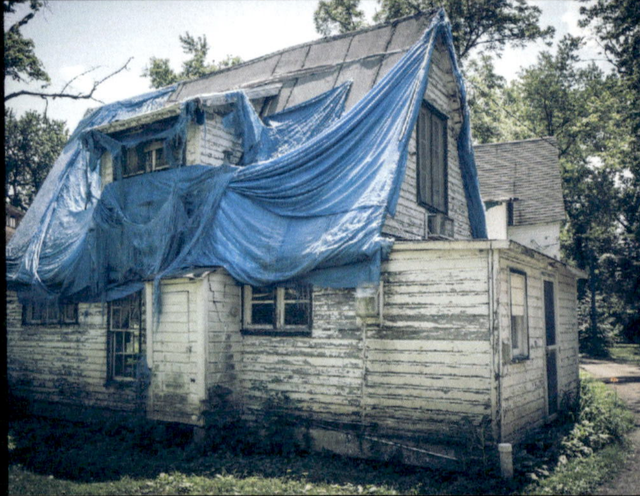

The Methodist Campground at 1900 E. Algonquin Road in Des Plaines, Illinois was added to the National Register of Historic Places in 2005. Severe flooding has made many cabins unlivable.

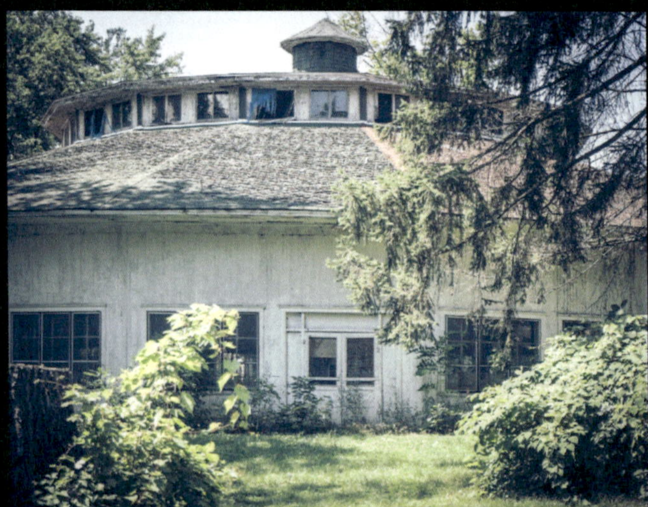

In 1860, Methodists began having tent meetings along the Des Plaines River, and after a few years the small spiritual community grew to 35 acres and contained a large tabernacle, approximately 100 cottages and a 30-room hotel.

EARLY YEARS

I bought my first "professional" DSLR camera in 2017. Before that, I took pictures on my iPhone, and before that, I had a succession of cheap digital and film cameras. Unfortunately, in my younger years I made low-resolution scans of many of my photos and threw the originals away in a misguided effort to "declutter" my life (I know… I know…).

Some originals, like the below black and white photo of a rural Indiana schoolhouse, remain. I grew up in Illinois but spent many holidays in Indiana because my mom's side of the family lived around Albion. My dad and I continued our explorations there. We even got permission to explore an abandoned farmhouse filled with old letters and whatever else the owners had left behind.

When I went to college at Eastern Illinois University in east-central Illinois, I continued to find and document these fast-fading places.

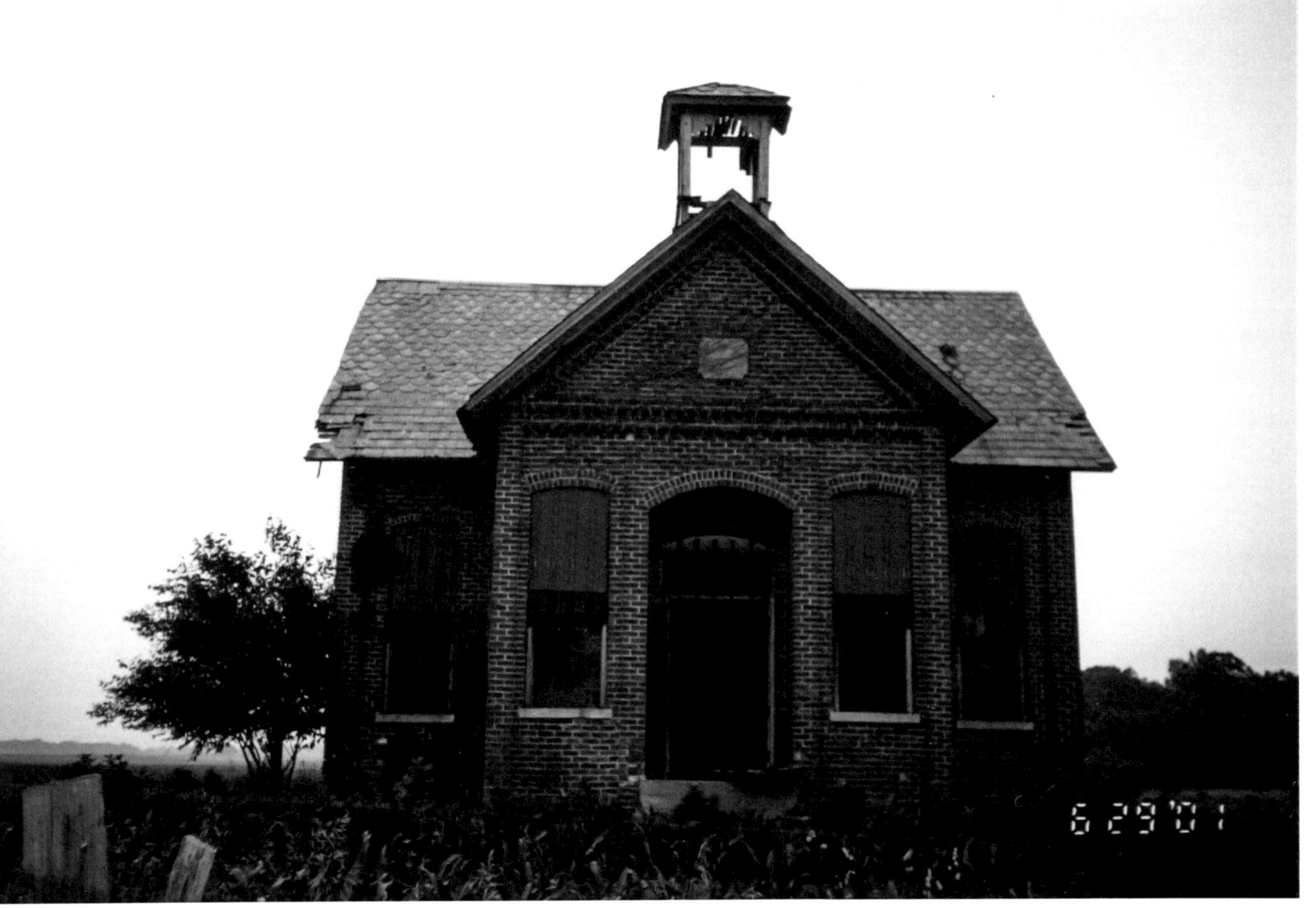

Dr. Harold C. Urey (1893-1981), born in Walkerton, Indiana, taught at this red brick, one-room school house in Noble County before moving on to win the Nobel Prize in Chemistry in 1934. I heard it has been demolished (unconfirmed).

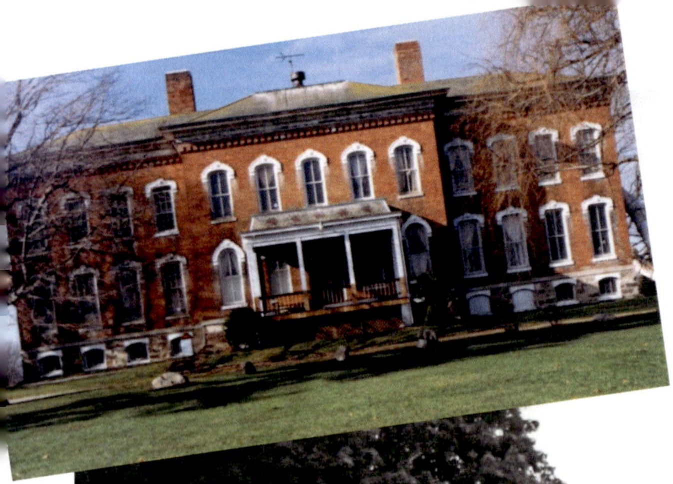

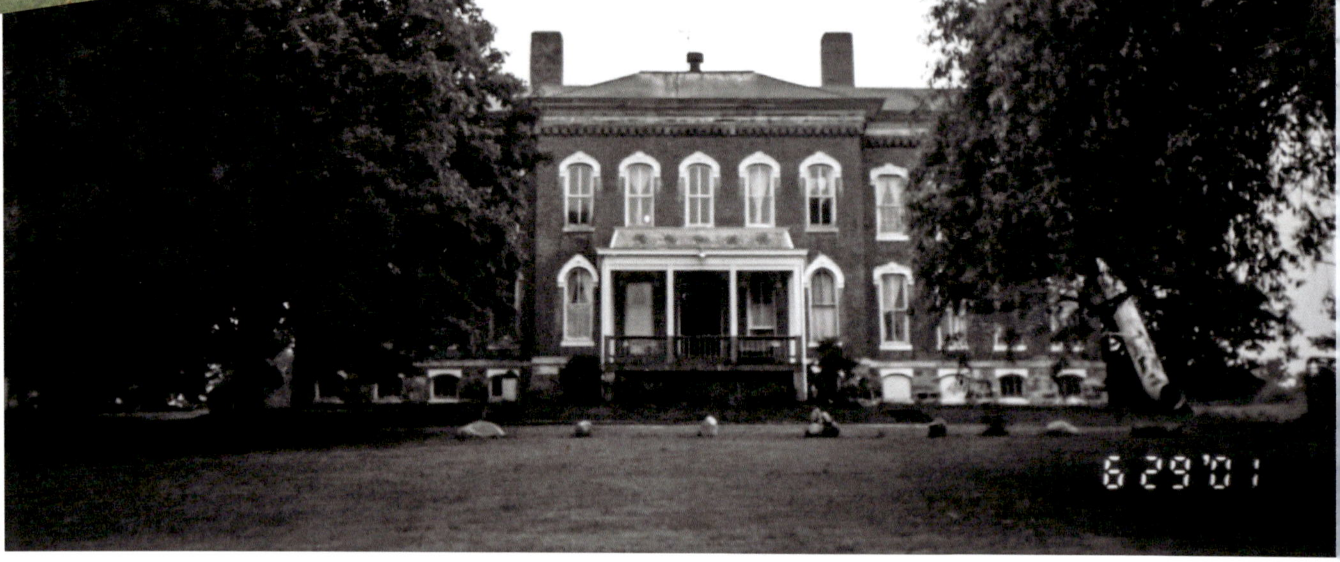

The Noble County Almshouse, at 4327 N 100 W northeast of Albion (41.4146, -85.4434), was built in 1871 and closed in 1957. It also served as a nursing home and apartments.

CLAYVILLE, ILLINOIS (1824-1850)

Clayville Historic Site in Cartwright Township, Sangamon County, Illinois is an interesting piece of abandonment. This stagecoach building is not original, but brought here in the 1960s as part of an effort to create an open-air museum around the Clayville Tavern, which was added to National Register of Historic Places in 1973. The museum closed in 1992, once again falling into abandonment and disrepair. When I visited, it was an "artificial" ghost town. Since 2010, however, it's been reopened.

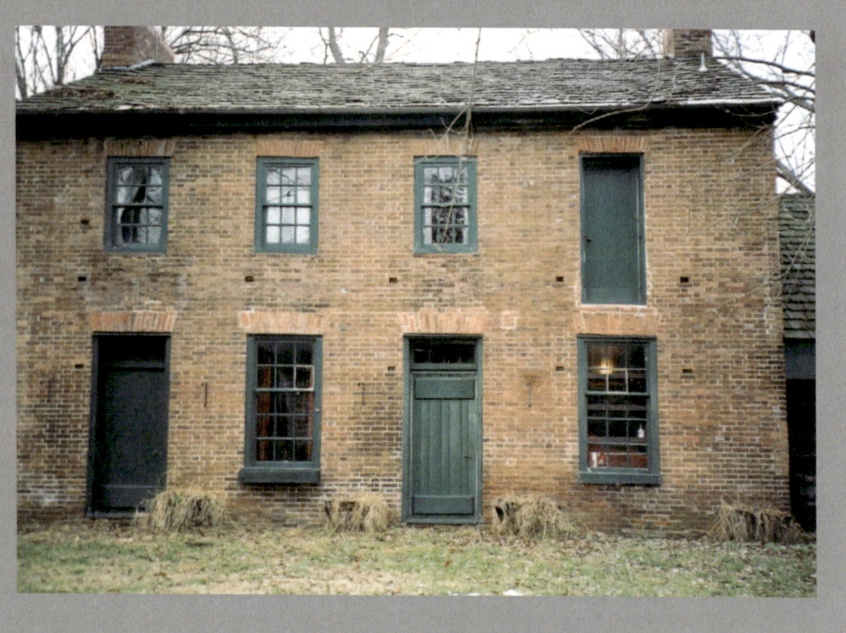

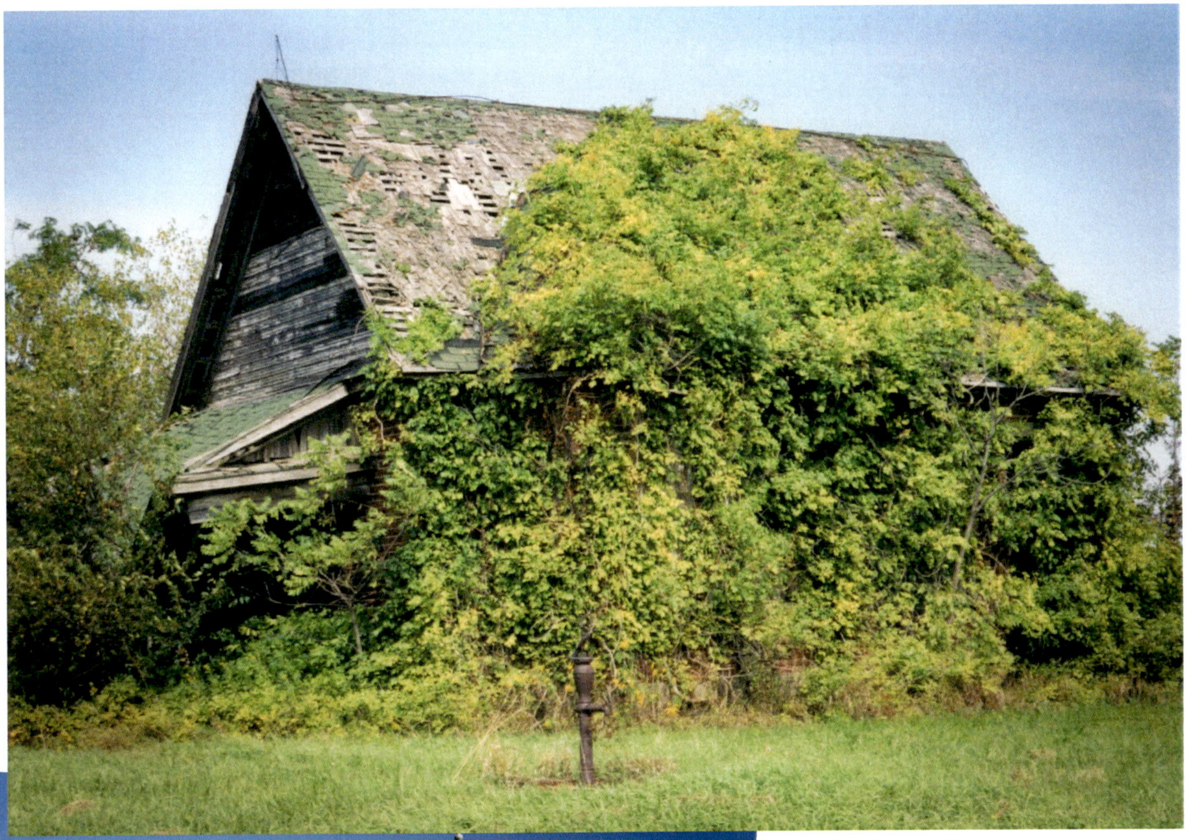

Old house or barn with a hand pump somewhere in rural Illinois.

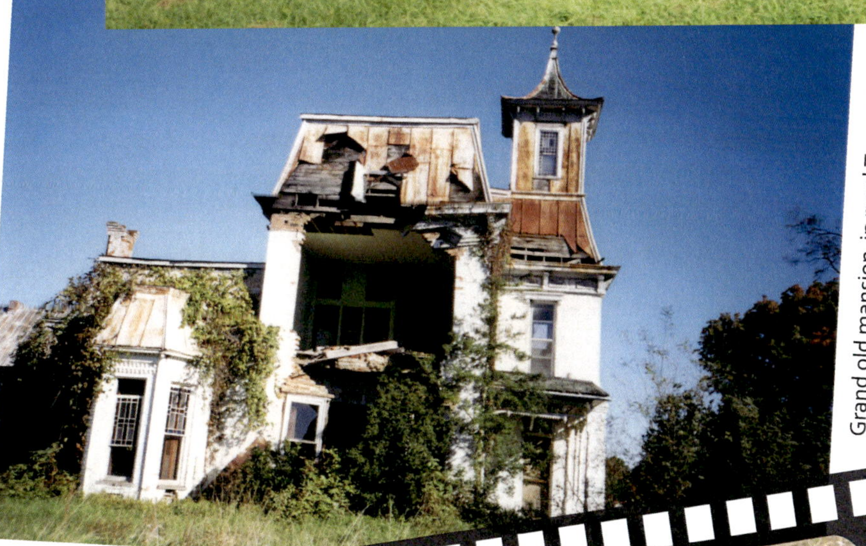

Grand old mansion in rural Tennessee.

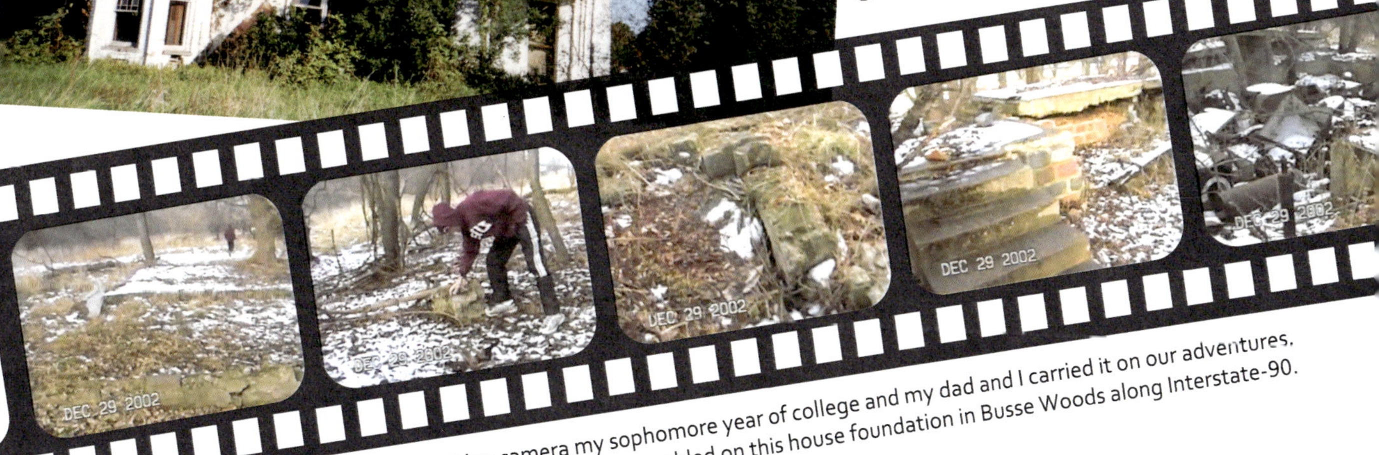

I bought a clunky VHS-C video camera my sophomore year of college and my dad and I carried it on our adventures. We stumbled on this house foundation in Busse Woods along Interstate-90.

ASHMORE ESTATES

Today, Ashmore Estates in Coles County, Illinois is internationally known, having appeared on TV shows like *Ghost Hunters* and *Ghost Adventures*, but when I visited in January 2001, it was just "that old abandoned asylum."

It was the beginning of my sophomore year at Eastern Illinois University. Two friends, both seniors, took me out there. When they were freshmen, "The Men of Adventure" wrote a satirical piece for the Halloween issue of the *Daily Eastern News* on how to make Ashmore Estates into a "highly illegal" Halloween escapade. "No one is really sure what this building once housed," they wrote. "But there are stories... We aren't sure if any of them are true or not, but they sure do make for three floors... of unadulterated fun."

Like countless others before us, my friends and I parked alongside the gravel road a few yards from the building and walked through a thin layer of snow on the fallow cornfield. Like the "Men of Adventure," I knew nothing about what this building was or what it had been. As we carefully explored its interior, any story about it seemed possible. It was years before I knew anything about its real history.

Built in 1916, Ashmore Estates was originally the almshouse on the Coles County Poor Farm. The poor farm operated from 1870 to 1959. Then, for 28 years, between 1959 and 1987, Ashmore Estates served Coles County as a care facility for the mentally disturbed and developmentally disabled. After its closure, local teens and students from Eastern Illinois University explored its empty corridors and gawked at what was left behind. They came away with stories ranging from the hair-raising to the absurd. It seemed like the 90-year-old building would sit empty, crumbling from disuse. Finally, in 2006, a man named Scott Kelley purchased it, cleaned it up, and turned it into a commercial haunted house.

I snapped the adjacent photo on a return visit in November 2001. I had no idea it would become an iconic photo of Ashmore Estates, especially after a violent storm destroyed the roof and irreversibly altered its appearance. Much to my annoyance, my photo has appeared all over the Internet and in publications, most of the time without my knowledge or permission.

Ashmore Estates has changed a lot over the decades, but in my mind it will always appear the way it did on those crisp, quiet autumn days.

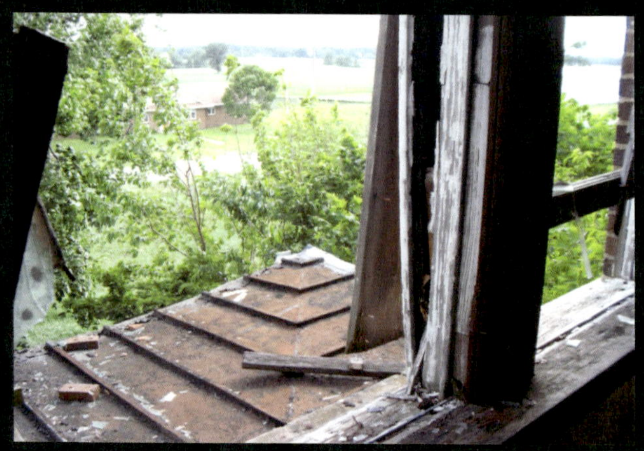

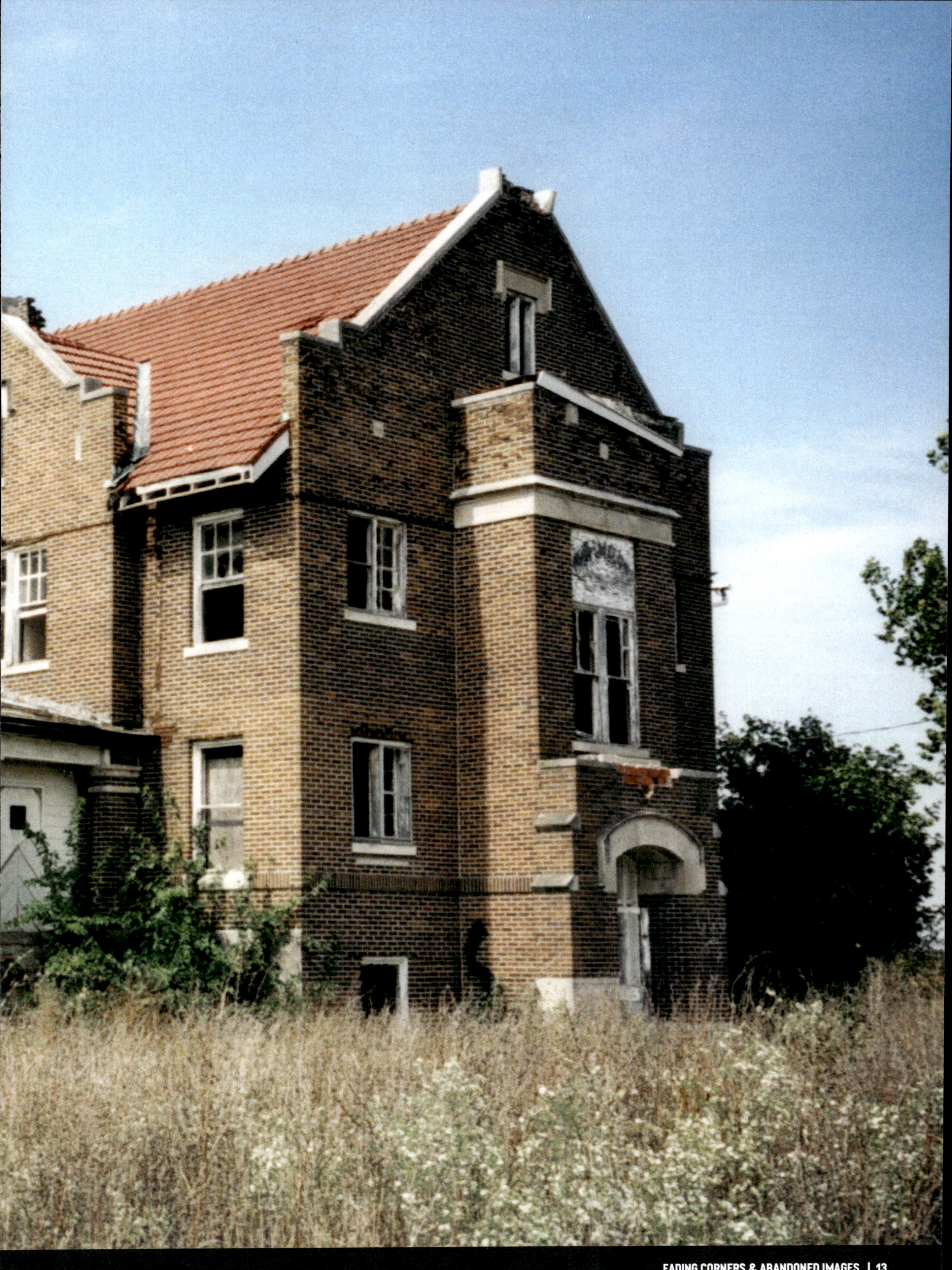

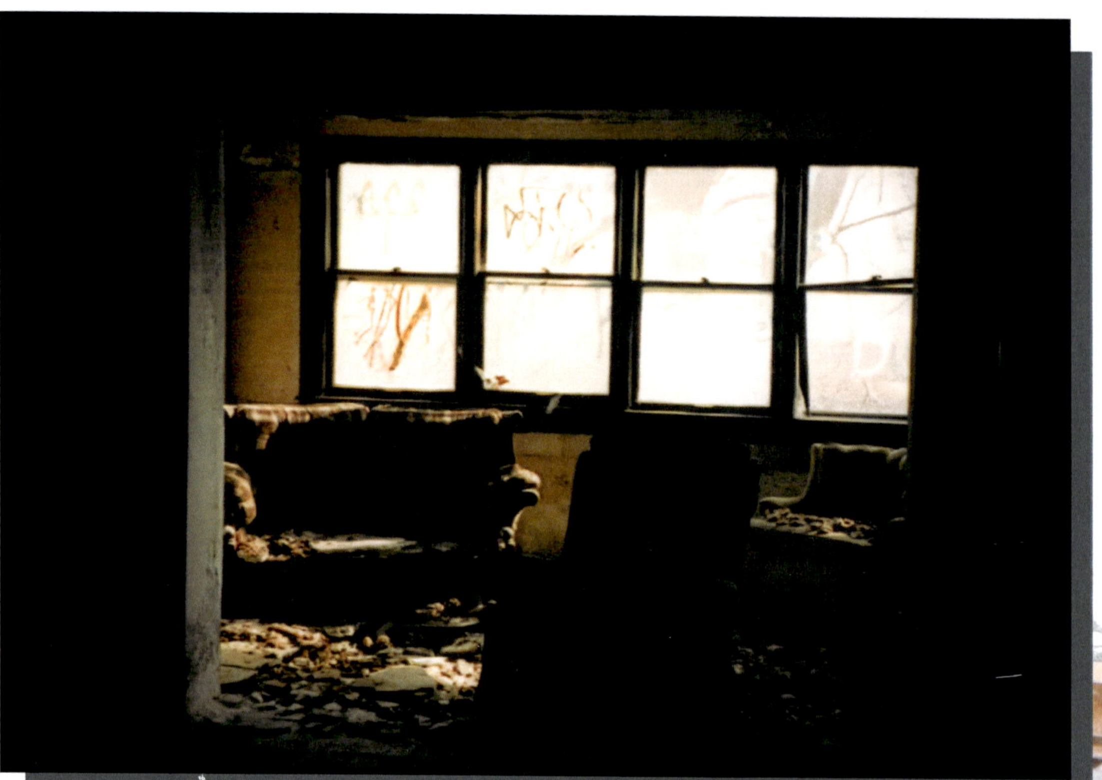

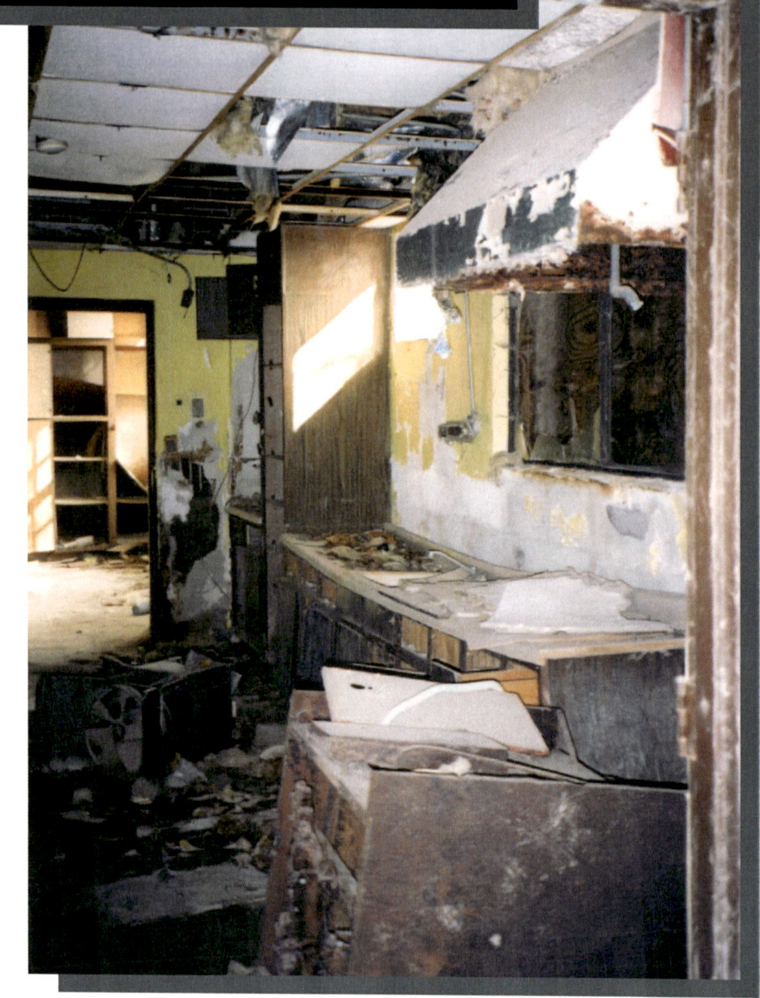

ASHMORE ESTATES (1916-?)

Since 2006, documentary filmmakers have flocked to Ashmore Estates and visitors have swapped stories of encountering specters and disembodied voices in its graffiti-covered halls. Stories of the ghost of an adolescent girl and a dapper man named Joe have joined tales of axe-murdering former patients in the litany of legends associated with this fascinating place.

National notoriety followed. In 2011, Ashmore Estates appeared in the fifth season premiere of the Travel Channel's *Ghost Adventures*, and in 2013 it was featured in an episode of the SyFy Channel's *Ghost Hunters*.

I gave my first public presentation at Ashmore Estates in 2006, made my first appearance on the local news, and my first appearance on cable TV when I was interviewed for *Ghost Adventures.* It would be difficult to point to any other single building that has left such a mark on my life.

ILLINOIS

Illinois sits at the crossroads of the Midwest. Most of the state is rural—small towns and farmland—but Chicago and its suburbs are among the largest urban areas in the country. Illinois' population growth has ground to a halt in recent decades, and it was the only Midwestern state to lose population in the 2020 census. It is the story of explosive growth, stagnation, and decline.

During that growth period in the first half of the twentieth century, large institutions sprung up all over Illinois, including state hospitals and military bases. Illinois had a system of poor farms and almshouses to care for the elderly and indigent. In the second half of the twentieth century, nearly all closed. Some buildings were repurposed, but most sat in decay, attracting urban explorers.

I missed the heyday of urbex in the 1990s, shortly after these institutions closed, but I was lucky enough to visit many of them a few years before they vanished under the wrecking ball forever. Sometimes I wasn't. In the winter of 2008, I attempted to visit the remains of Villa de Chantal Catholic School in Rock Island, only to find an empty lot.

Since 2007, Illinois has lost multiple destinations popular with legend trippers and urban explorers:

- Lindbergh School on Shoe Factory Road in Hoffman Estates (2007)
- Villa de Chantal in Rock Island (2008)
- Sacred Heart Chapel at Barat College in Lake Forest (2008)
- Sunset Haven outside Carbondale (2013)
- Manteno State Hospital's Morgan Cottage in Manteno (2015)
- Mennonite Hospital/Electrolux in Bloomington (2015)
- White Hall at Chanute Air Force Base in Rantoul (2015)
- Peoria State Hospital's Bowen Building in Bartonville (2017)

Each of these locations was a historic building in Illinois, and each was home to popular legends and ghost stories. The loss of these irreplaceable landmarks is unfortunate, and as I've since learned, avoidable. Organizations in other states have been successful in preserving historic sites like these and raising money to maintain them and share their history through tours and events (see the chapter on "Dark Tourism").

I lived in Illinois for 33 years, and never imagined I would leave. Life had other plans, however, and in 2014 I would change careers and travel the country, finding many more places that caught my interest.

PEORIA STATE HOSPITAL (1902-2017)

Peoria State Hospital (originally known as the Illinois Hospital for the Incurable Insane) began its life in 1885, but no patients were ever housed or treated in the original building and it was torn down in 1897.

The institution was rebuilt and reopened in 1902 with a new name and a new superintendent. Now called Peoria State Hospital, a progressive physician named Dr. George A. Zeller took over the facility and instituted new, more humane treatments for mentally ill patients. Small cottages were built to house the patients and a dorm housed the full- time staff.

Like most of these hospitals, it eventually closed and was overrun by vandals, urban explorers, and vagrants. In 2012, an attempt was made to rehabilitate the main Bowen Building and open it for tours. It appeared on the SyFy Channel's *Ghost Hunters* in 2013 and Destination America's *Ghost Asylum* in 2016. I was interviewed for a documentary about Peoria State called *For the Incurable Insane*. The Bowen Building was demolished in 2017.

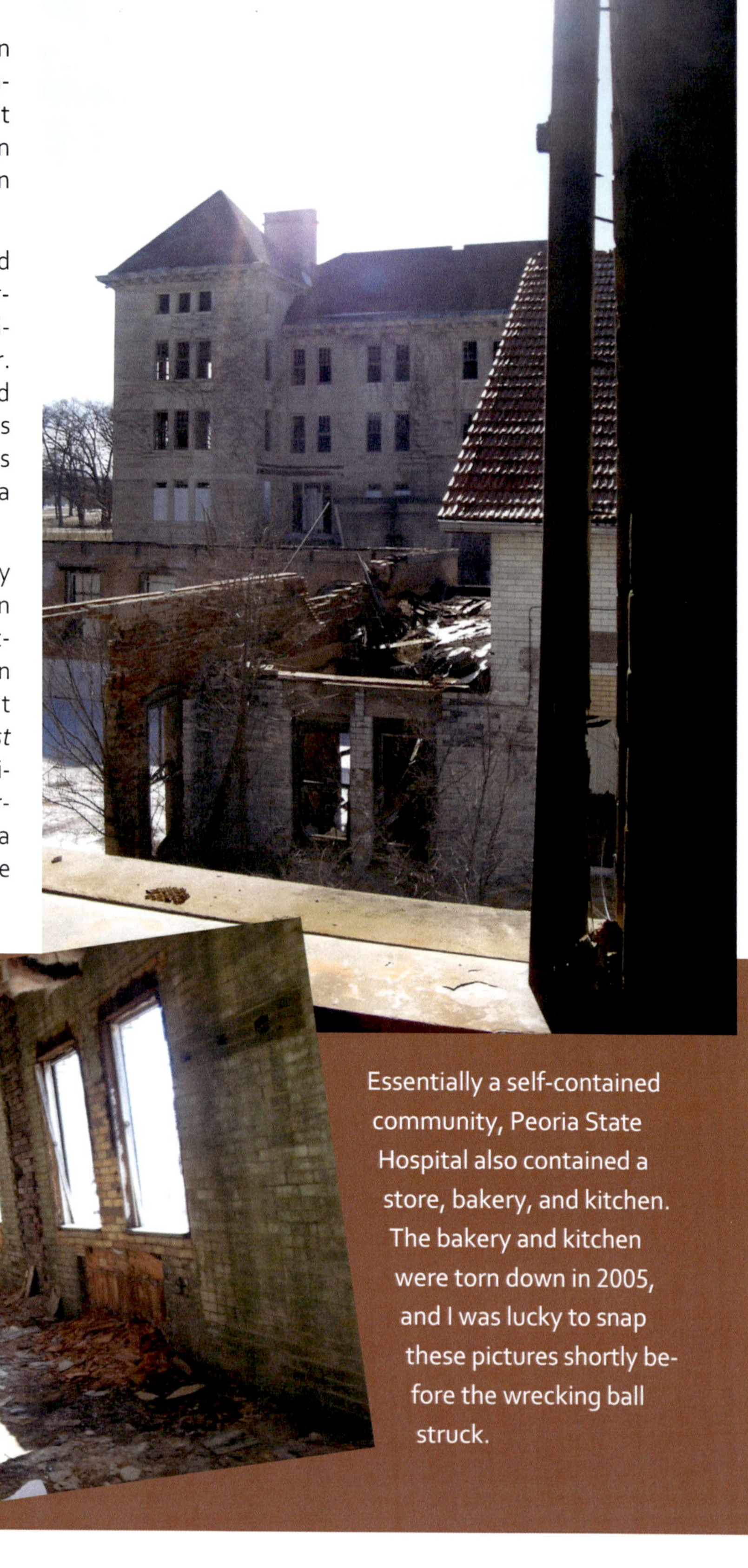

Essentially a self-contained community, Peoria State Hospital also contained a store, bakery, and kitchen. The bakery and kitchen were torn down in 2005, and I was lucky to snap these pictures shortly before the wrecking ball struck.

"Don't shoot 'em, Chanute 'em..."

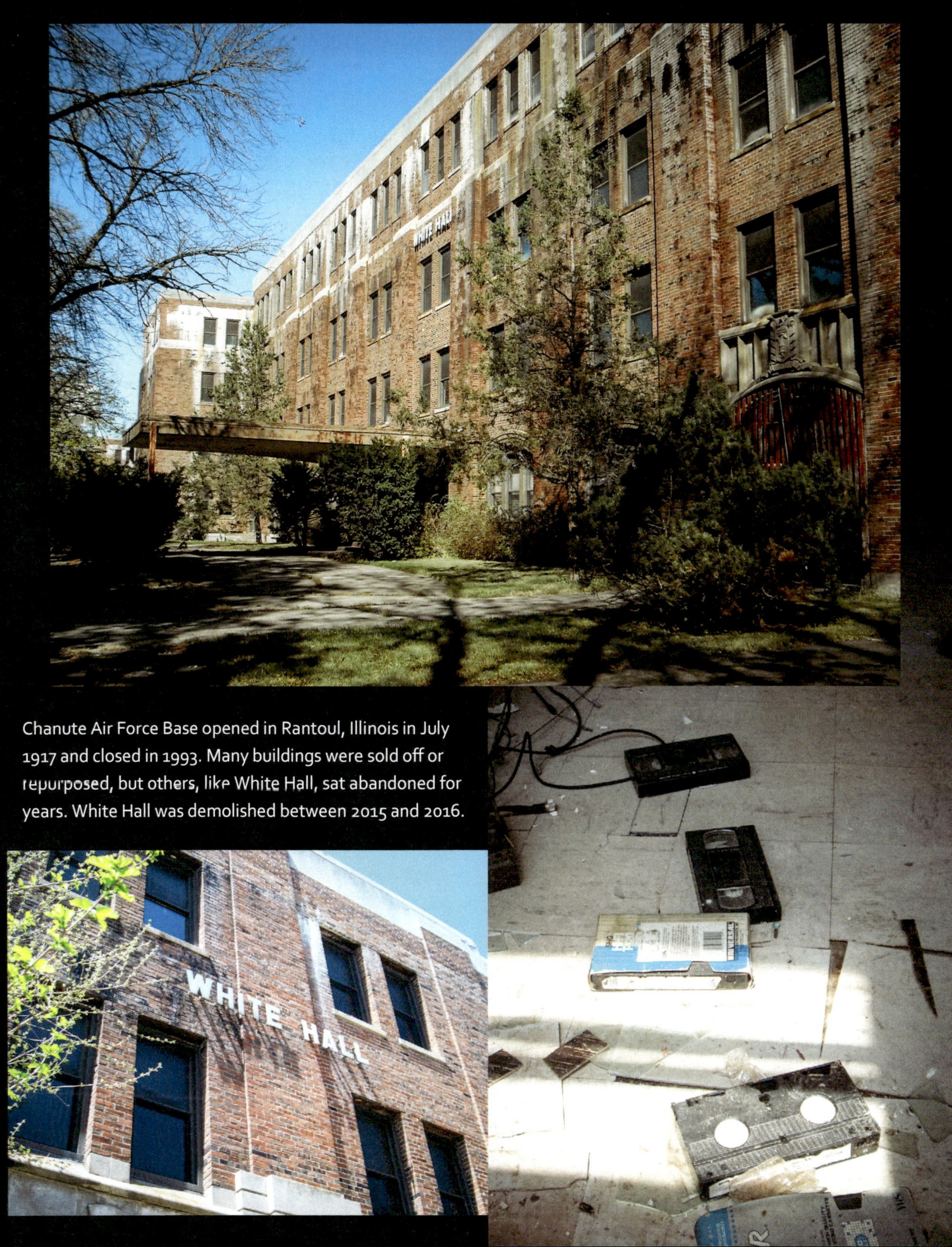

Chanute Air Force Base opened in Rantoul, Illinois in July 1917 and closed in 1993. Many buildings were sold off or repurposed, but others, like White Hall, sat abandoned for years. White Hall was demolished between 2015 and 2016.

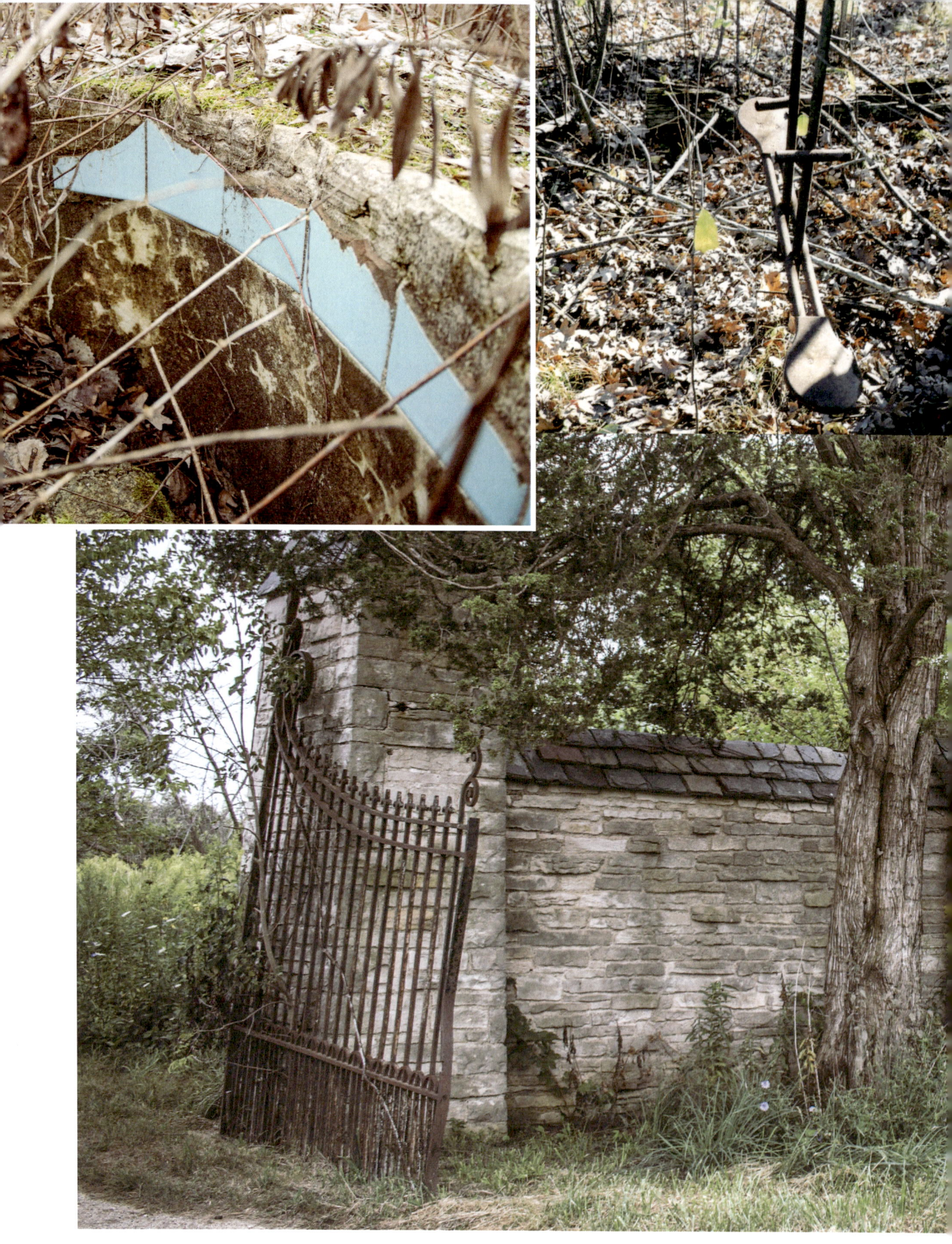

INDEPENDENCE GROVE

The story of Independence Grove in Libertyville, Illinois began in 1925 when Katharine Doddridge Kreigh Budd, wife of Britton I. Budd, passed away. Britton Budd was a railroad tycoon, and he aspired to open a charitable orphanage in his wife's name.

He chose a picturesque property along the Des Plaines River and set to work. Construction on the Katharine K. Budd Memorial Home for Children began in the spring of 1926. The camp was originally designed to accommodate 150 children in ten separate cottages. A swimming pool, chapel, and a home for Episcopalian nuns were added later.

During World War 2, ownership of the camp passed to the Catholic Archdiocese of Chicago. In 1955, the archdiocese rechristened it St. Francis Boys Camp. It ran for another three decades until it was sold to the Lake County Forest Preserve. The Forest Preserve quickly made plans to tear down the old camp and reclaim the area as a nature preserve. The 100-acre site was absorbed into over 1,000 acres of land that became known as Independence Grove.

Remnants remained, however—most notably, the camp's beautifully gothic iron gates—but the woods were filled with cement foundations and artifacts of every variety. I first explored this site in 2001 and returned every few years, each time discovering something new. Though no buildings remain standing, you never know what is waiting to be found just below the surface.

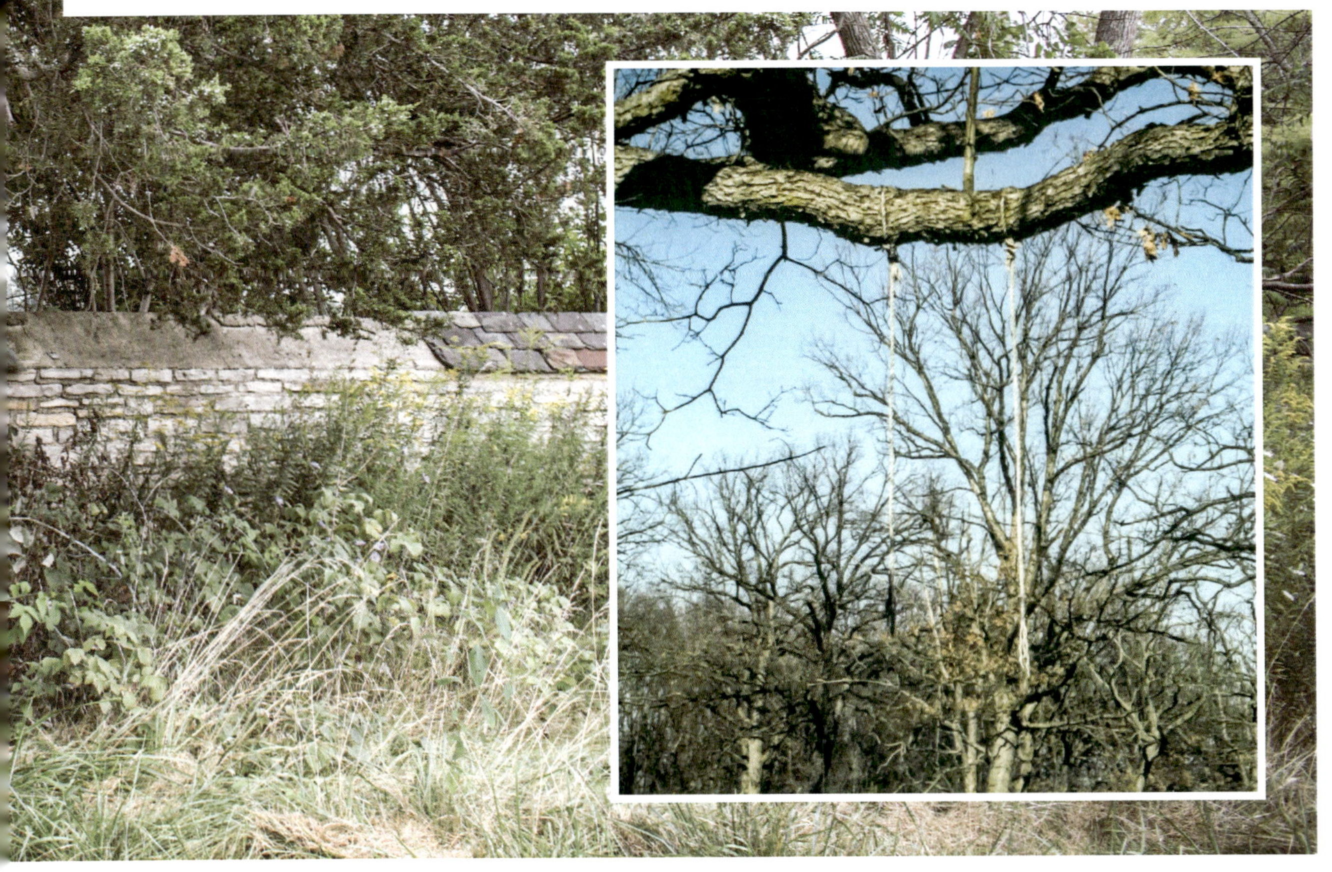

MANTENO STATE HOSPITAL

Manteno State Hospital, one of two former mental health facilities in Kankakee County, Illinois, opened its doors in the early 1930s. Like Peoria State Hospital, Manteno State Hospital was originally laid out in a "cottage plan," which meant the patients were housed in a series of separate buildings rather than in one single institution.

It took several years after the purchase of the property in 1927 for the sprawling mental hospital to be completed. When it first opened, Manteno accommodated 5,500 patients and 760 staff.

Manteno State Hospital was later renamed Manteno Mental Health Center, and closed in 1985 along with many of such facilities in Illinois. Its campus was divided up and sold off. The north side of campus became a veteran's home.

Manteno has attracted many curiosity seekers since its closure, including its share of ghost hunters. Accounts of ghostly sounds and encounters have filtered down from those adventurous—or foolhardy—enough to explore the old tunnels and buildings.

Morgan Cottage (photo below) was the last remaining abandoned building on the former hospital campus. For years, urban explorers, vandals, and amateur paranormal investigators sought out the building as the last remnant of the old hospital they could safely explore. By May 2015, the building had been lost to the bulldozers.

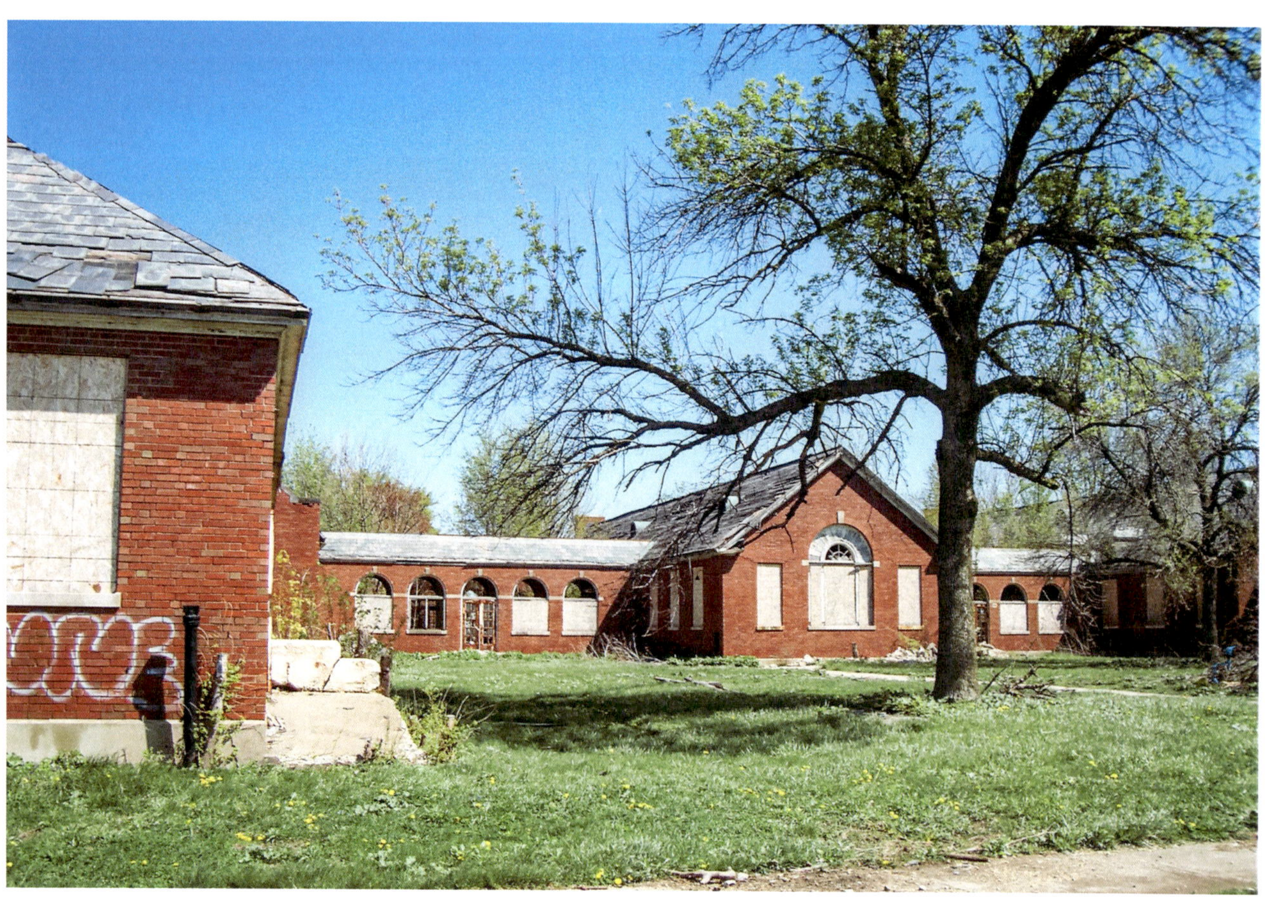

In 1939, 384 patients and staff came down with typhoid fever and 47 died. Panic gripped the hospital and dozens of support staff fled. Archie Bowen, director of Illinois' Public Welfare Department, was held liable for the incident in court, but his conviction was later overturned.

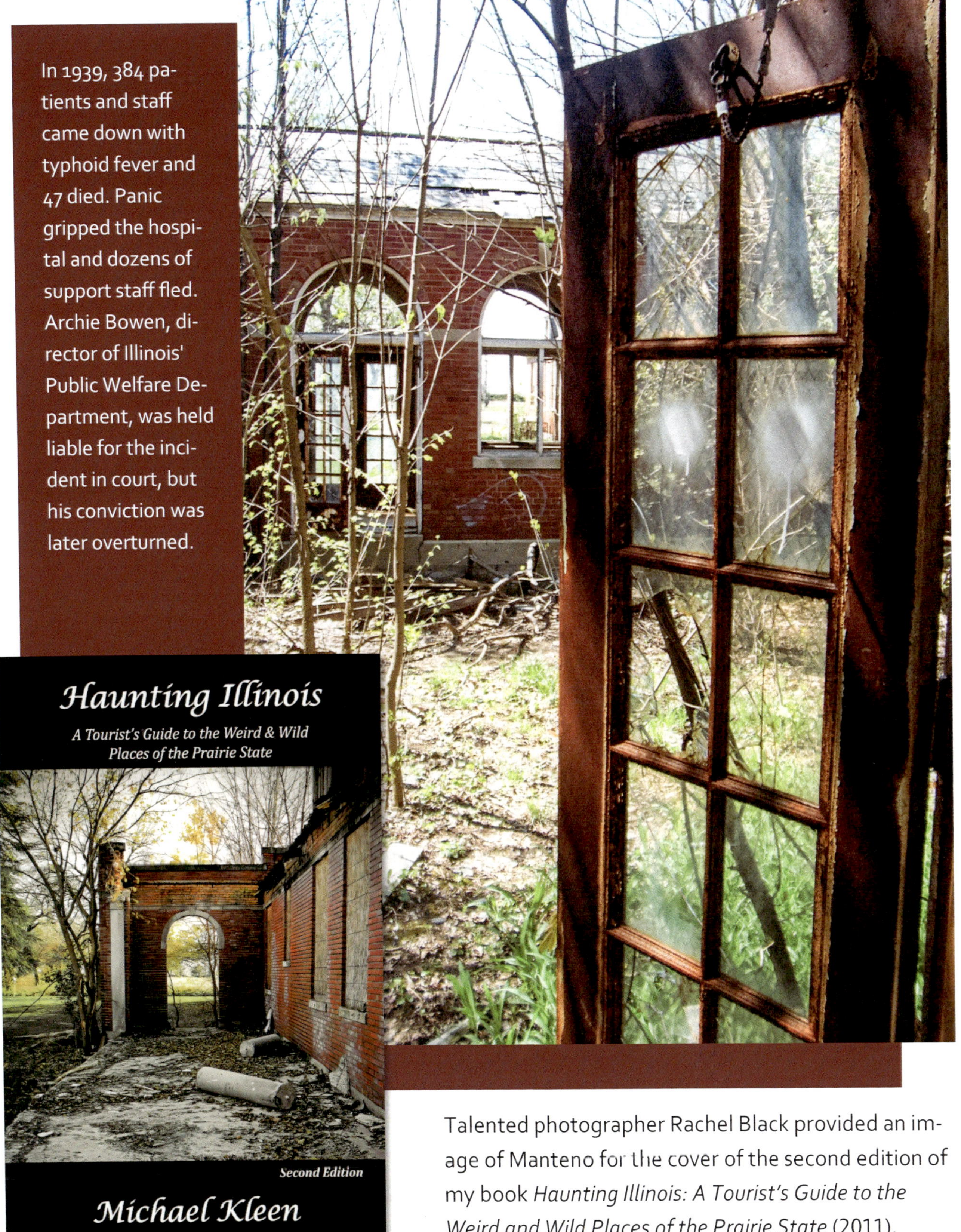

Talented photographer Rachel Black provided an image of Manteno for the cover of the second edition of my book *Haunting Illinois: A Tourist's Guide to the Weird and Wild Places of the Prairie State* (2011).

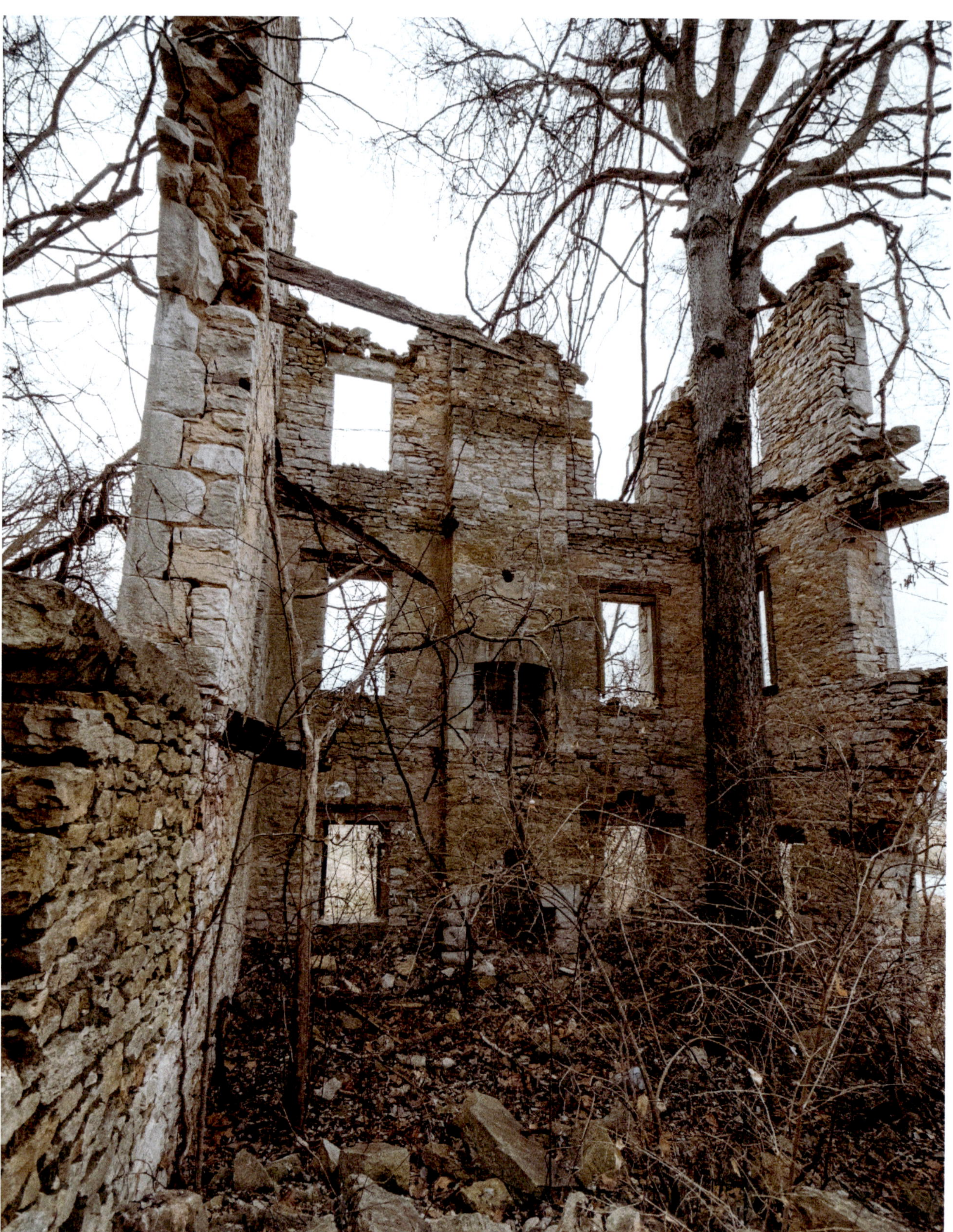

Ruins of the Azariah Sweetin Mansion, near the intersection of River Road and 430E in Greene County.

Stephen Miles Family Mausoleum in Eagle Cliff Cemetery, Monroe County.

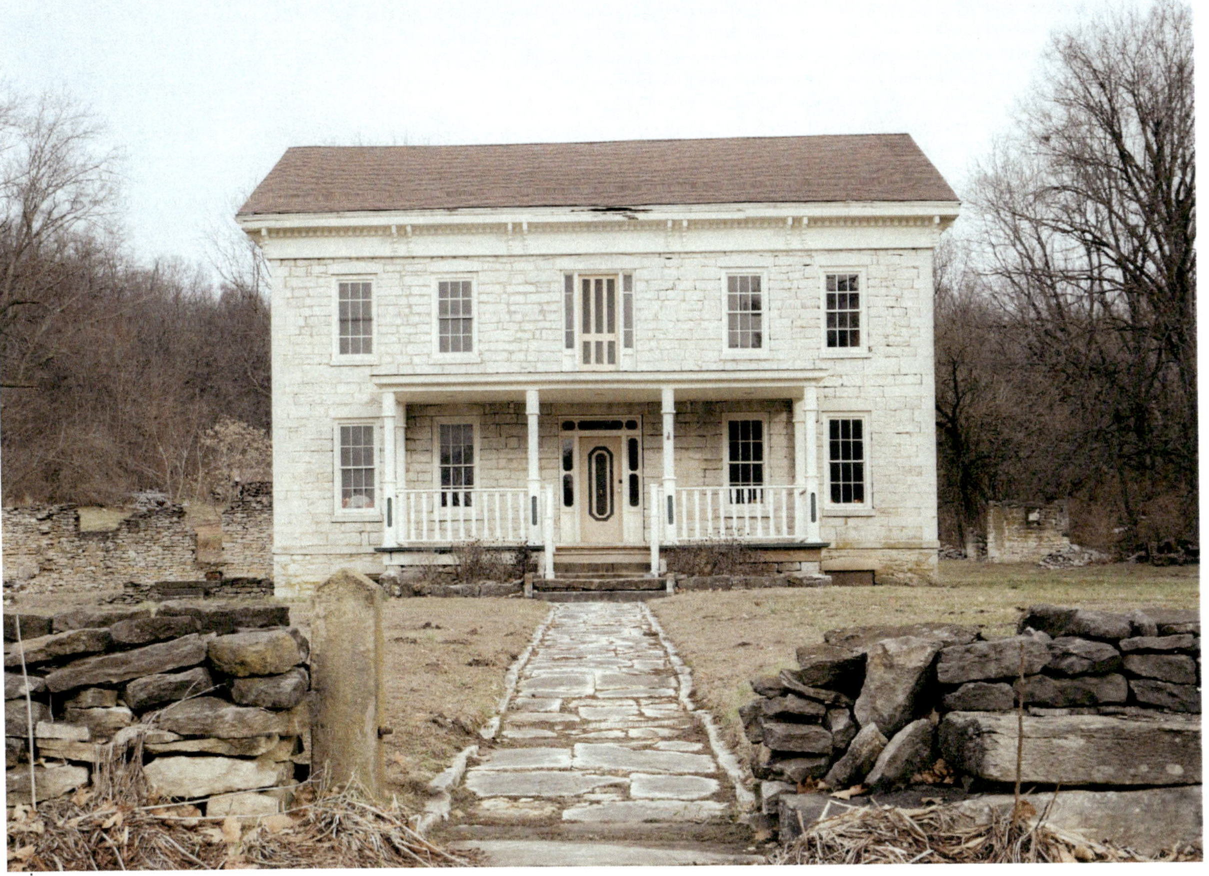

James J. Eldred Home, near the intersection of 1300N and River Road in Greene County.

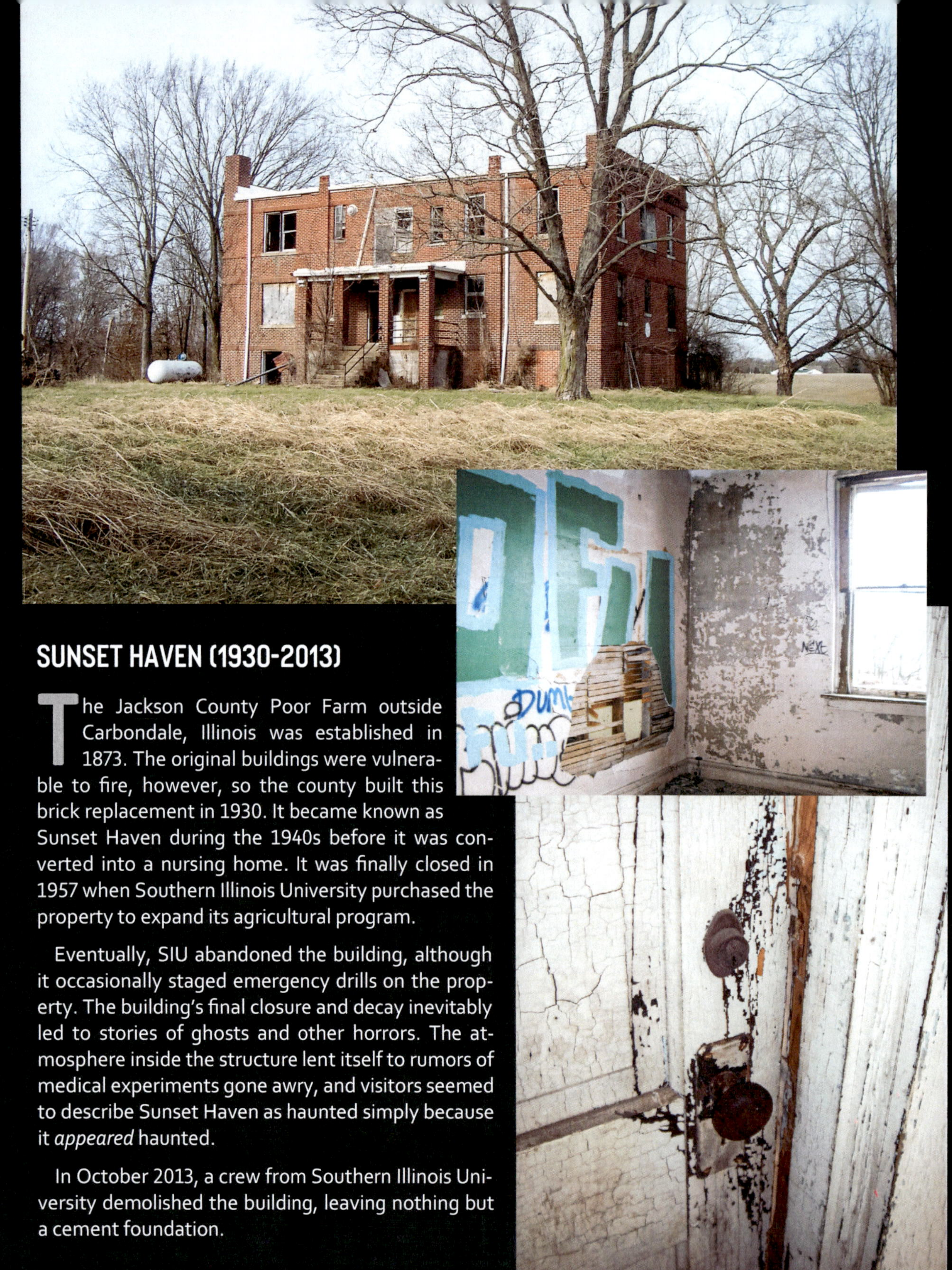

SUNSET HAVEN (1930-2013)

The Jackson County Poor Farm outside Carbondale, Illinois was established in 1873. The original buildings were vulnerable to fire, however, so the county built this brick replacement in 1930. It became known as Sunset Haven during the 1940s before it was converted into a nursing home. It was finally closed in 1957 when Southern Illinois University purchased the property to expand its agricultural program.

Eventually, SIU abandoned the building, although it occasionally staged emergency drills on the property. The building's final closure and decay inevitably led to stories of ghosts and other horrors. The atmosphere inside the structure lent itself to rumors of medical experiments gone awry, and visitors seemed to describe Sunset Haven as haunted simply because it *appeared* haunted.

In October 2013, a crew from Southern Illinois University demolished the building, leaving nothing but a cement foundation.

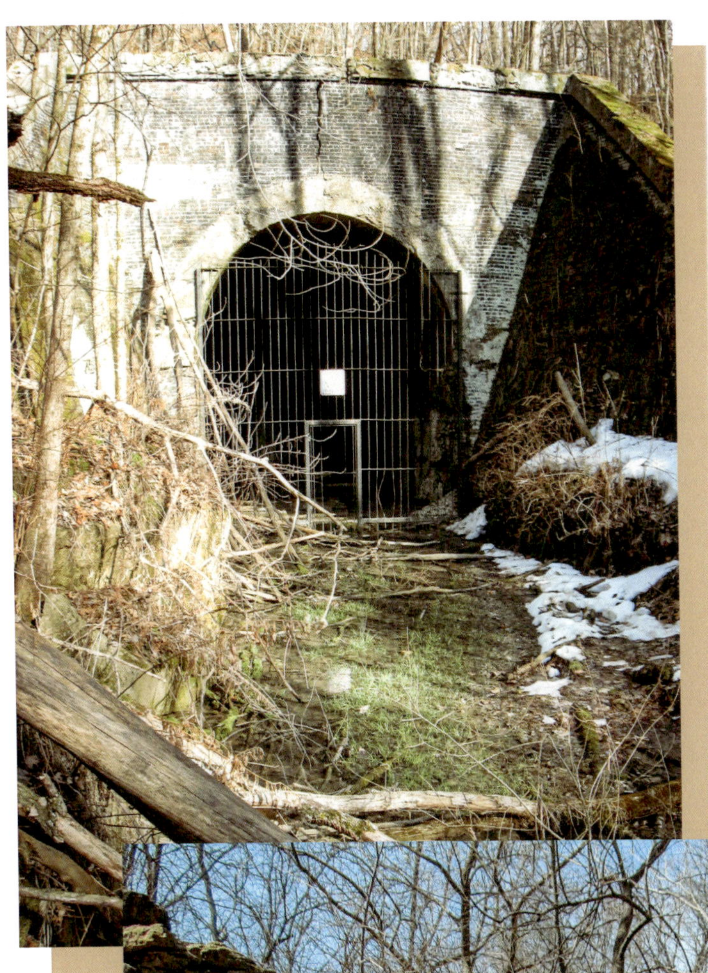

WINSTON TUNNEL

At 2,493 feet, the Winston Tunnel in Jo Daviess County was the longest railroad tunnel in Illinois. It was built in 1888 for the Minnesota and Northwestern Railroad, a line that ran from Chicago to Minneapolis, Omaha, and Kansas City. It took 350 workmen more than nine months to complete the tunnel. Shortly after, the Minnesota and Northwestern became known as the "Chicago Great Western Railway."

The Winston Tunnel was abandoned in 1972. The old pump house was torn down in 2007, but its brick walls still remain. One end of the tunnel is completely covered by dirt and debris, and the other is sealed by a large iron gate. The site is currently maintained by the Illinois Department of Natural Resources.

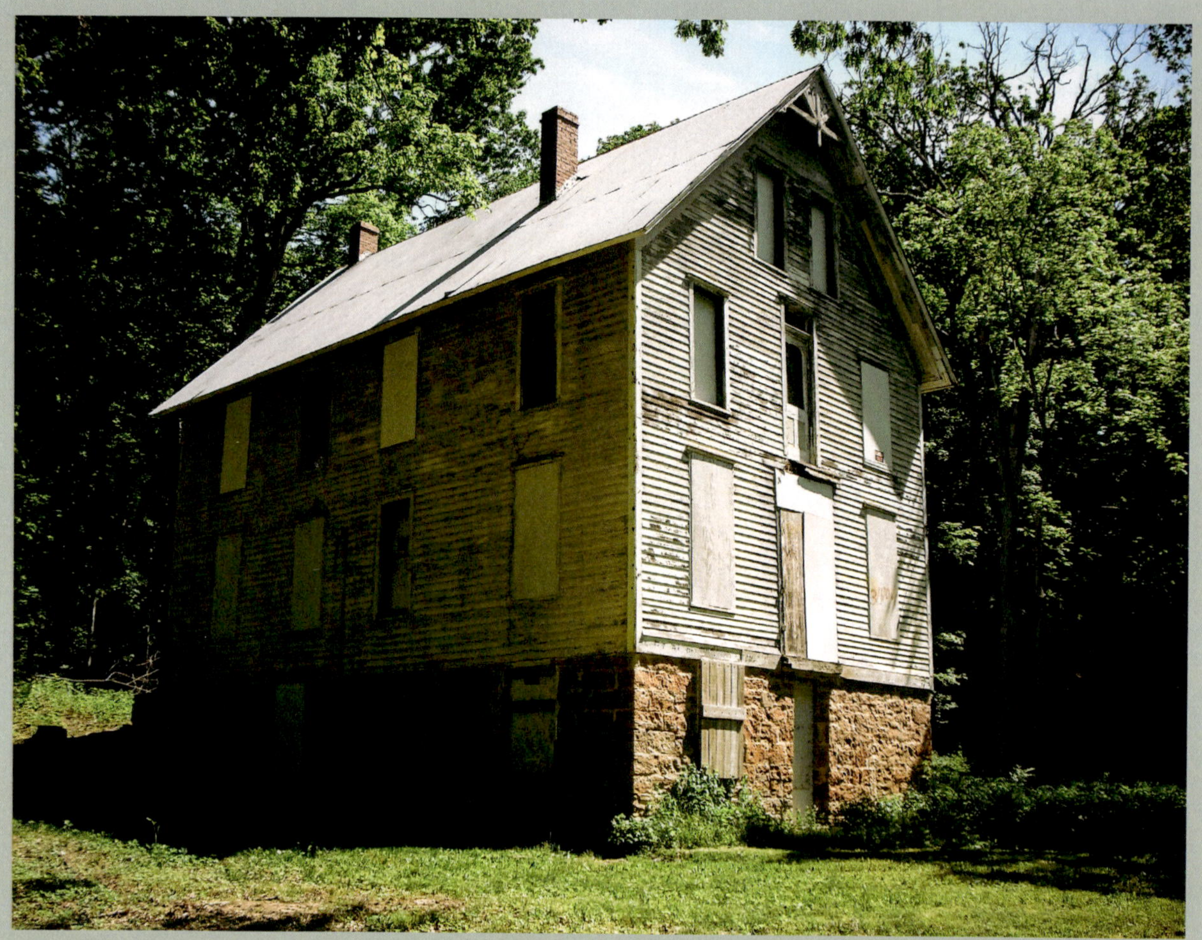

VISHNU SPRINGS

Vishnu Springs was a once-thriving resort community west of the town of Colchester in McDonough County. An entrepreneur named Darius Hicks inherited the land. He recognized the natural spring's healing properties and built a hotel he called the Capital Hotel. Other people soon arrived to live and work there, but the isolated nature of the resort impeded its growth.

During the early 1900s, several deadly incidents (including an employee crushed to death by the carousel) and scandals tarnished the community, and when Darius Hicks committed suicide in 1908, no one remained who was willing to invest their time and energy into maintaining the resort.

During the 1970s, a group of hippies made a short-lived attempt to turn it into a commune. Today, all that remains is the old hotel—a shadow of what it once was. Olga Kay Kennedy, a Western Illinois University alumnus, inherited Vishnu Springs from her grandparents and gifted it to the university in 2003. All 140 acres were turned into a wildlife sanctuary and access to the site is restricted.

HARTFORD CASTLE

Hartford Castle is the colloquial name for a mansion called Lakeview that formerly stood on a tract of land just outside of Hartford, Illinois, across the river from St. Louis in Madison County. It was built by Benjamin Biszant. The last owners abandoned it in the 1960s. In 1972, vandals destroyed the interior, and a fire ravaged the grounds a short time later. Today, not much remains besides some cement foundations and this old gazebo.

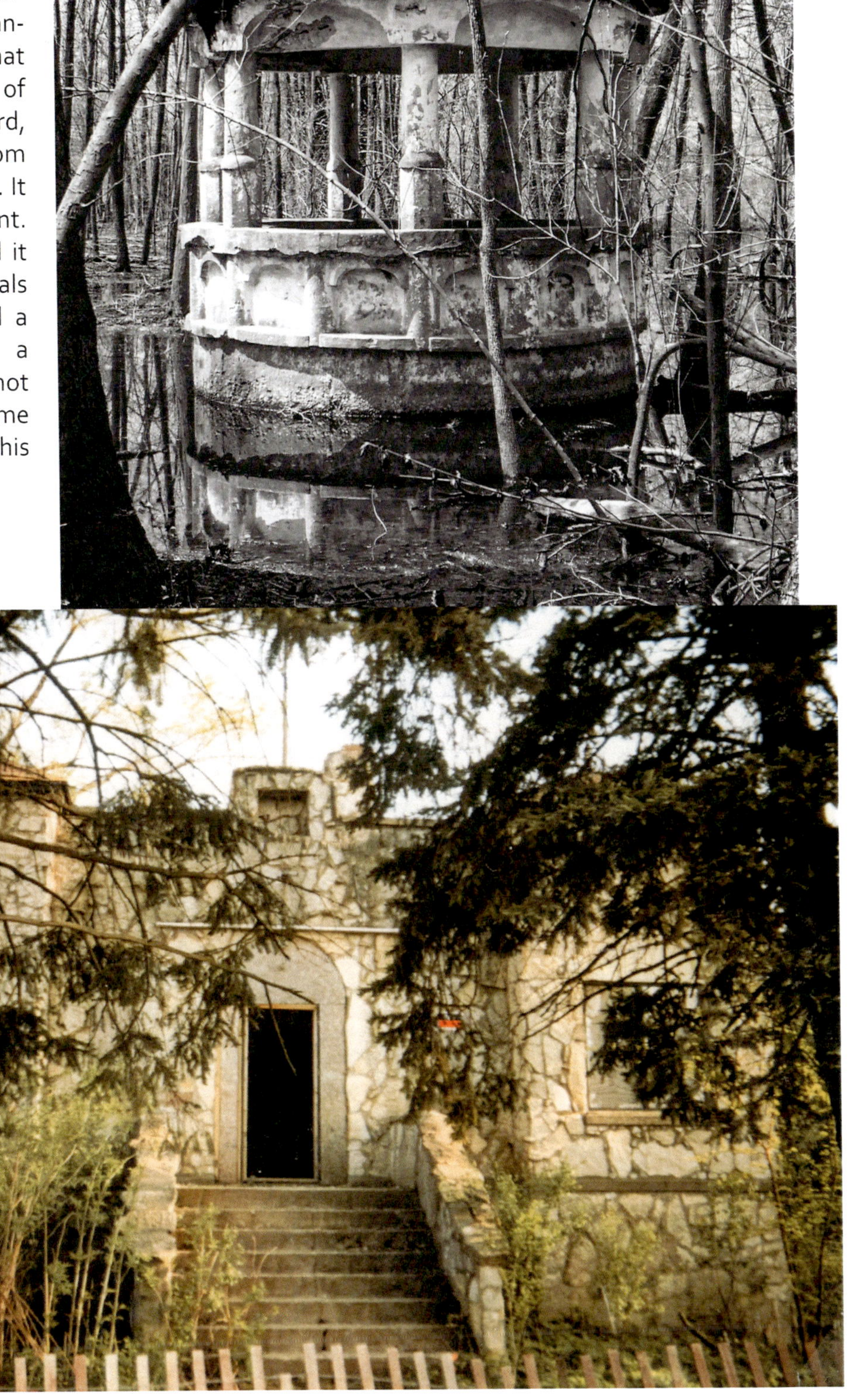

LINDBERGH SCHOOL

(1929 - 2007)

The historic Charles A. Lindbergh School, named after the famed aviator, was built along Shoe Factory Road in Hoffman Estates in 1929. Despite a determined preservation campaign, it was demolished in 2007.

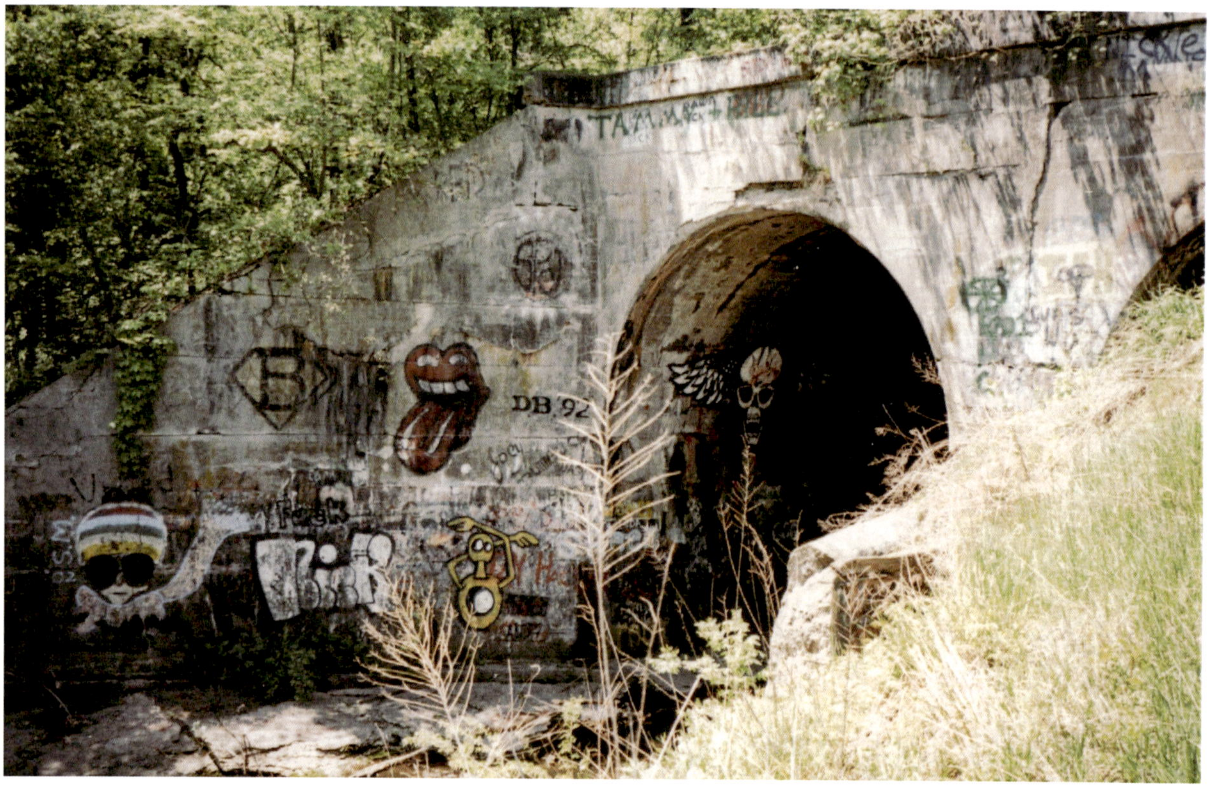

"Double Arches" bridge along 700 N is a defunct railroad bridge over Opossum Creek five miles south of Pana, Illinois.

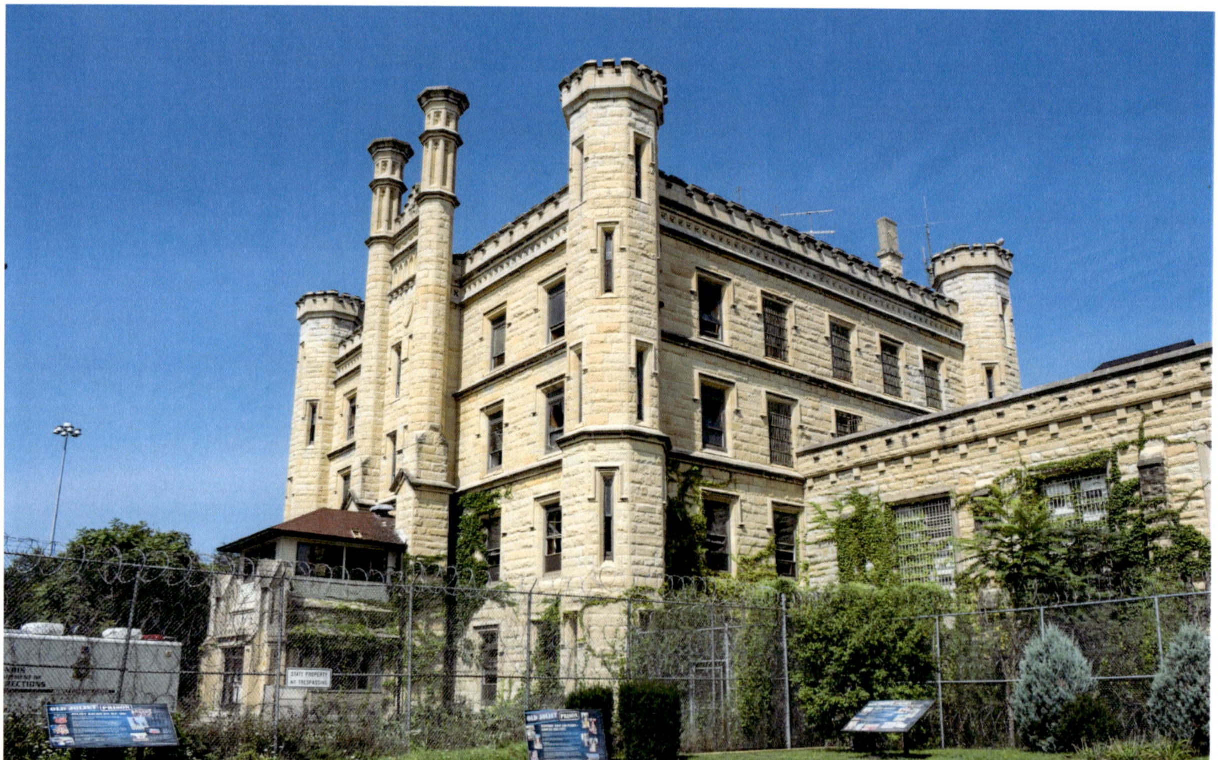

The former Joliet Correctional Center at 1125 Collins Street in Joliet, Illinois, opened in 1858 and closed in 2002. It sat abandoned for many years, until being purchased by the city in 2017 and opened for tours.

ARIZONA

The American southwest—the "Wild West"—is a harsh, unforgiving environment, but it was also filled with precious metals. This combination led to gold rushes and "boomtowns", towns that rose with the discovery of a silver vein and fell when it ran dry. This boom and bust cycle left behind dozens of ghost towns and abandoned mines and other sites scattered throughout the desert.

It's a history and environment very different from where I grew up, so whenever I had an opportunity to visit, I jumped at it. I lived in southern Arizona for several months while I was serving in the Army, and I made the most of that time exploring my surroundings. The following are a few of those sites, preserved in the San Pedro Riparian National Conservation Area. Preservationists have only recently saved these sites from destruction.

During World War 2, the Army used one ghost town as a training ground, damaging or demolishing many of its buildings. When I visited Fairbank, staff told me people used to sneak up to the old cemetery, vandalize it, and dig up graves. Thankfully, that no longer happens, and you can safely visit these ruins and imagine what life was like for people living there in the 1880s.

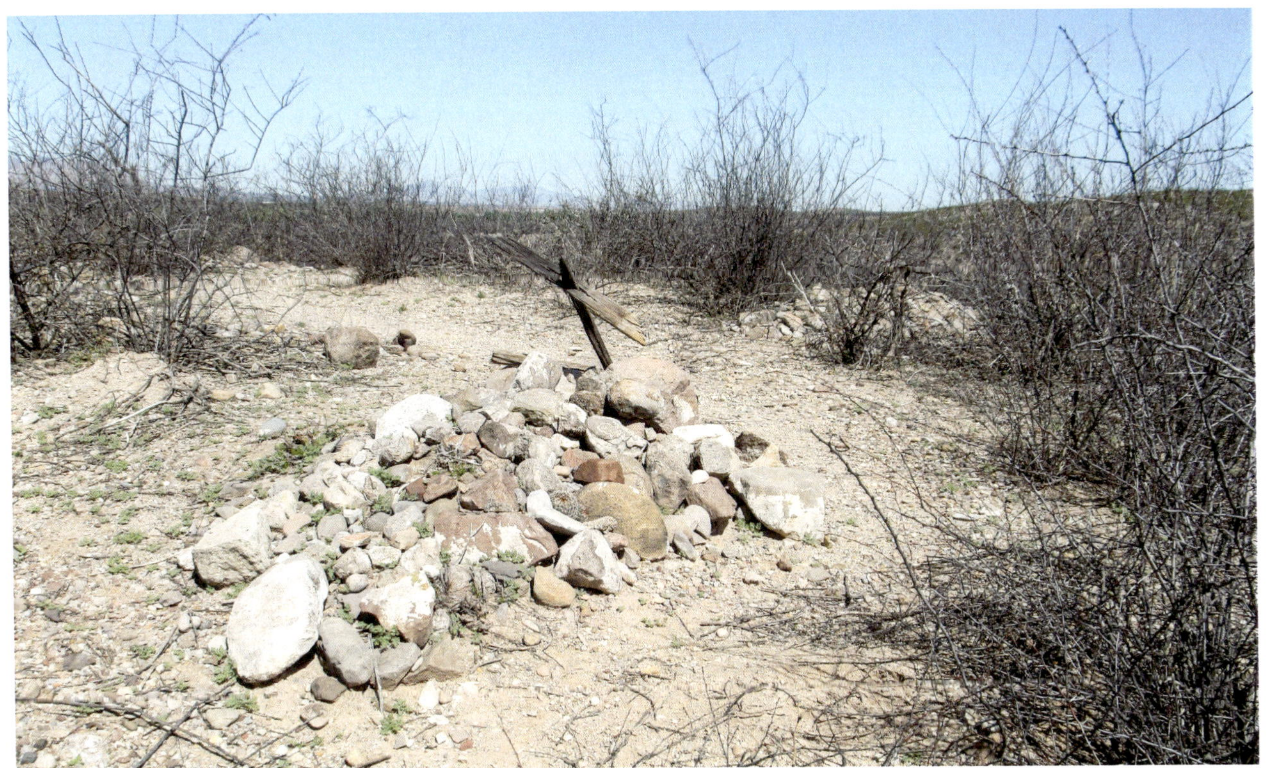

The old Fairbank Cemetery (31.7297, -110.1868) behind Fairbank Historic Townsite in Cochise County, Arizona.

BLOODY BRUNCKOW CABIN

Crumbling adobe walls overlook a San Pedro River tributary. Ants and snakes burrow into the rocky soil, past the bleached bones of unfortunate prospectors and outlaws resting in shallow graves. At night, a cold chill descends on the desert floor of the San Pedro Riparian National Conservation Area. Located south of Charleston Road between Tombstone and Sierra Vista, Arizona, this place has been described as "the bloodiest cabin in Arizona history." In 1858, T.F. White and Fredrick Brunckow sought their fortunes in these hills. Since then, as many as 22 deaths have been reported in or near the cabin.

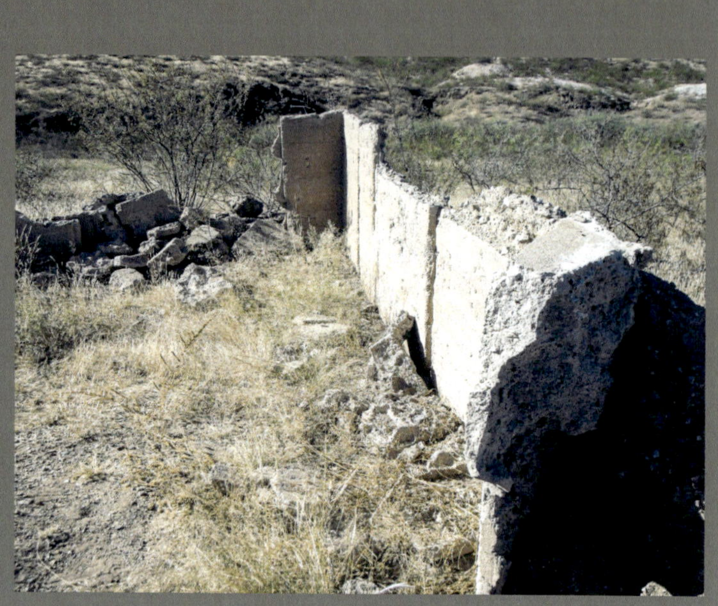

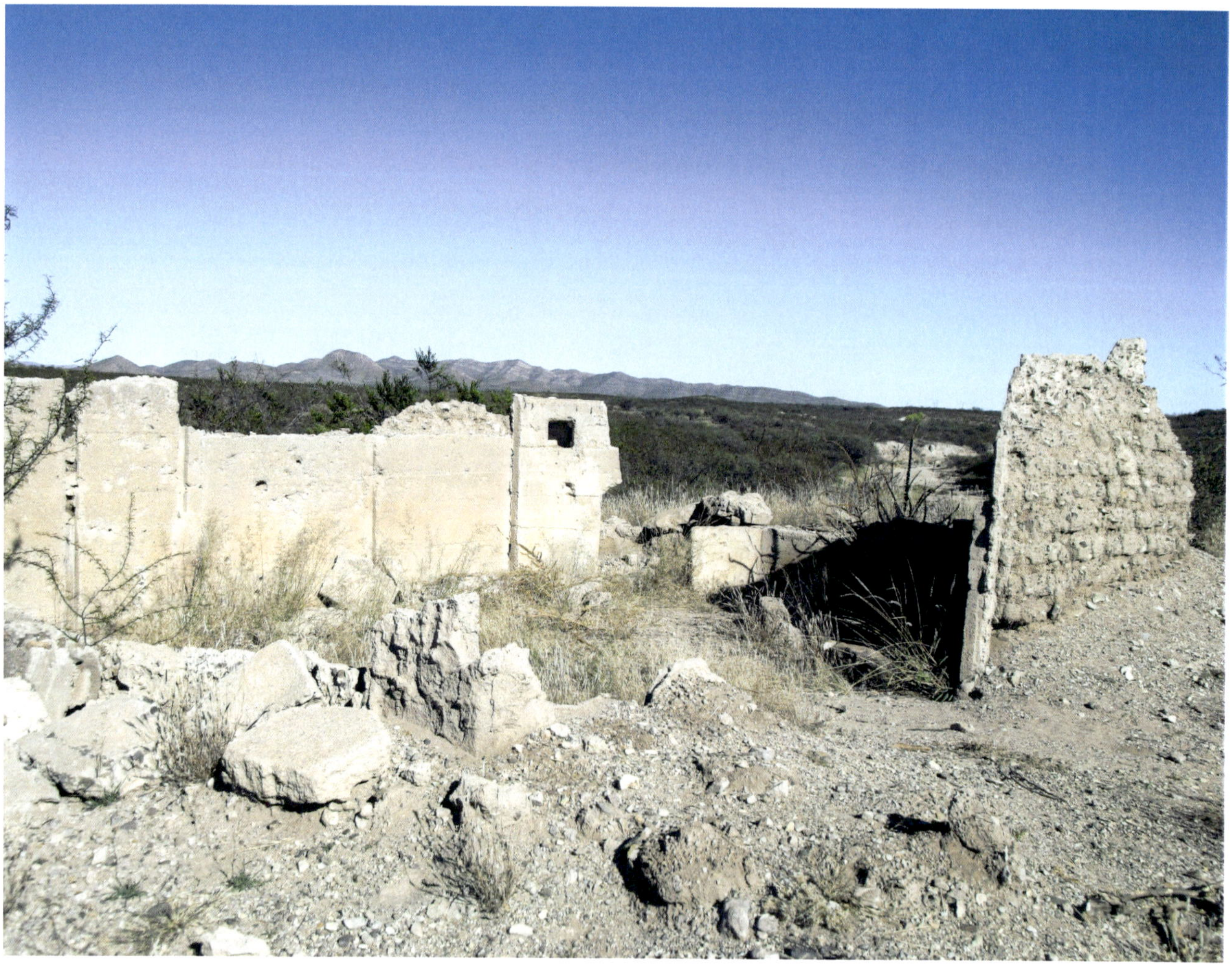

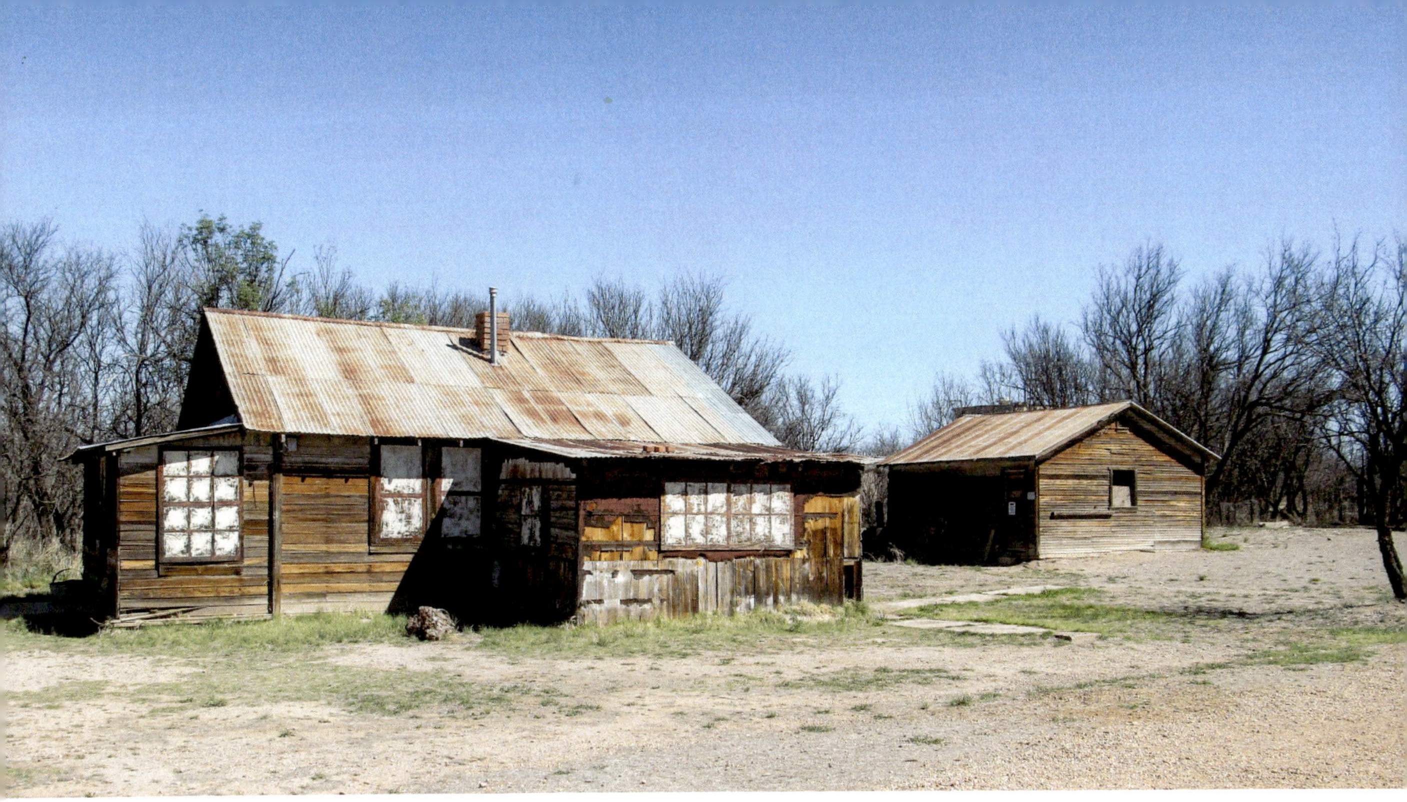

FAIRBANK GHOST TOWN

A forgotten cemetery on a sunbaked hill in the desert and tumbleweed drifting through dusty, deserted streets all bring to mind the quintessential southwestern ghost town. Located off State Route 82 along the San Pedro River in Cochise County, Arizona, Fairbank is just such a ghost town. It grew up around the nearest rail stop to Tombstone and was first settled in 1881. It never had more than 100 residents. The town began to die in the early 20th century, and by 1970, only a small gas station remained.

In 1986, the Bureau of Land Management created the San Pedro Riparian National Conservation Area. Today, the remains of Fairbank have benefited from tourist activity and a few of the original buildings have been preserved.

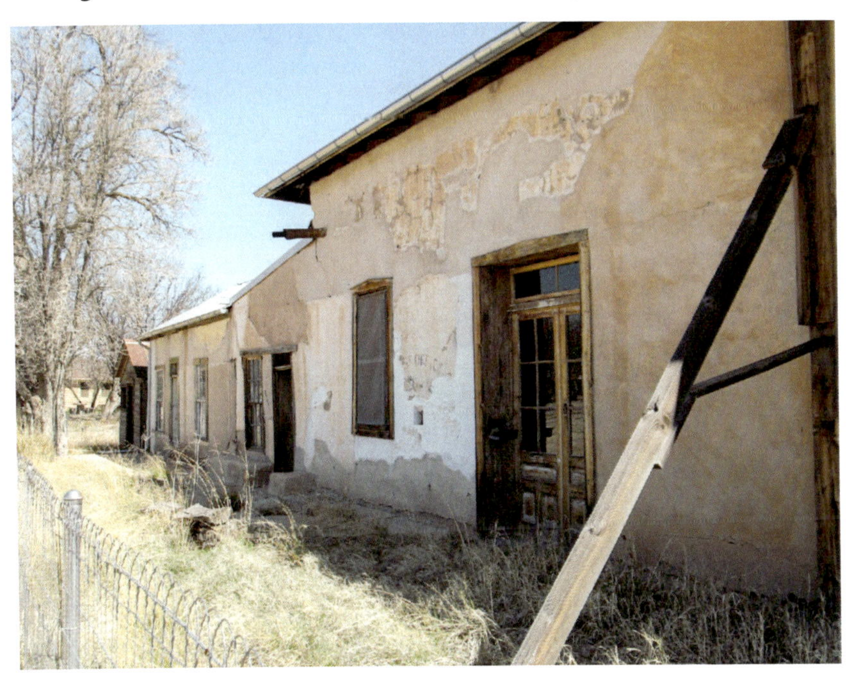

The old Fairbank Cemetery is located about a half mile up a trail and is heavily vandalized. Only a few of the original graves remain, marked by piles of stones, wooden crosses, and iron fencing.

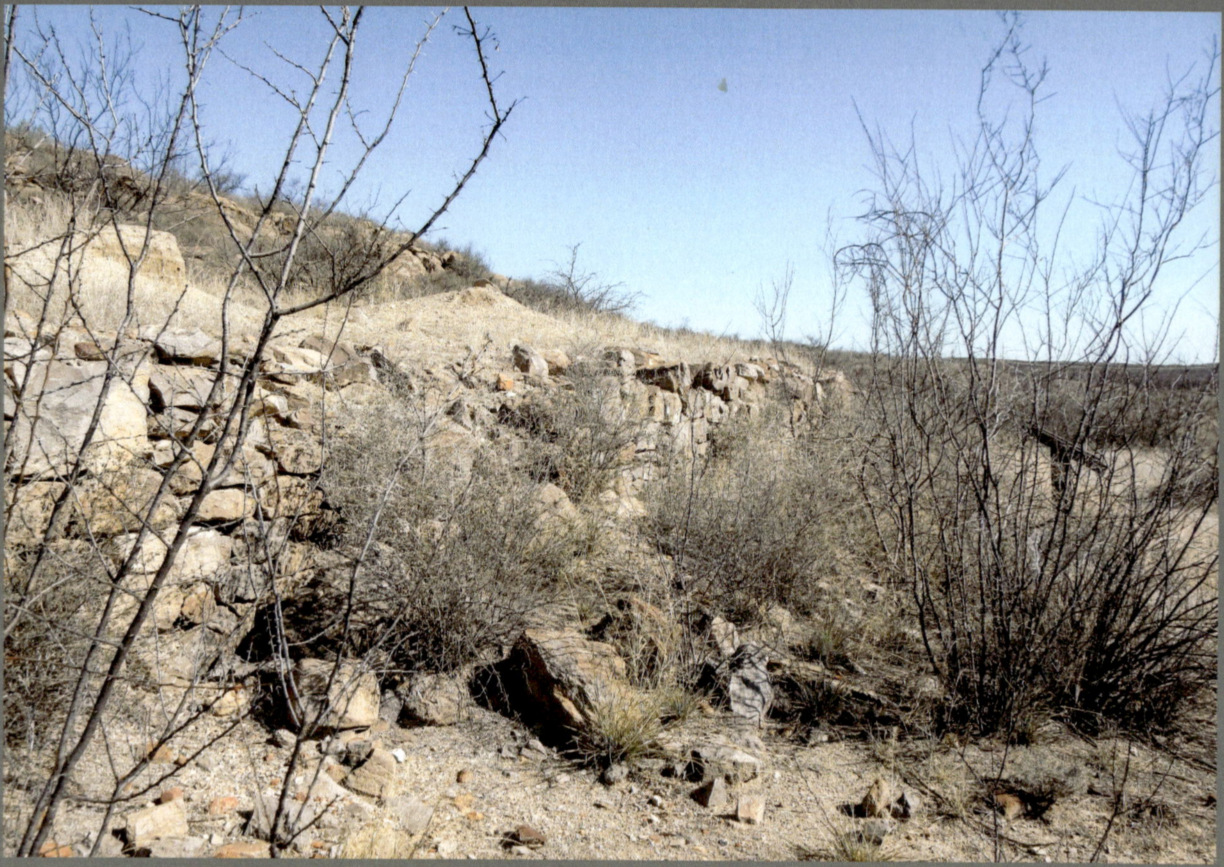

MILLVILLE RUINS

In their heyday, the twin towns of Millville and Charleston in southeastern Arizona had a lawless reputation. Located on opposite sides of the San Pedro River, about nine miles southwest of Tombstone, Millville and Charleston were home to some of the Wild West's most notorious figures. Outlaw Frank Stilwell, for example, once owned a saloon in Charleston. Stilwell was a deputy sheriff in Tombstone, Arizona for Cochise County Sheriff Johnny Behan and was suspected of killing Morgan Earp on March 18, 1882.

The Tombstone Mill and Mining Company and the Corbin Mill and Mining Company owned the mills of Millville. These mills processed silver ore from the mines around Tombstone, and from 1881 to 1882 processed almost $1.4 million in silver. When the mines dried up, the people moved on. Today, most of Charleston is gone and only a few stone walls remain of Millville.

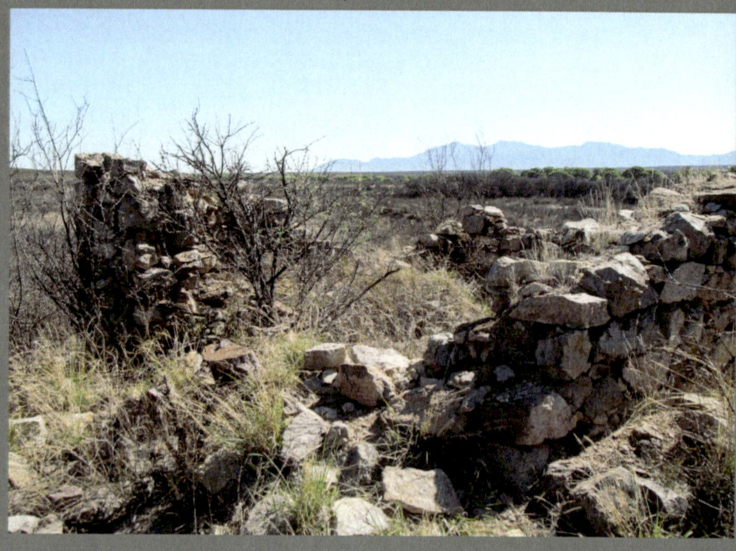

DARK TOURISM

Dark Tourism is the commodification of legend tripping. In one way or another, nearly all the places in this book are the subject of legend tripping. Author Lisa Hefner Heitz defines the practice as "visits by young people to a locally famous site that is known to be haunted or a hangout for monsters and other supernatural creatures." Others have described it as "a usually furtive [secret] nocturnal pilgrimage to a site which is alleged to have been the scene of some tragic, horrific, and possibly supernatural event or haunting."

Cemeteries (particularly unusual monuments within them), old bridges and tunnels, and of course, abandoned places all fit the bill. Somewhere along the line, entrepreneurs figured out they could profit from this practice by restricting access to a site and charging an entrance fee. The Villisca Axe Murder House in Iowa, Lizzie Borden House in Massachusetts, and Waverly Hills Sanatorium in Kentucky are all prominent examples.

Often, profits are reinvested into restoration and interpretation of the site, leaving a portion of it "as it was" and turning the remainder into a museum. This has the benefit of preserving the site but also allowing visitors to have an experience as though they are exploring an abandoned or restricted place without risking fines for trespassing.

I think this is a wonderful way to raise money for the preservation of historic sites, particularly if they are connected to something tragic or unsavory. My home state of Illinois has a bad track record when it comes to dark tourism. Local officials balk at the subject and would rather see these places torn down than turned into tourist attractions.

New York is one state that's gotten it right. The Haunted History Trail of New York State is an effort by dozens of public and private organizations, including New York State Tourism (creator of the popular "I Love New York" campaign), and many others. Their website and brochure offers a guide to over 30 different locations across the state, many of which have appeared on paranormal-themed television shows. The website also has an audio tour, haunted road trips, and a calendar of events.

Kelly Rapone of the Genesee County Chamber of Commerce's Tourism program came up with the idea in 2013 as a way to help market Rolling Hills Asylum.

There is always concern that promoting dark tourism attracts vandalism and other criminal activity. No one can stop people with bad intentions from doing bad things, but what you can do is remove opportunities for mischief in a controlled, carefully supervised environment in which people can satisfy their curiosity about the unknown.

The following are just a few of the "dark tourist" destinations that I've visited over the years that don't fit into any other chapter.

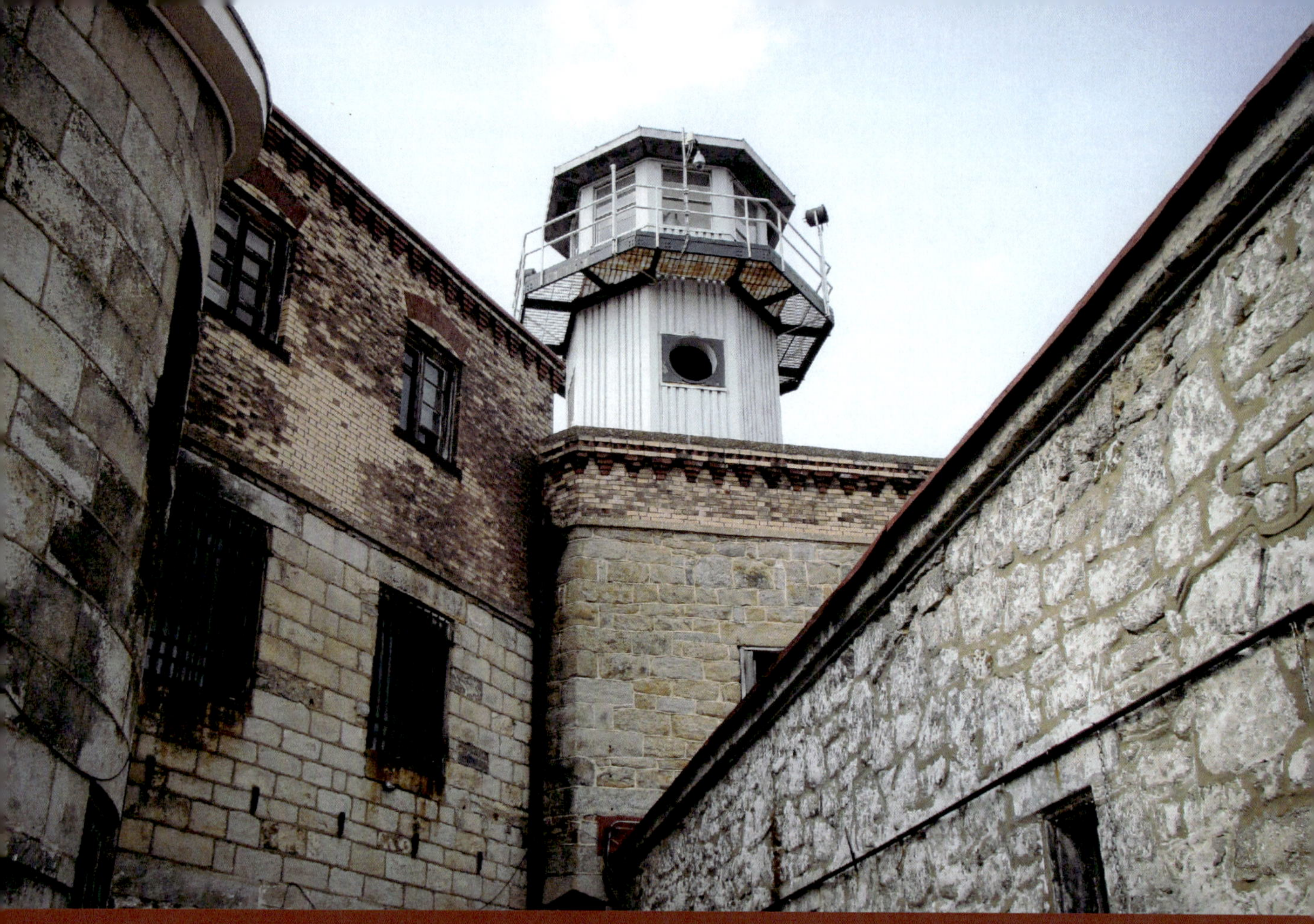

EASTERN STATE PENITENTIARY - PHILADELPHIA, PA

Some may consider it ironic that the world's first true penitentiary was built not only in the Land of the Free, but in the City of Brotherly Love. The Gothic Revival exterior of Eastern State Penitentiary inspired fear for over a century. Situated in the heart of modern Philadelphia, Pennsylvania, it stood as a reminder of what fate awaited those who ran afoul of the law. It is no surprise that more than a few ghosts are believed to lurk behind its thick stone walls.

Eastern State Penitentiary is located at 2027 Fairmount Avenue in the Fairmount neighborhood. Fairmount used to be a farming community outside the City of Philadelphia, but was incorporated into the city in the 19th century. Eastern State was designed by architect John Haviland and built in 1829. A man named Charles Williams was its first prisoner. The prison became so famous that it was one of two places Charles Dickens wanted to see when he visited Philadelphia in 1842.

The system enforced at the prison became known as the "Pennsylvania Model." In contrast to New York State's "Auburn System", which emphasized punishment, the Pennsylvania Model advocated solitary confinement, isolation, reflection, and quiet labor. This Quaker-inspired system was meant to instill penitence in the prisoners, hence the name "penitentiary."

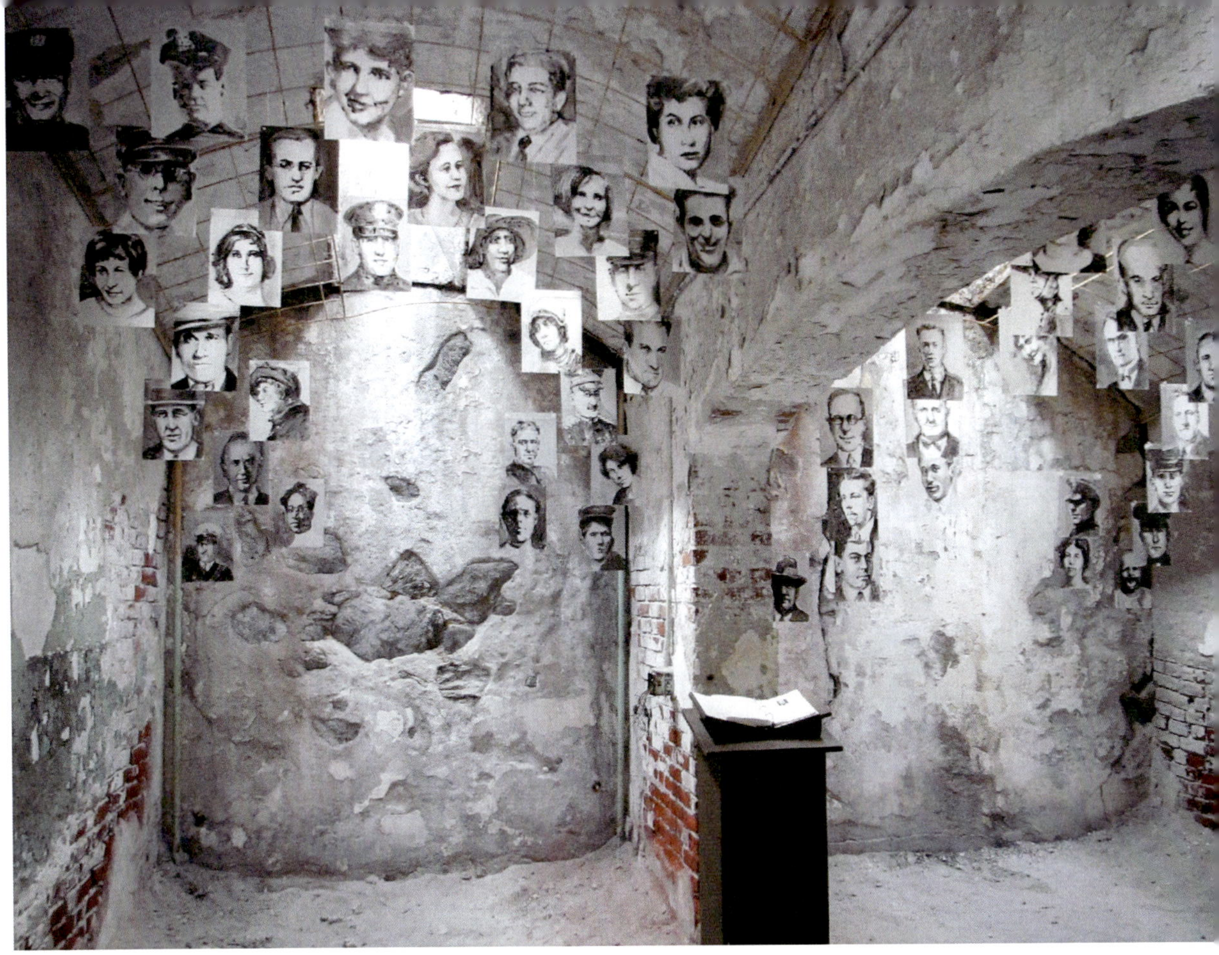

Today, the prison hosts daily tours and special events. Art installations can be found scattered throughout the grounds and in some of the cells, and the museum holds a wealth of information about the US prison system.

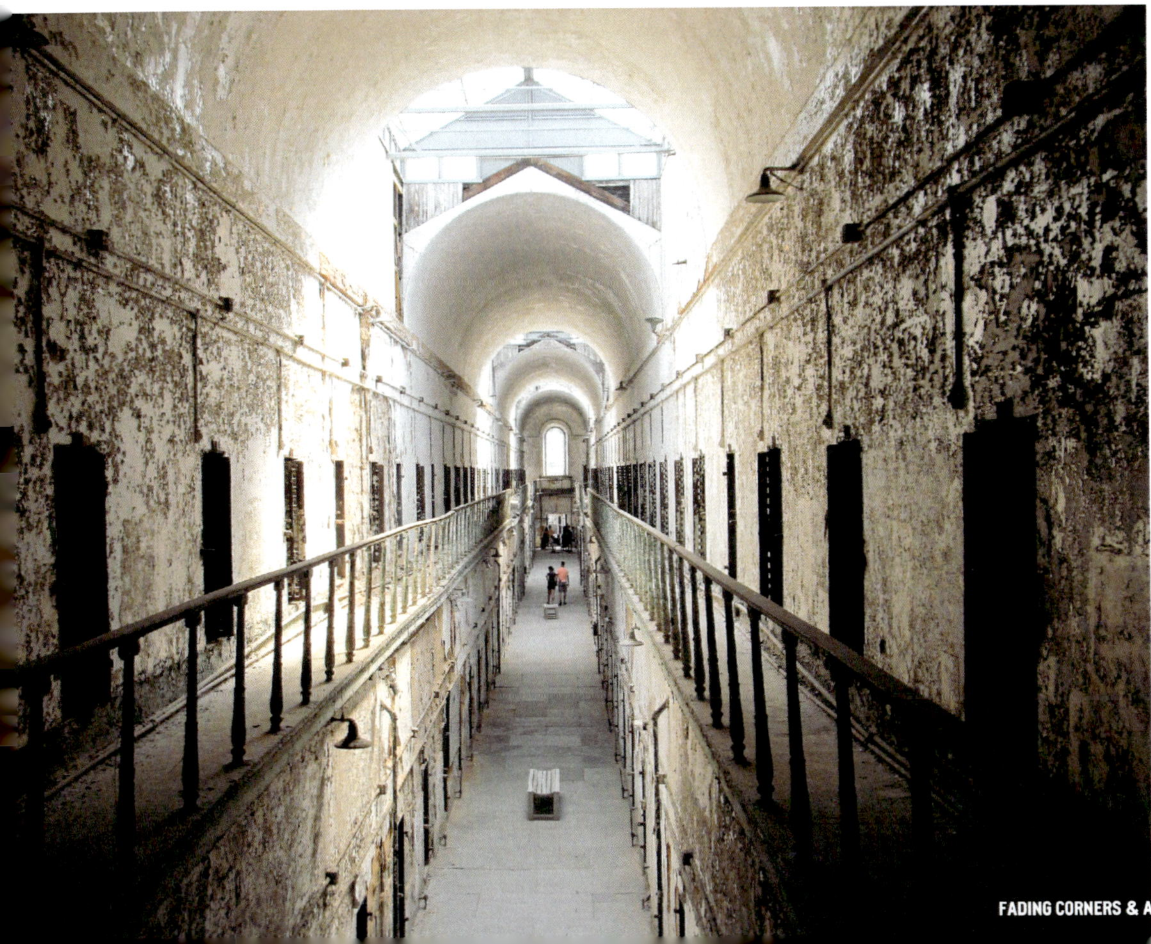

Eastern State Penitentiary closed in 1971 and stood abandoned for the next 23 years. Its decaying corridors, overgrown prison yard, and history of agony lent itself to ghost stories.

OHIO STATE REFORMATORY - MANSFIELD, OH

Built between 1896 and 1910, the Ohio State Reformatory in Mansfield served as a detention center for young, petty criminals. The first inmates were admitted in 1896, and they helped construct the Romanesque Revival building. The reformatory closed in 1990 and was used most famously in the filming of *The Shawshank Redemption* (1994). Today it is open for tours.

The old superintendent's office is widely believed to be haunted by the ghosts of Helen and Warden Glattke. Visitors often experience strong feelings of dread, anger, and fear throughout the former reformatory.

One form of punishment was to send prisoners to solitary confinement in "the hole"—a dark and claustrophobic room—for an indeterminate amount of time. Several violent episodes occurred at the prison, and there have been around 200 documented deaths. On February 6, 1960, in Cell #13, East Cell Block, a prisoner named James Lockhart stole lighter fluid and set himself on fire. He burned to death at the age of 22.

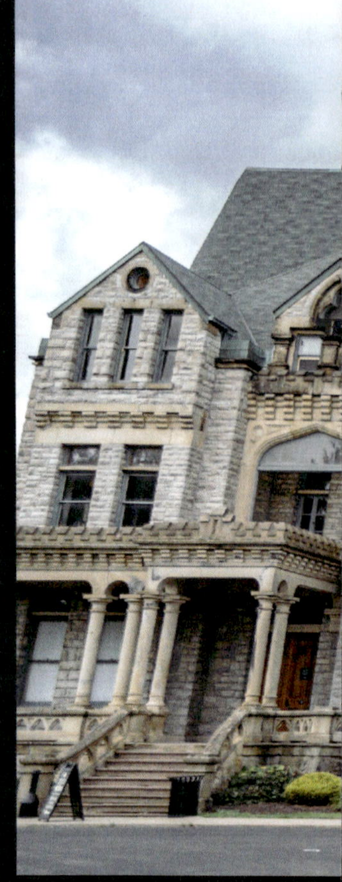

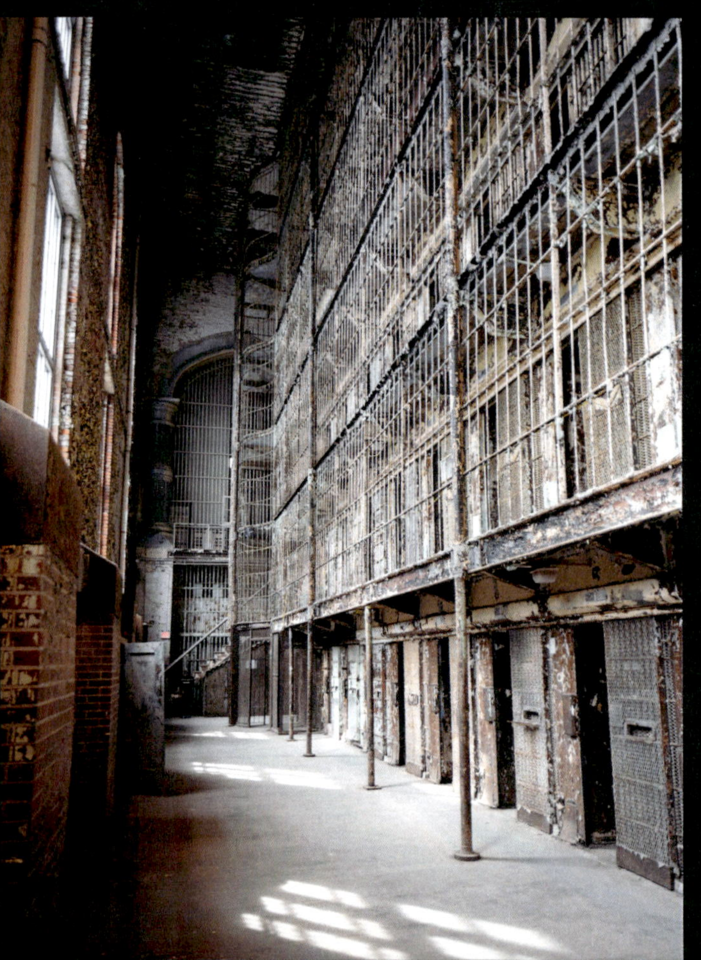

It's easy to see why people believe this prison is haunted, and why it was ultimately shut down for inhumane conditions. I can't imagine being crammed into a small cell so far off the ground for years on end. Before I took the tour, they didn't warn me about how high up I'd be walking along a narrow, rickety metal walkway in the cell blocks.

The first part of the tour has more of a "museum" feel to it, with displays and artifacts behind glass, but the farther you go, the more abandoned and isolated things become. You walk through numerous empty rooms, left "as is" with cracking tile and peeling paint. It is a genuinely creepy and disconcerting experience.

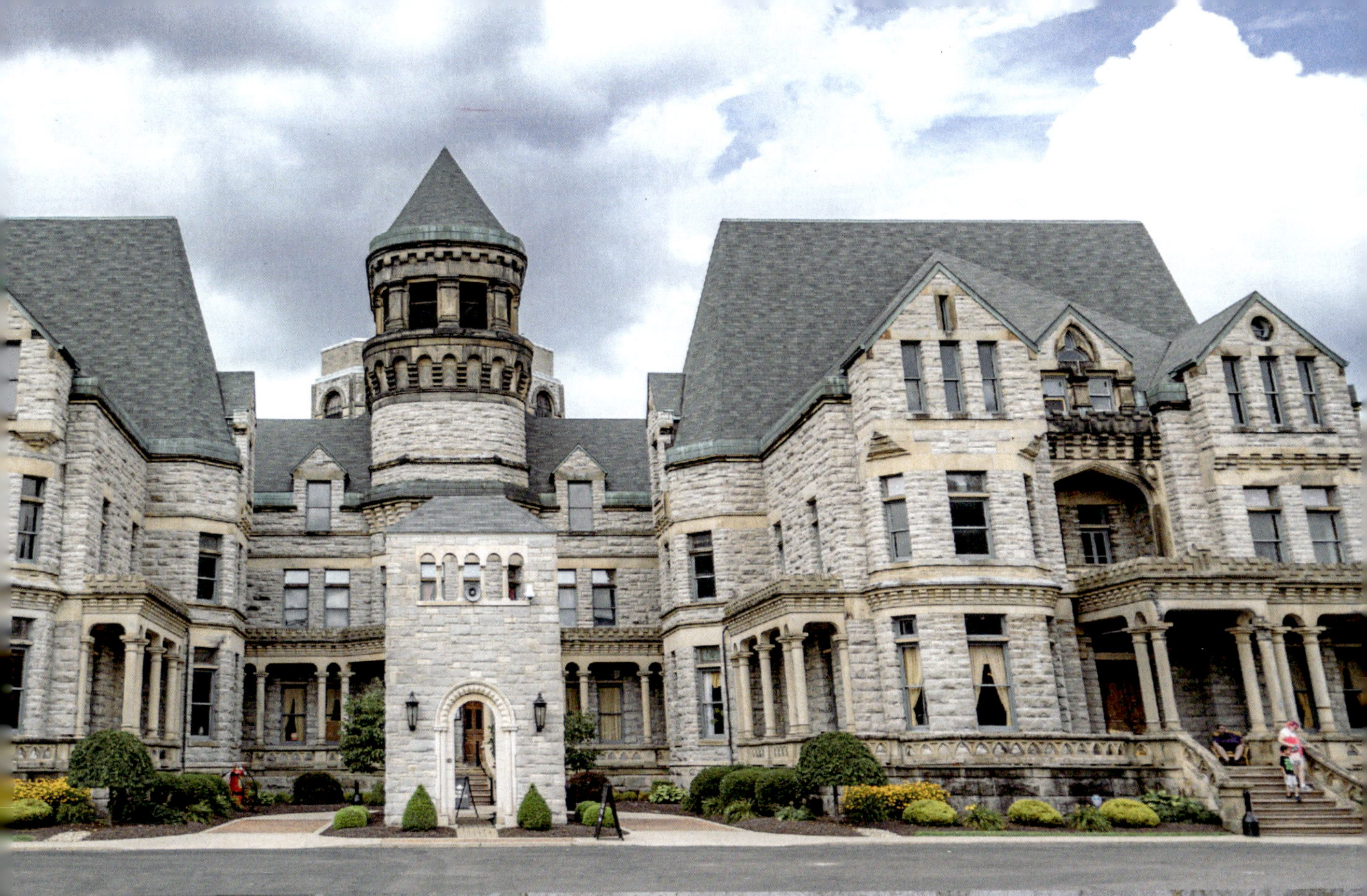

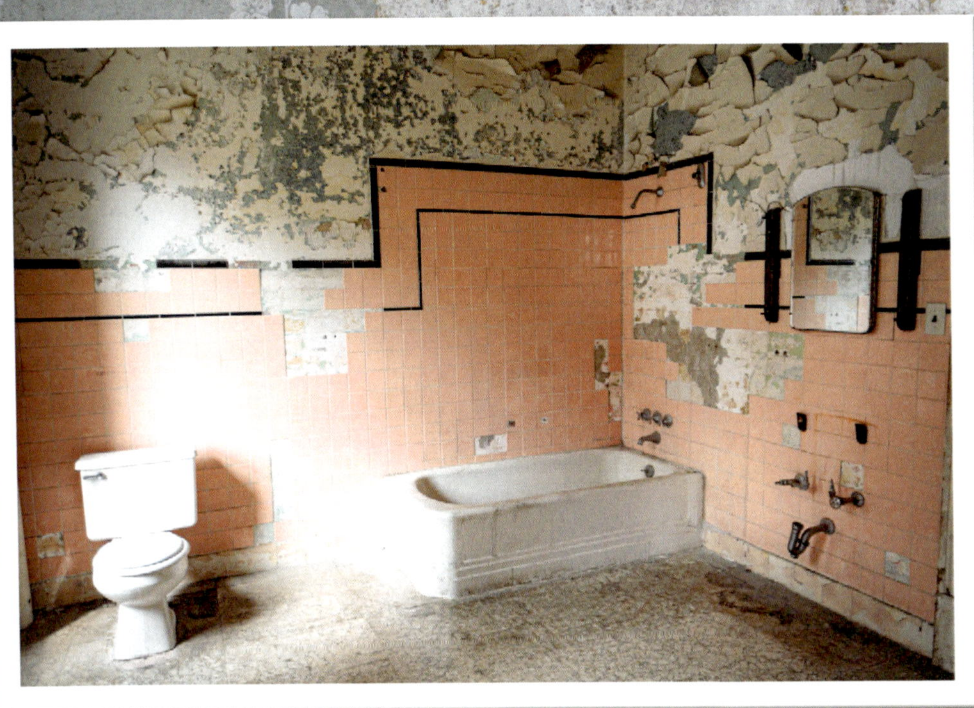

TRANS-ALLEGHENY LUNATIC ASYLUM - WESTON, WV

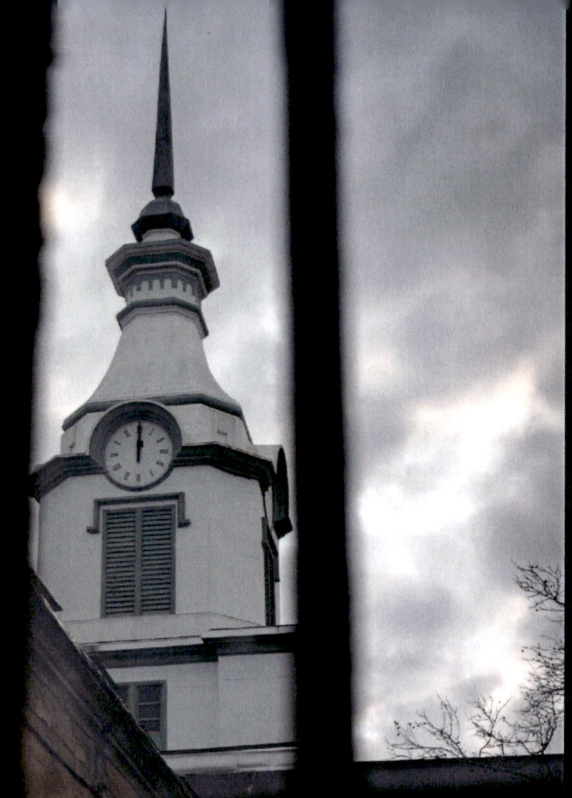

Designed by architect Richard Snowden Andrews in Gothic and Tudor Revival styles, construction on the Trans-Allegheny Lunatic Asylum in Weston, West Virginia began in 1858. Its main building was laid out according to the Kirkbride plan, brainchild of Thomas Story Kirkbride. Kirkbride theorized that exposure to natural light and fresh air would aid in curing the mentally ill, so he designed a long, narrow hospital with staggered wings extending outward from the center.

In 1861, the Civil War interrupted construction on Virginia's new asylum as Union troops seized its construction funds from a local bank. When West Virginia seceded from Virginia in 1863 and was admitted to the Union, the new state government renamed it the West Virginia Hospital for the Insane. Construction on the sprawling grounds wasn't completed until 1881.

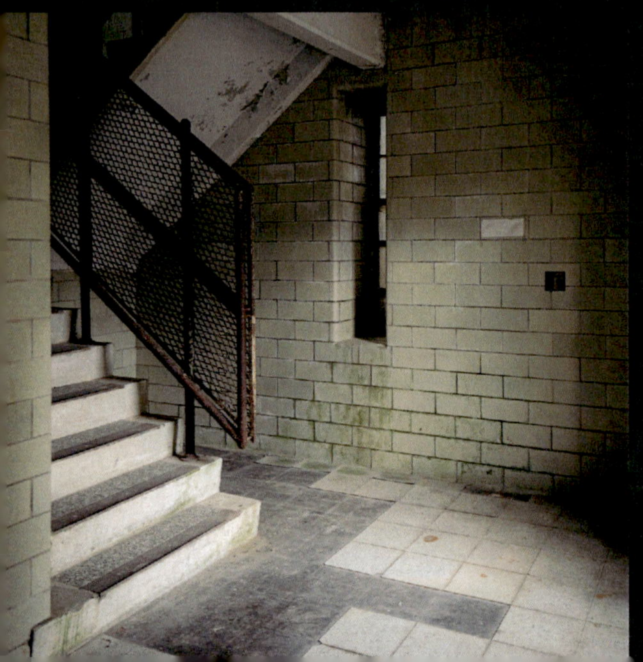

Conditions slowly deteriorated into a horror show. During the 1950s, its population peaked at a staggering 2,600 patients, with state and medical officials resorting to lobotomy to reduce overcrowding. A lobotomy was designed to make patients docile by severing connections in the frontal lobe of the brain. It's believed over a thousand lobotomies were performed there.

Like many large psychiatric hospitals, Weston State Hospital (as it came to be called) closed in the 1990s. It was added to the National Register of Historic Places in 1978 and the Weston Hospital Main Building was designated a National Historic Landmark in 1990. Preservation efforts bore fruit in 2007 when Joe Jordan purchased the building for $1.5 million and opened it for tours.

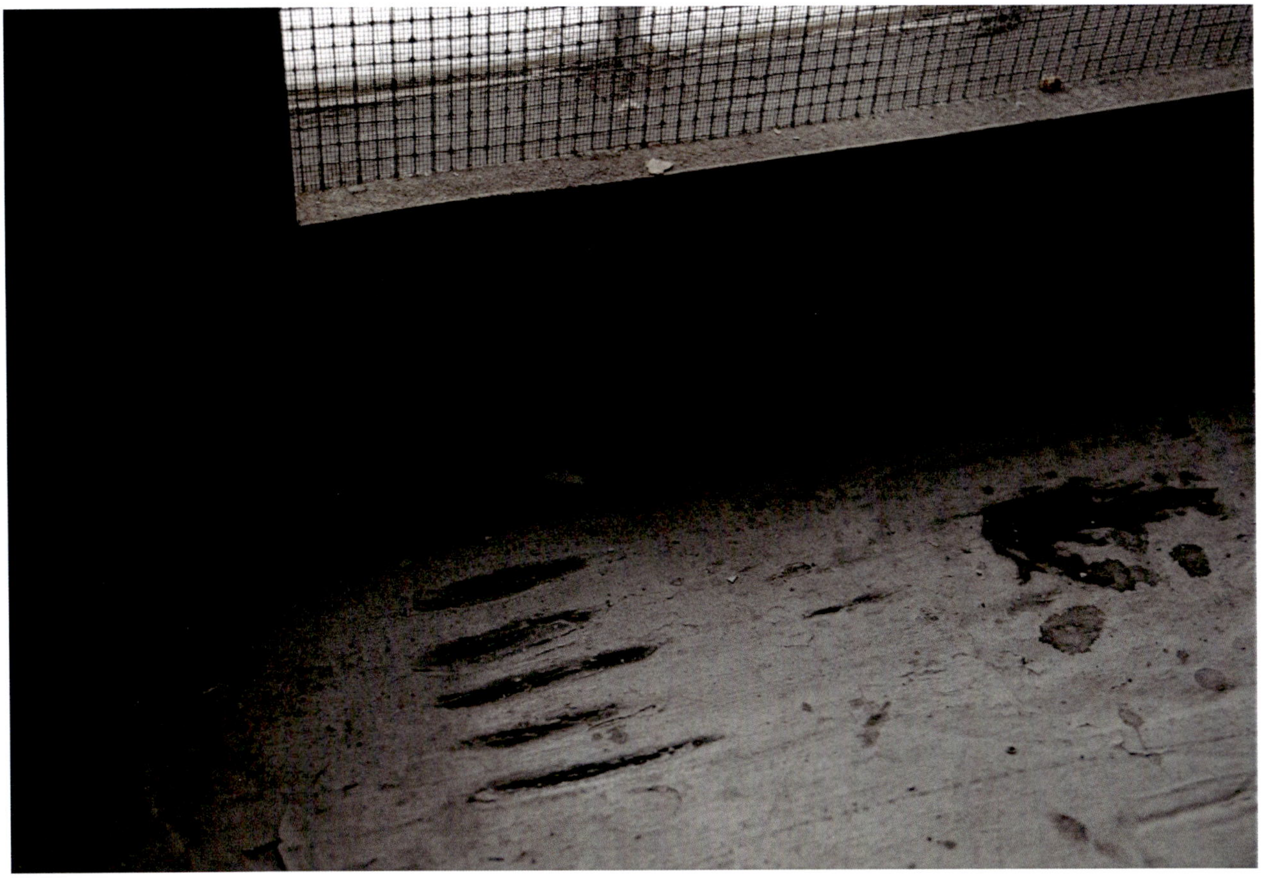

Whether or not you believe the numerous reports of paranormal activity, the opportunity to explore the history, architecture, and artifacts of the building is well worth the drive.

Trans-Allegheny Lunatic Asylum has appeared in a cornucopia of TV shows, including Travel Channel's *Ghost Stories*, *Paranormal Challenge*, and *Ghost Adventures*, Syfy's *Ghost Hunters*, and Destination America's *Paranormal Lockdown*, making it one of the most famous destinations for ghost hunting and dark tourism in America.

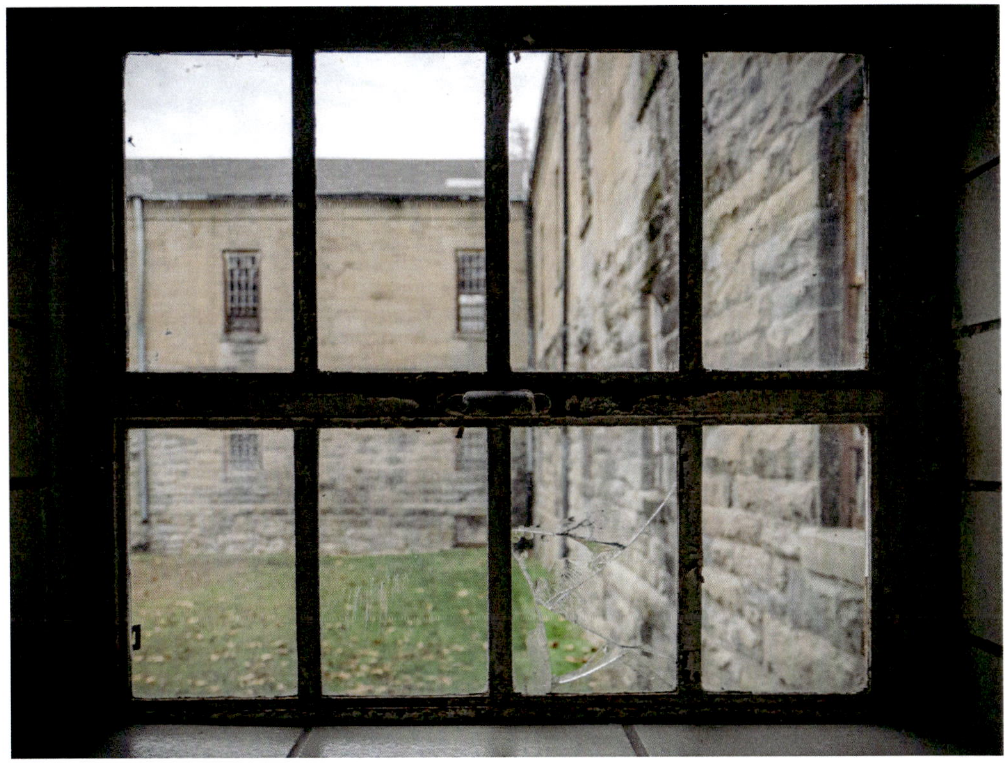

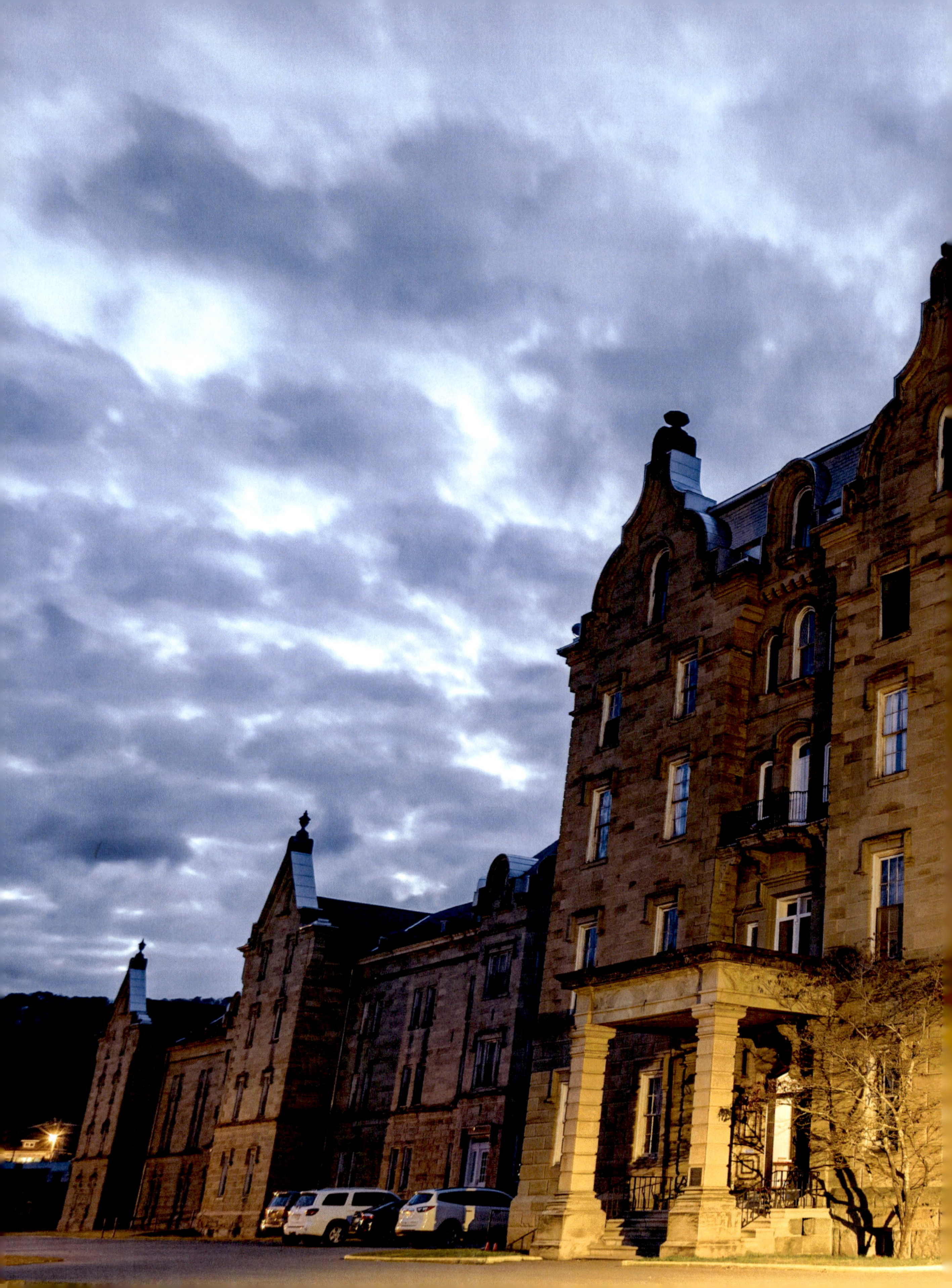

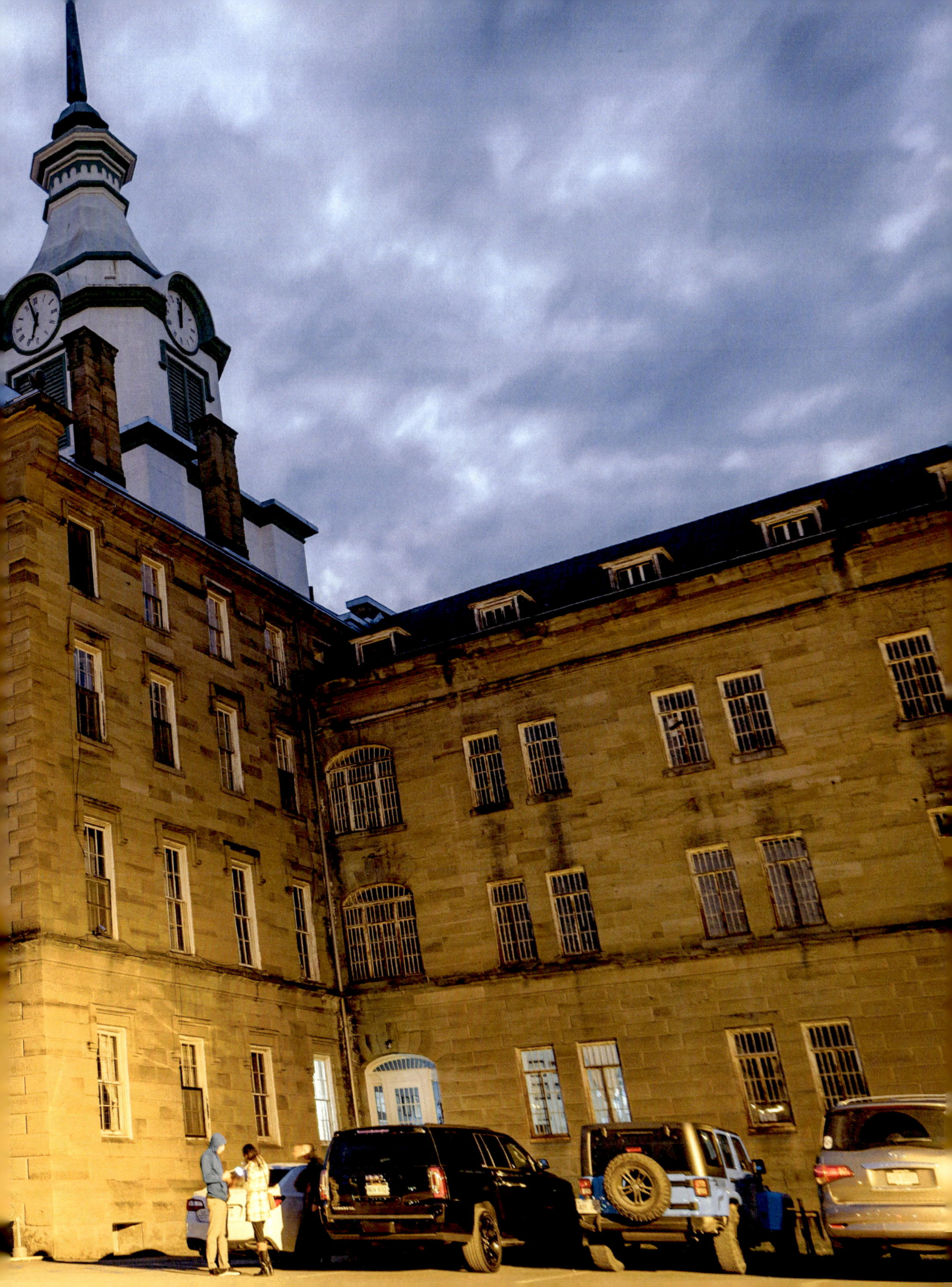

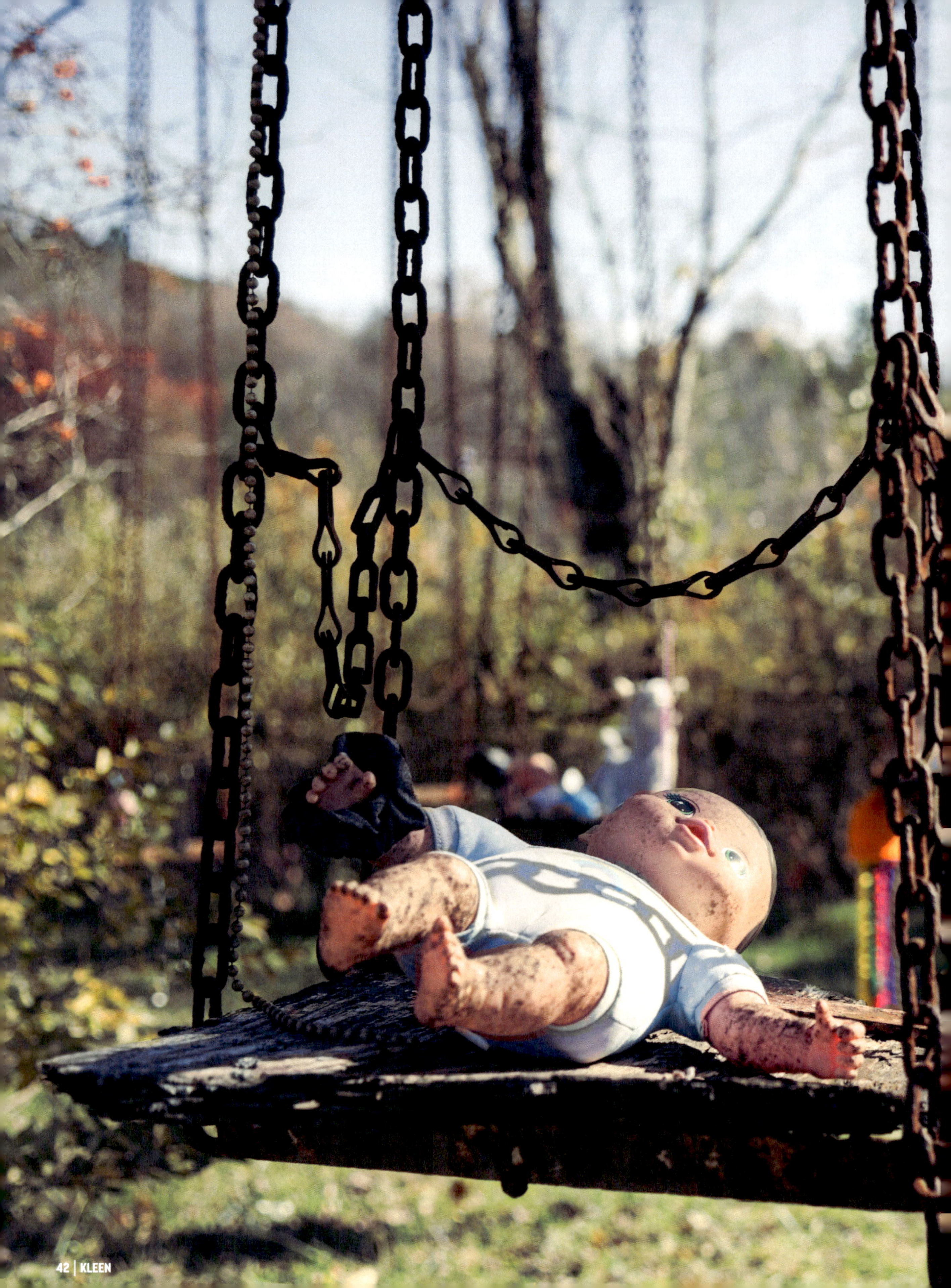

LAKE SHAWNEE AMUSEMENT PARK - PRINCETON, WV

What comes to mind when you imagine a spooky, abandoned amusement park? Was it built on an American Indian burial ground, or near the site of a Colonial-Era massacre? If yes, then you may be thinking of Lake Shawnee Amusement Park in Mercer County, West Virginia.

Lake Shawnee is a small, manmade lake along the Bluestone National Scenic River. In the mid-eighteenth century, the Shawnee lived in the Ohio region and had some settlements in the northern Shenandoah Valley. They resented white colonists moving into western Virginia, what they considered their hunting grounds, a sentiment which eventually led to the Northwest Indian War (1785–1795).

In 1783, a Shawnee raiding party attacked the homestead of Mitchell and Phoebe Clay, first white settlers of Mercer County, killing two of their children. Their graves are still on the property.

Why, 143 years later, a man named Conley Trigg Snidow thought this would be a great place for an amusement park is anyone's guess. But build it he did. Snidow's resort operated from 1926 to 1967, the year following the death of an adolescent girl on the rotating swing ride. Accidents claimed the lives of two other guests over the years.

A former employee named Gaylord White tried to reopen the park in the late 1980s, but failed after two years. It was White who accidentally uncovered the American Indian burial ground on the property.

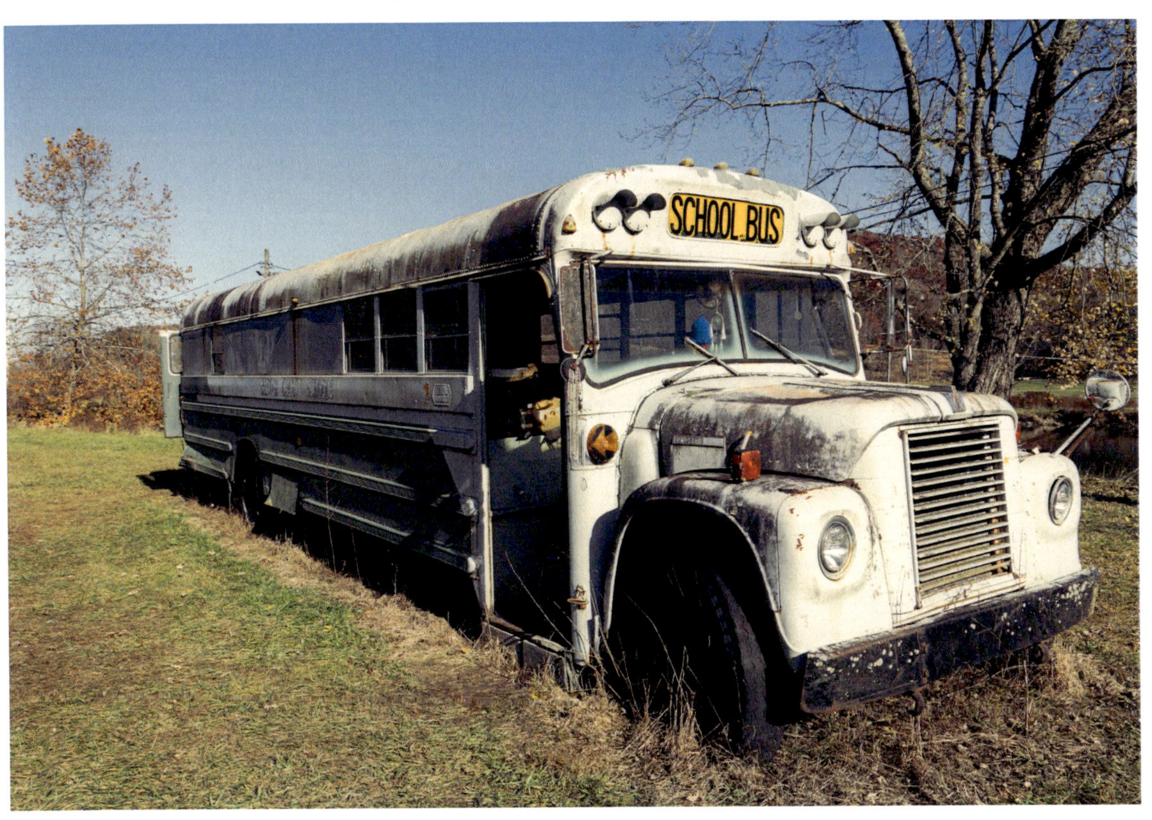

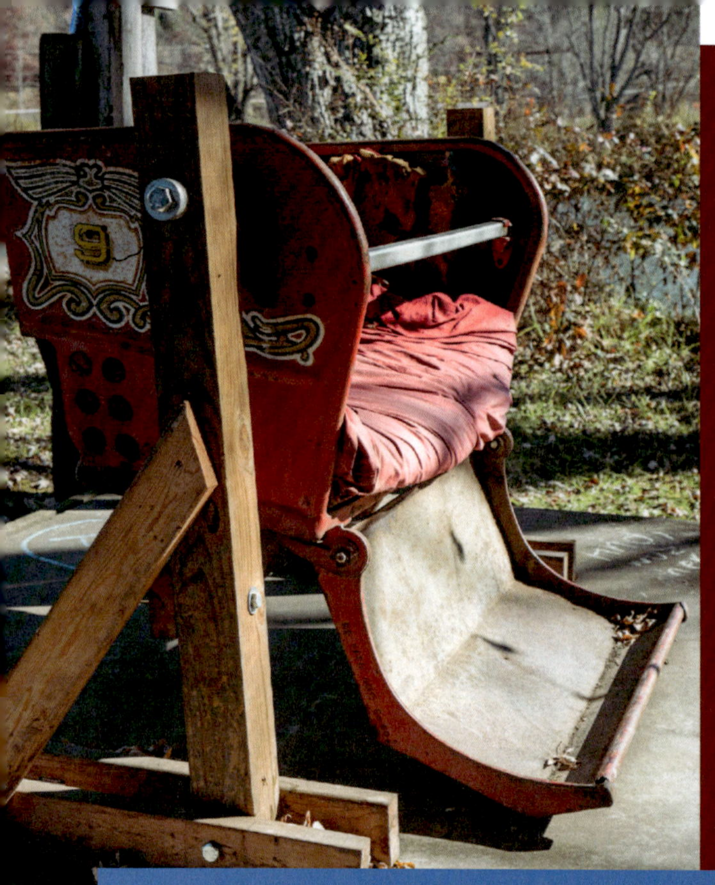

With so much tragedy connected to the property over many decades, is it any wonder some people call it cursed? Whether or not you believe in ghosts or the paranormal, the juxtaposition of macabre history with the fun, carefree spirit of carnival and amusement is enough to send shivers up the spines of even the most skeptical visitor.

This Appalachian retreat has thrilled visitors for nearly a century, both as a functional amusement park and after. It has consistently played host to curiosity seekers looking to catch a glimpse of the ghosts of children rumored to play around the lake. TV shows like *Ghost Lab*, *Scariest Places on Earth*, *Most Terrifying Places in America*, and *Portals to Hell* have made this destination famous around the world.

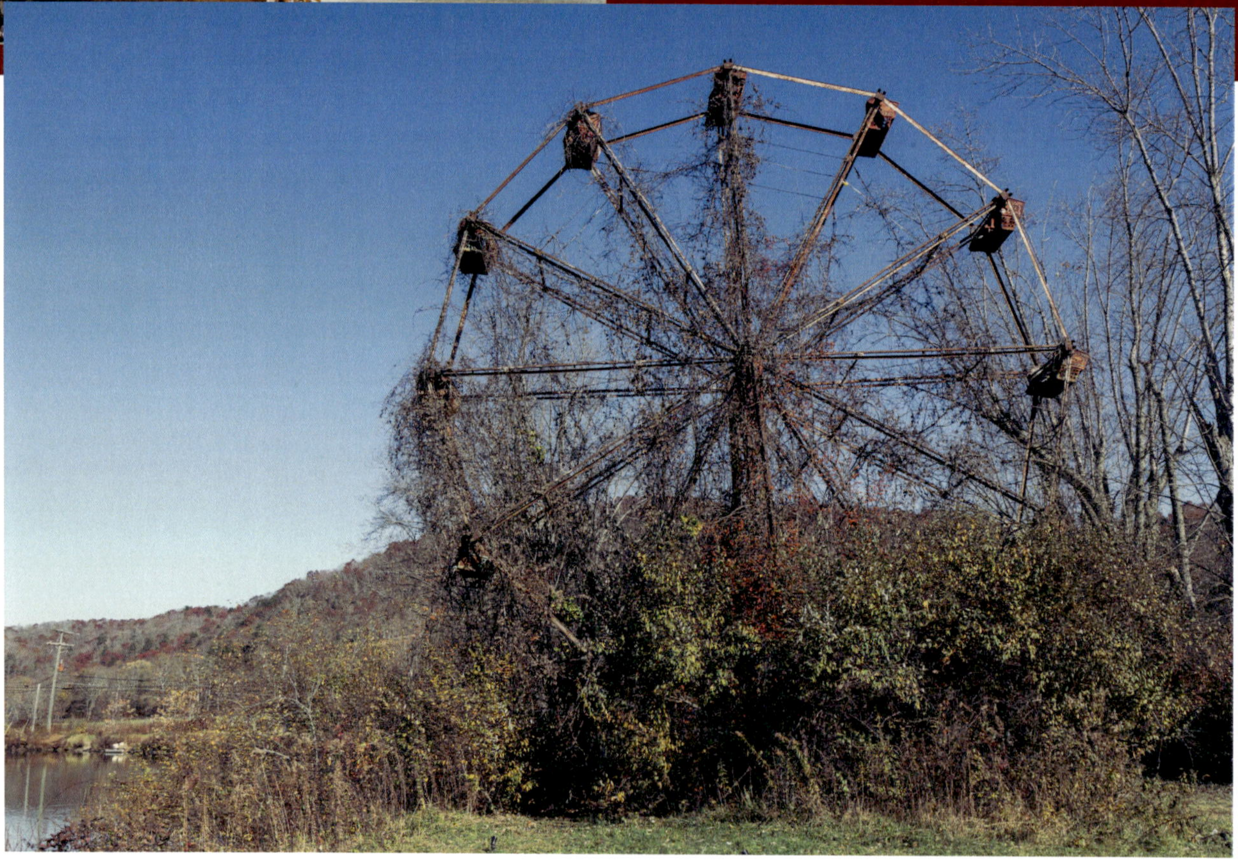

Lake Shawnee's rusted Ferris wheel has become iconic on its own, with numerous photos appearing on the Internet. Low-angle photography exaggerates the size (it's actually quite small).

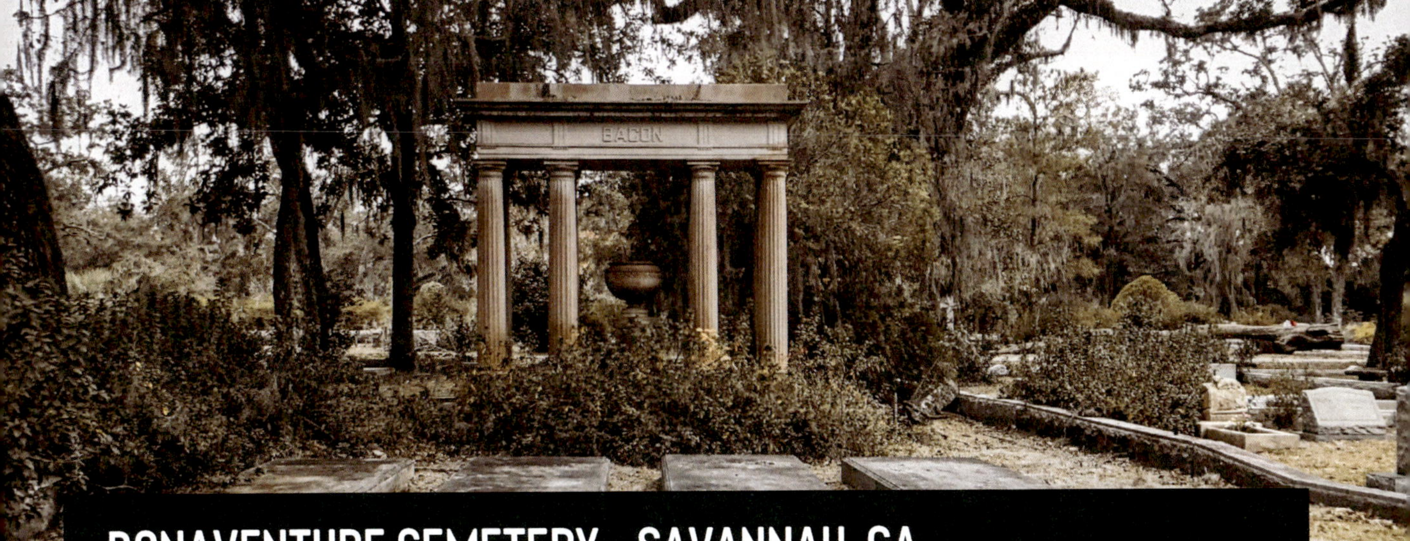

BONAVENTURE CEMETERY - SAVANNAH, GA

Live oak trees adorned with Spanish moss line the roadways of an old and neglected necropolis. Ferns engulf mournful statues, while branches lay where they fell. Bonaventure Cemetery is a setting made for dark romance and Gothic ghost tales. Its history and its legends have lured visitors for more than 170 years.

The haunting, picturesque scenery led one statue, called "Bird Girl," to appear on the cover of John Berendt's novel *Midnight in the Garden of Good and Evil* (1994). The subsequent popularity of the novel and movie starring Kevin Spacey and John Cusack made Bonaventure Cemetery a magnet for tourists.

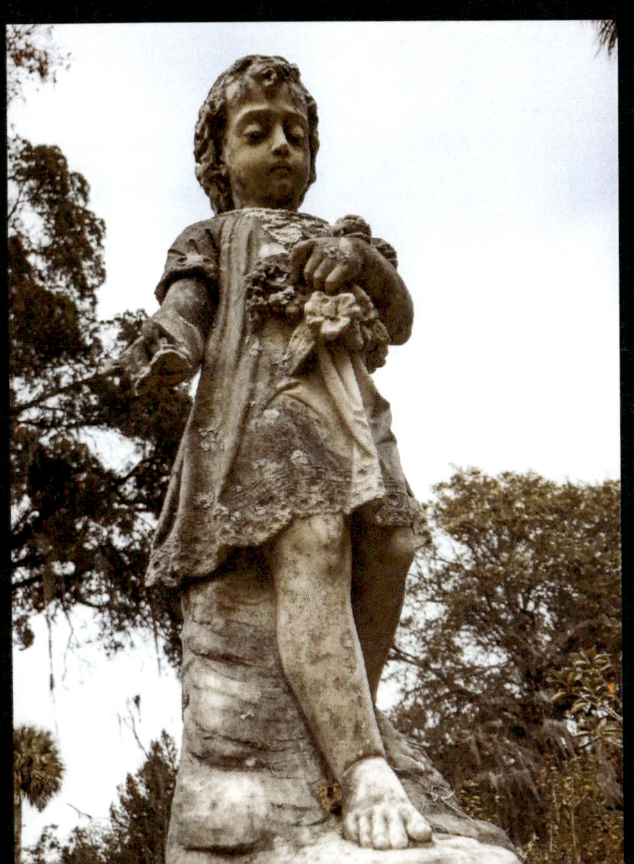

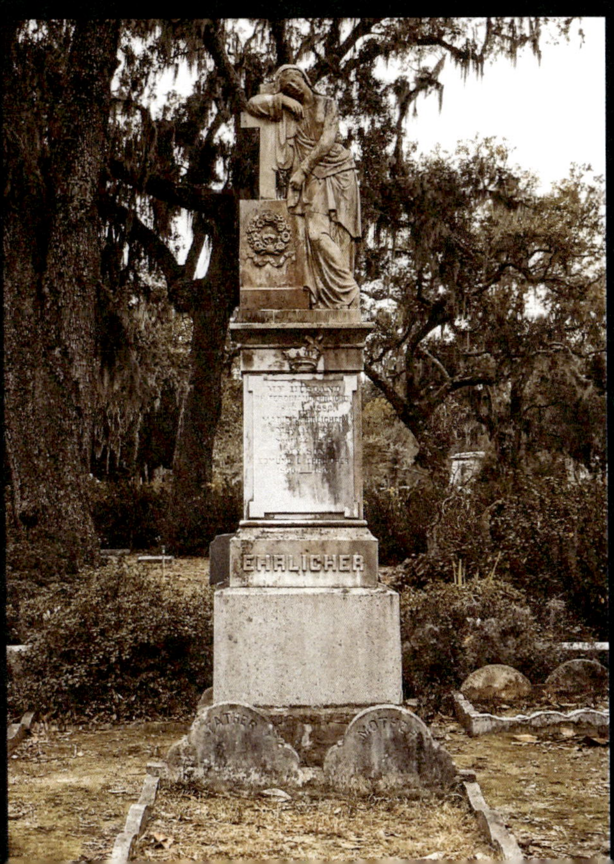

KORESHAN STATE HISTORIC SITE - ESTERO, FL

Deep in the pine flat woods of southeast Florida, a group of religious believers sought to build a new Jerusalem on the Gulf Coast. These followers of Dr. Cyrus Teed, called Koreshans, believed the earth and universe were contained within a concave sphere.

Cyrus Teed was born in 1839 in New York. He quickly gained an interest in science and medicine and opened a clinic in Utica. During one of his experiments, he was electrocuted and claimed a divine spirit had told him that he was the Messiah. He changed his name to Koresh and began to gather followers.

Dr. Teed and his followers settled near Estero, Florida in 1894. At its peak, their New Jerusalem was home to 250 people. Today, it is a ghost town maintained as the Koreshan State Historic Site. The last resident of the Koreshan Unity died in 1981. What remains of their community is a wonderful place to visit along the Gulf Coast. Just, perhaps, not after dark.

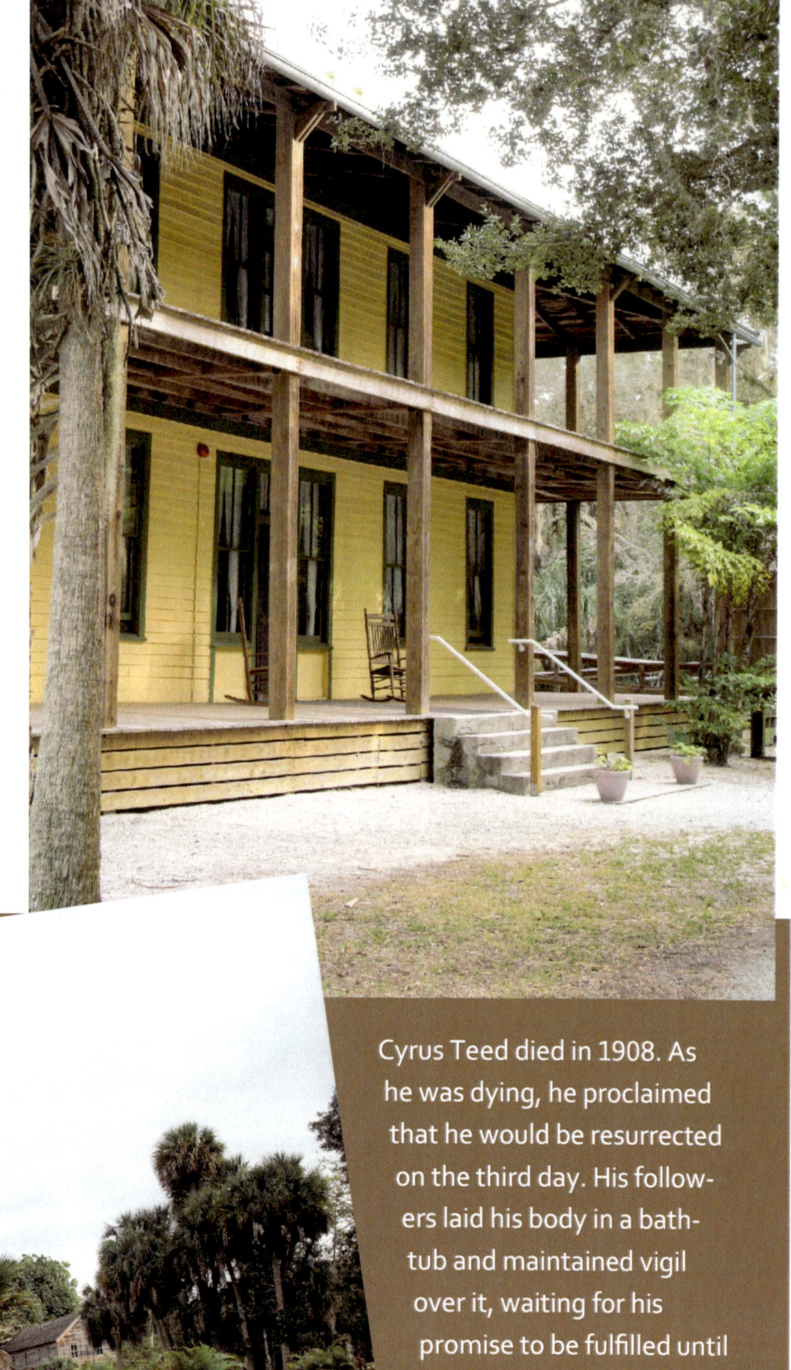

Cyrus Teed died in 1908. As he was dying, he proclaimed that he would be resurrected on the third day. His followers laid his body in a bathtub and maintained vigil over it, waiting for his promise to be fulfilled until county health inspectors insisted they bury his rapidly decomposing body.

IRAQ

The Republic of Iraq has a long history stretching back millennia. Its capital, Baghdad, was founded in AD 762, a thousand years before the United States was even conceived by our Founding Fathers. As a specialist in the U.S. Army, 2-22 Infantry Battalion, I was deployed to Iraq for roughly nine months from the fall of 2015 to summer of 2016 to support the fight against the Islamic State of Iraq and Syria (ISIS).

Saddam Hussein and his secular socialist Ba'ath Party ruled Iraq from 1979 to 2003. We fought two wars against his regime: the Gulf War (1990–1991) and the Invasion of Iraq in 2003. I was in college during the Invasion of Iraq and didn't join the Army until 2014, but the physical, social, and political scars from that conflict remained. We battled a strong insurgency until 2011. Then, when ISIS (or Daesh as Arabs call them) seized large swaths of northern and central Iraq, we returned to help the new Iraqi government fight these enemies.

The Iraqi Ba'ath Party headquarters was located in a large building in central Baghdad, what became known as the Green Zone after U.S. troops occupied the capital. It was bombed in 1990 and 2003. Then, during the occupation, it was used as a barracks despite the destruction and debris. U.S. soldiers weren't allowed to stray far due to the volatile situation, but I did have the opportunity to explore this unique location.

In the end, the Iraqis were able to defeat ISIS and reclaim their country, though sometimes it seems like the next conflict is right around the corner.

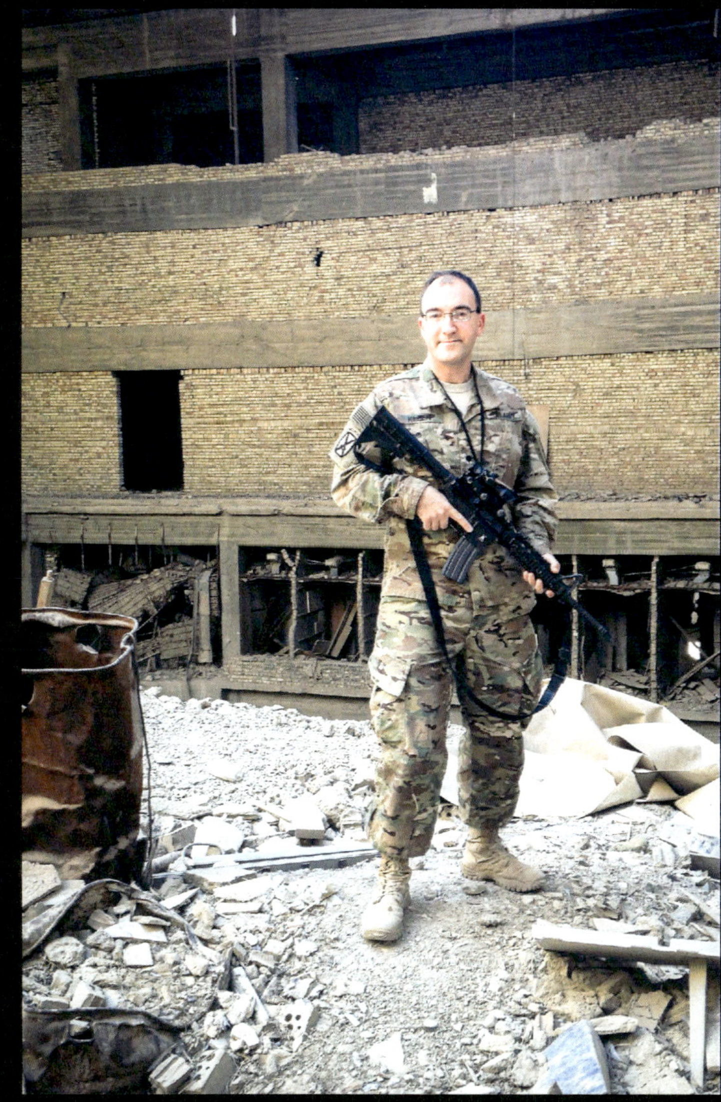

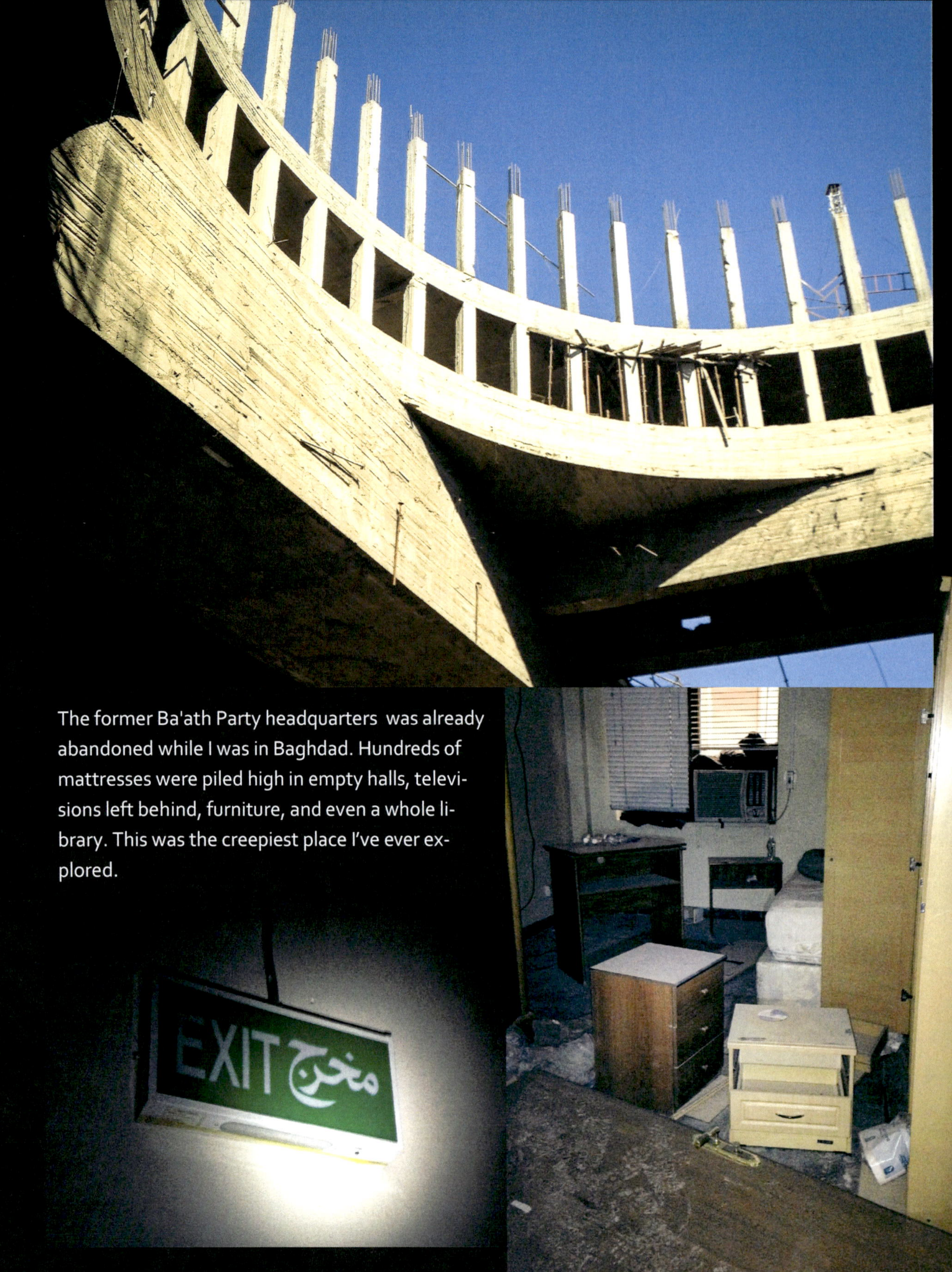

The former Ba'ath Party headquarters was already abandoned while I was in Baghdad. Hundreds of mattresses were piled high in empty halls, televisions left behind, furniture, and even a whole library. This was the creepiest place I've ever explored.

NEW YORK

I was stationed at Fort Drum in Upstate New York for three years, interrupted by one deployment to Iraq. In the same way most people think of Chicago when you tell them you're from Illinois, before I moved to New York, I imagined New York City. Yes, of course I was aware the state was enormous and much more than the five boroughs, but I wasn't prepared for the vast stretches of wilderness and wild beauty.

Whether it's the Finger Lakes, 1000 Islands, Adirondacks, or the Hudson Valley, New York State has thousands of square miles to explore. Its colonial history stretches back to the 1500s and its land was fought over by the Iroquois, French, British, and Dutch, and later, the American colonists. Remnants of these empires can be found in surprising places.

More modern ruins dot the landscape as well, all as unique as the far-flung regions of the Empire State itself. Ghost towns of the Adirondacks and decaying Catskill resorts equally excite the impulse to explore. For the most part, New Yorkers seem content to let the moldering structures lie, creating public parks around them or allowing them to simply decay, out of sight, out of mind. It's easy for these places to be swallowed up by the vast acreage.

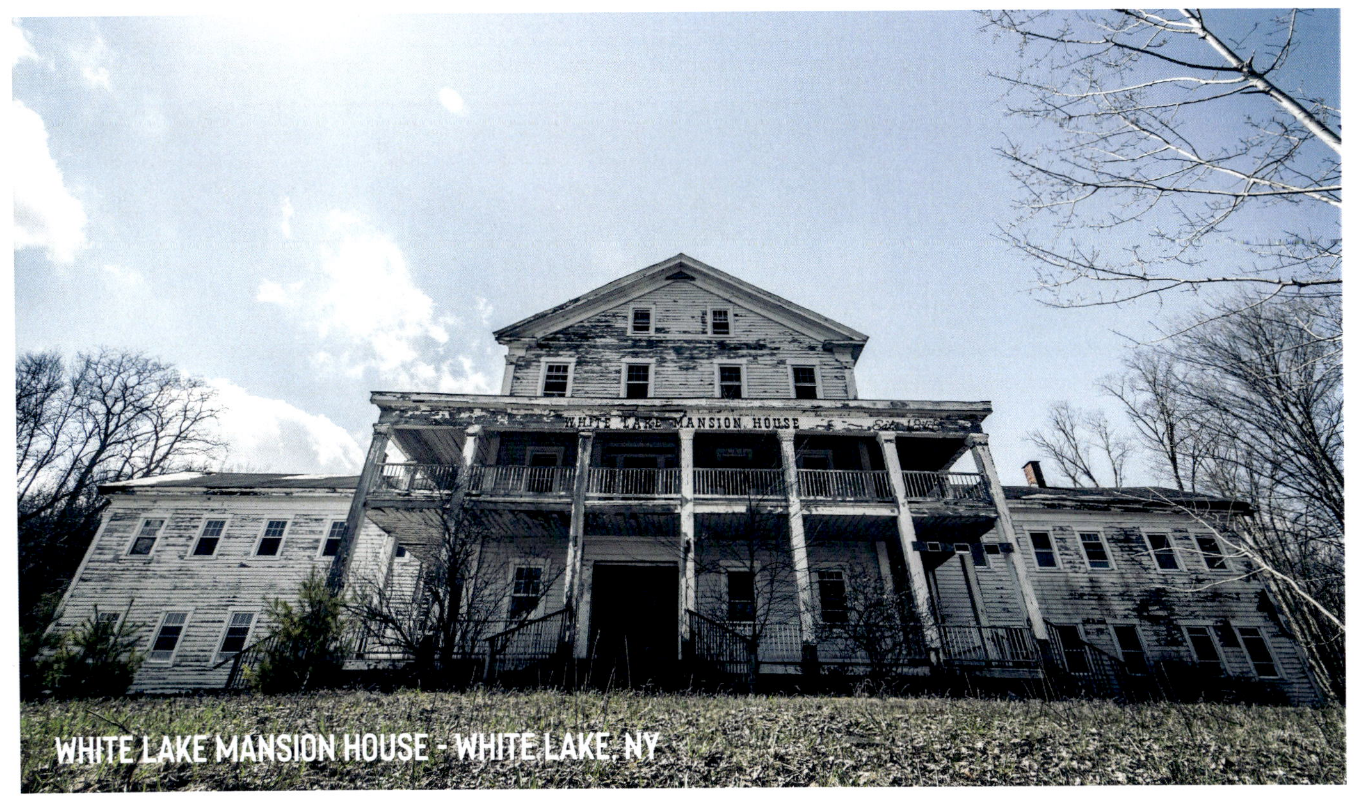

WHITE LAKE MANSION HOUSE - WHITE LAKE, NY

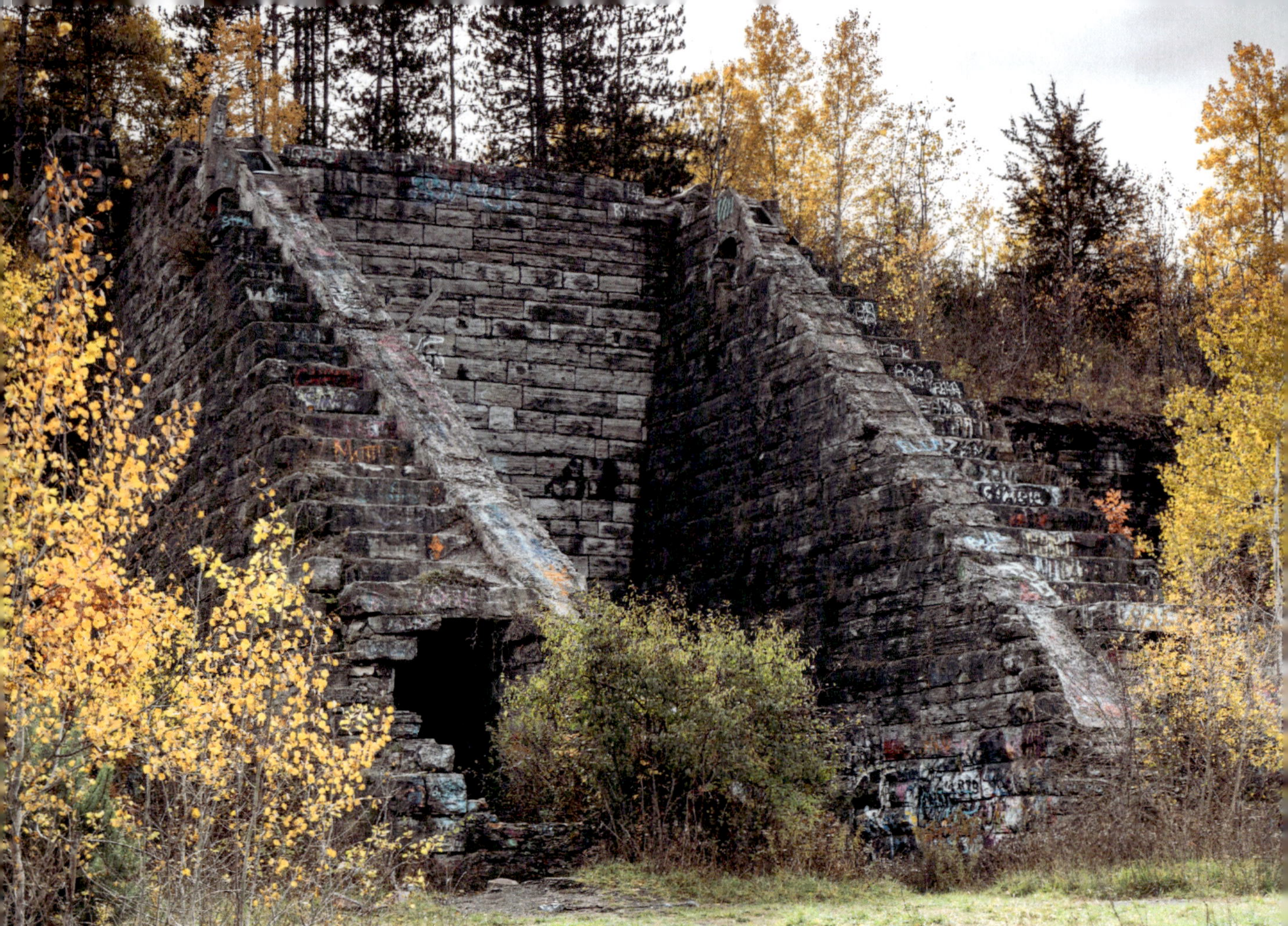

SPLIT ROCK QUARRY

On July 2, 1918, a terrible explosion at a munitions factory outside Syracuse, New York claimed the lives of more than 50 workers, injuring dozens more. Fifteen men were incinerated beyond recognition and over 20 reported missing and presumed dead. Today, Split Rock Quarry is largely abandoned, taken over by hikers, urban explorers, curiosity seekers, and partiers.

Evidence of late night excursions abound. Dark, graffiti-covered tunnels excite the imagination. This sinister reputation led the site to be featured on the Travel Channel's *Destination Fear* in October 2012.

Split Rock Quarry was originally built by the Solvay Process Company, founded in 1880. It manufactured soda ash through the Solvay Process, which combines salt brine and limestone. The limestone was quarried at Split Rock near Onondaga, New York and pulverized in a giant rock crusher.

During World War I, the company was involved in making TNT for munitions for the U.S. government. It was engaged in that effort when it exploded. Though the victims were not killed in battle, their service to this country and to the war effort was just as important as the soldiers fighting at the front lines.

Since its closure, some visitors have reported strange encounters in the abandoned quarry at night. Eyewitnesses report strange lights and glowing green and yellow apparitions.

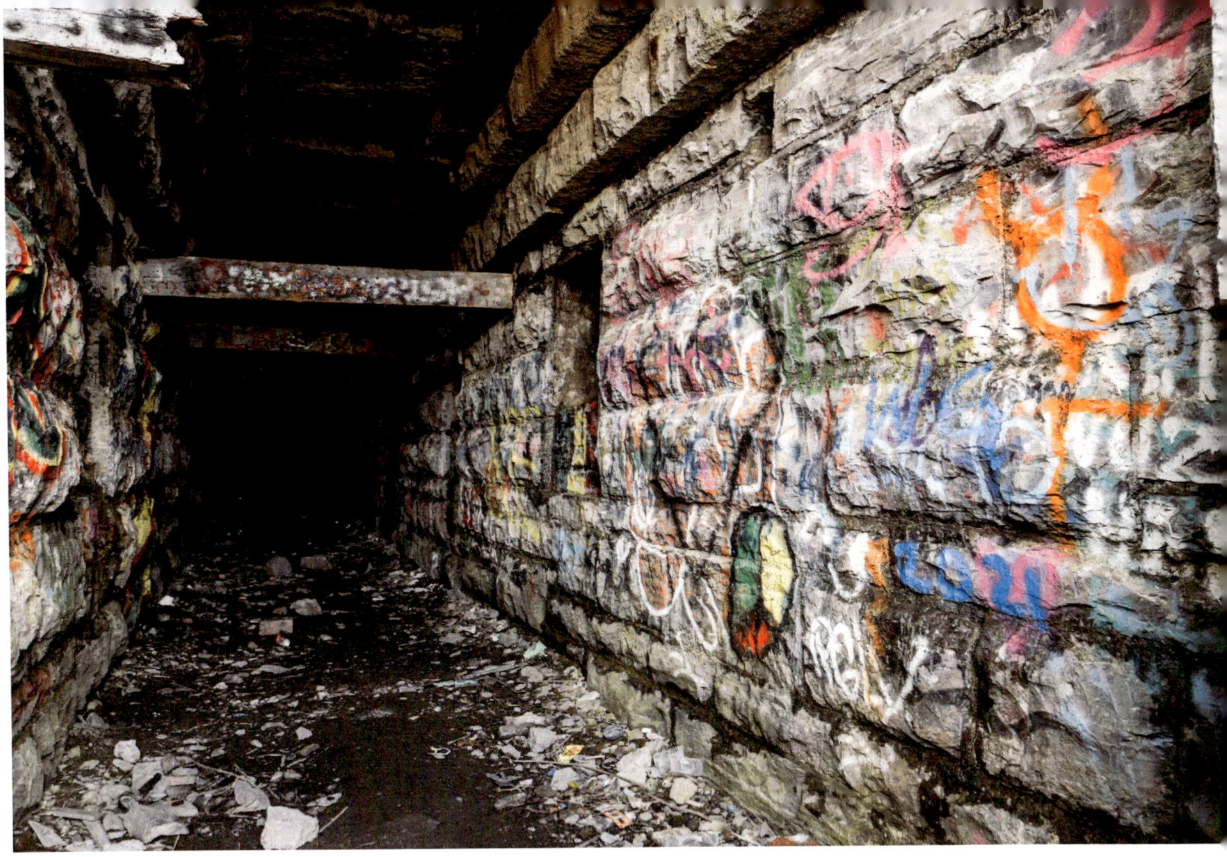

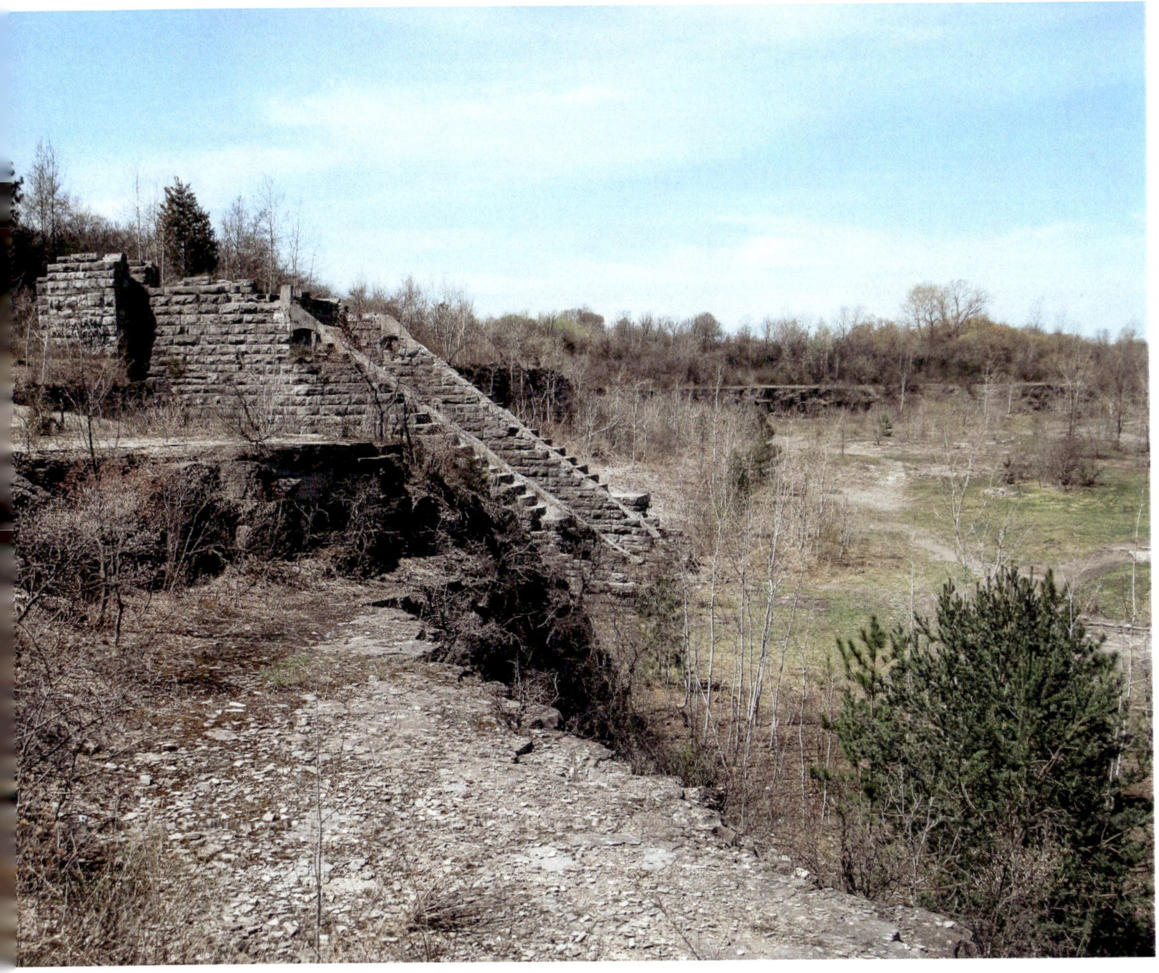

With its peaceful setting, it is easy to forget the tragedy that occurred here nearly a century ago. Please be respectful when visiting. This was, after all, the final resting place for over 50 men.

MACINTYRE IRON FURNACE - ADIRONDACK MOUNTAINS

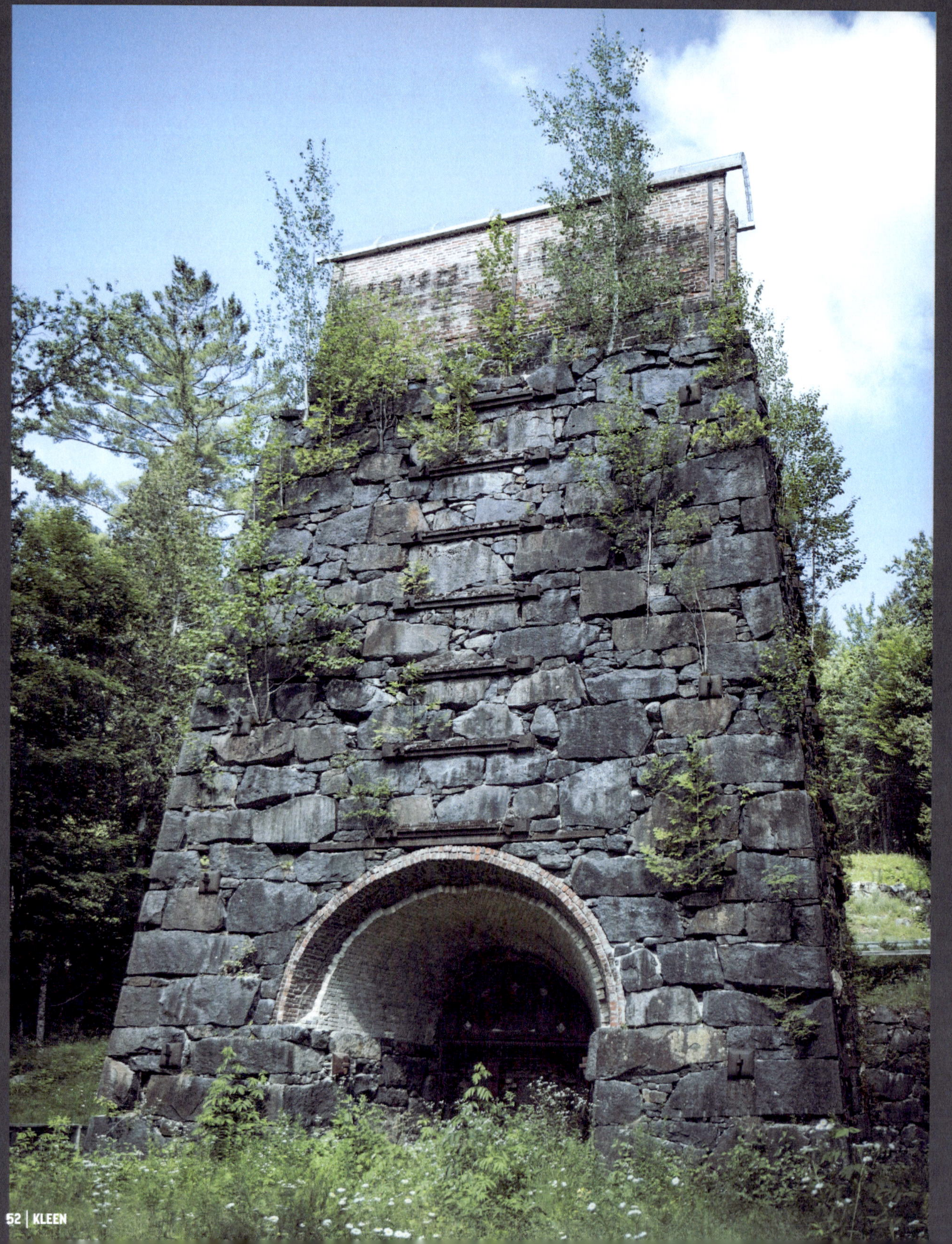

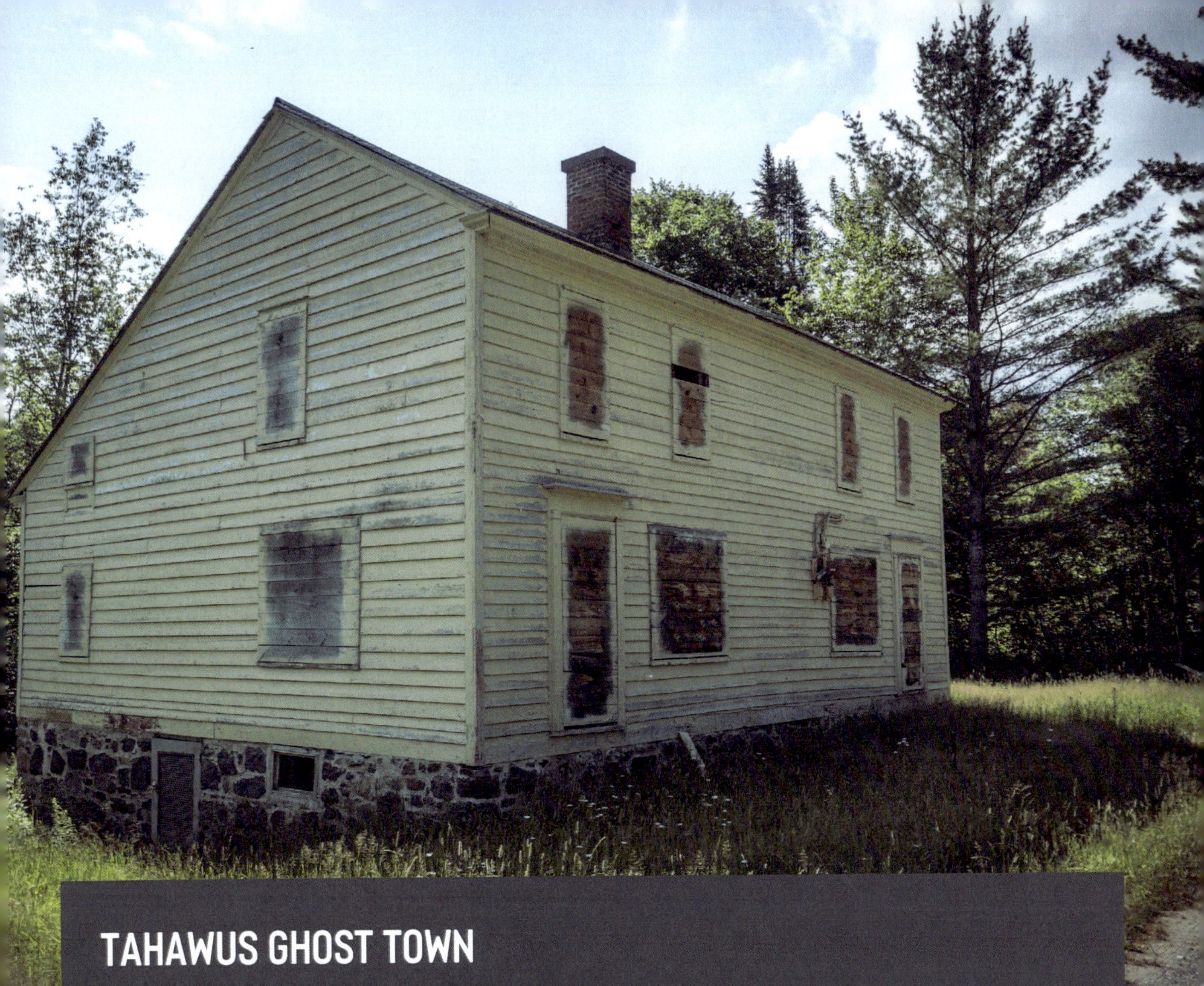

TAHAWUS GHOST TOWN

On September 6, 1901, Anarchist Leon Czolgosz shot President William McKinley in the stomach in Buffalo, New York. As McKinley lay in agony, Vice President Theodore Roosevelt, who was vacationing in Vermont, left to be at his side, but stayed with family at the Tahawus Club in the Adirondack Mountains along the way.

The Tahawus Club ruins can still be seen today, at the Upper Works Trailhead at the end of Upper Works Road (County Road 25) in Adirondack Park, Essex County, New York. The sportman's club was built on the ruins of an older town called Adirondac, which businessmen Archibald McIntyre and David Henderson built for their iron miners and lasted from 1826 to 1853. A titanium mine opened in 1940, and the newly christened town of Tahawus grew to over 80 buildings.

That mine closed in the 1980s, however, and the structures quickly deteriorated. Today, not much remains of this ghost town. Beautifully illustrated interpretive signs explaining the area's history have been erected at the site, and one building, called the MacNaughton Cottage, has been preserved.

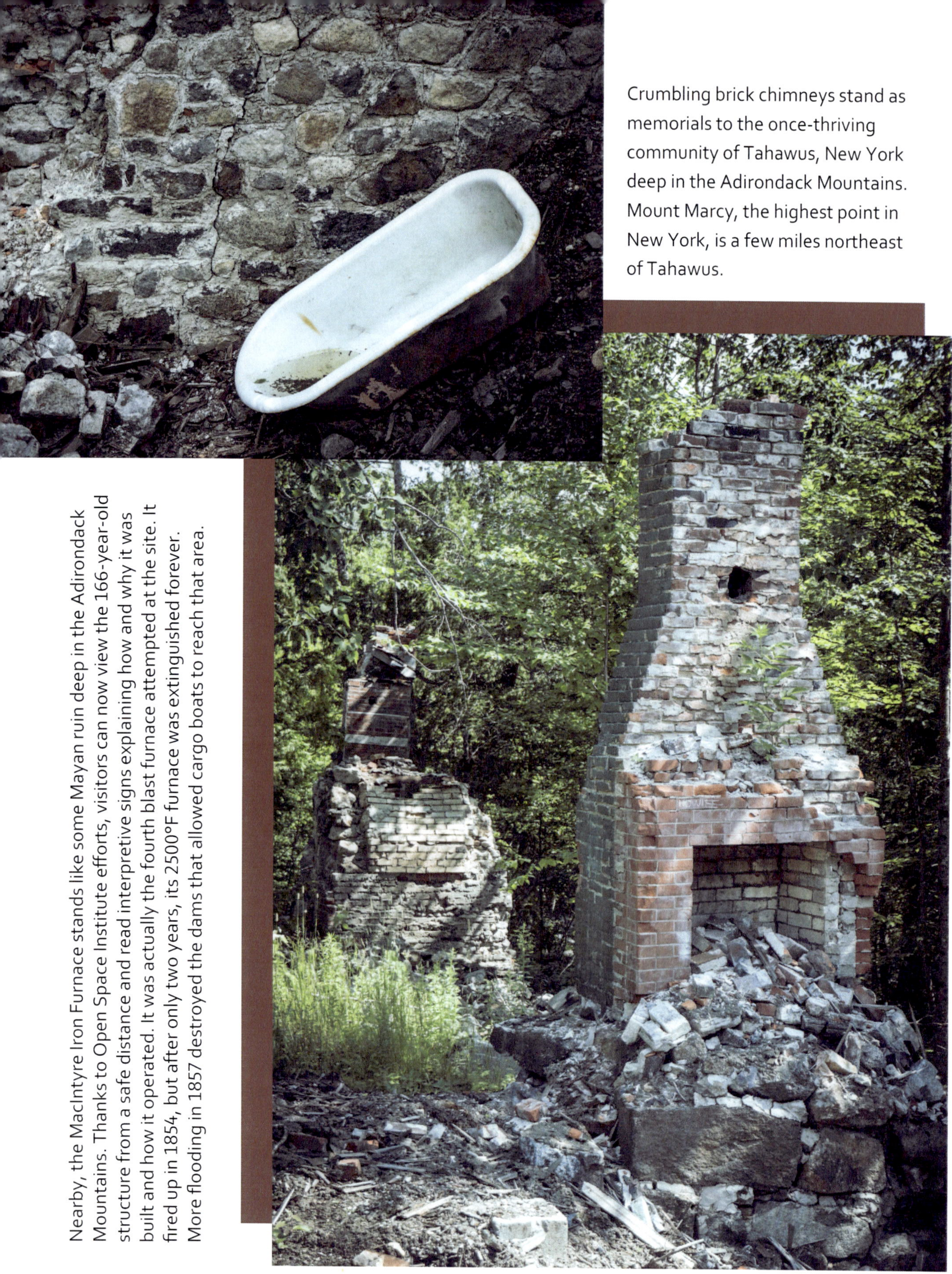

Crumbling brick chimneys stand as memorials to the once-thriving community of Tahawus, New York deep in the Adirondack Mountains. Mount Marcy, the highest point in New York, is a few miles northeast of Tahawus.

Nearby, the MacIntyre Iron Furnace stands like some Mayan ruin deep in the Adirondack Mountains. Thanks to Open Space Institute efforts, visitors can now view the 166-year-old structure from a safe distance and read interpretive signs explaining how and why it was built and how it operated. It was actually the fourth blast furnace attempted at the site. It fired up in 1854, but after only two years, its 2500°F furnace was extinguished forever. More flooding in 1857 destroyed the dams that allowed cargo boats to reach that area.

SHANLEY HOTEL

Built in 1895 and rumored to have been a brothel and speakeasy during Prohibition, the Shanley Hotel on Main Street in Napanoch, New York has gained a reputation for the unusual.

Napanoch is a hamlet in Ulster County, which straddles the Shawangunk Mountains and Hudson River Valley.

James and Beatrice Shanley bought the hotel in 1906 and welcomed many prominent guests, including Thomas Edison and Eleanor Roosevelt. Tragedy followed, however.

All three Shanley children died as infants, as well as the hotel barber's daughter and Beatrice's sister, who died of influenza. James Shanley died in 1937.

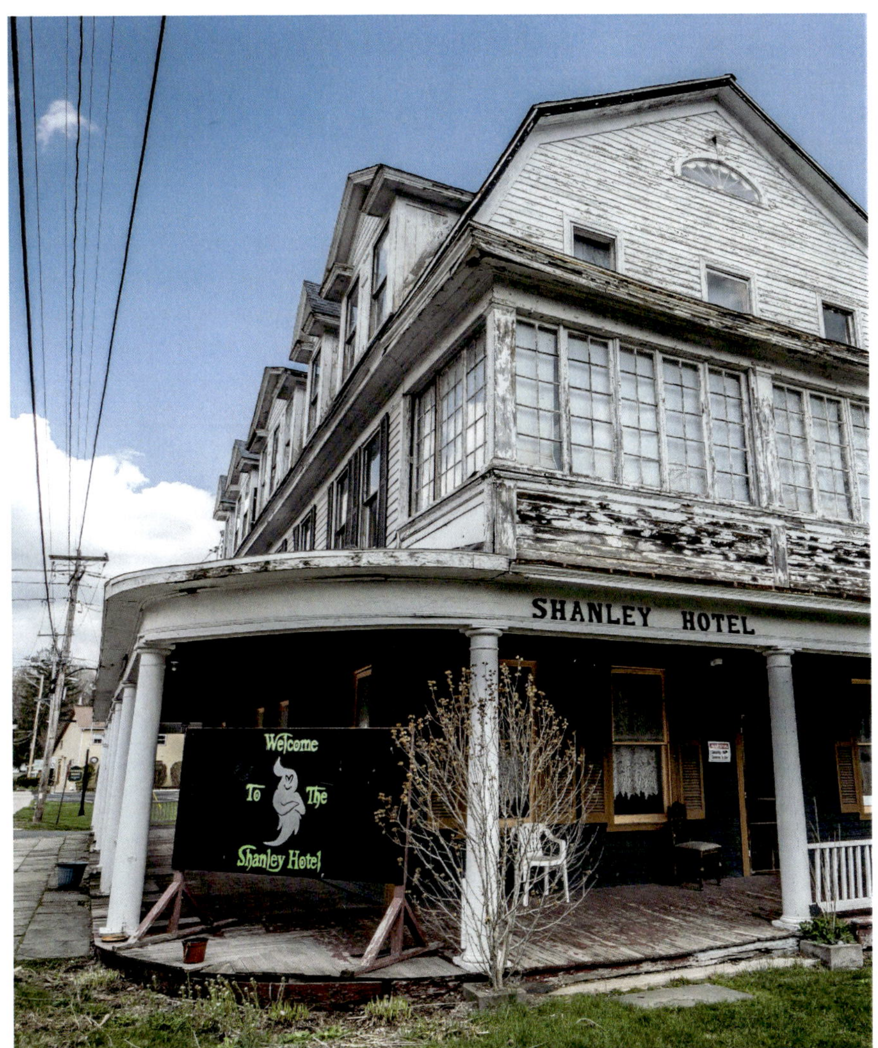

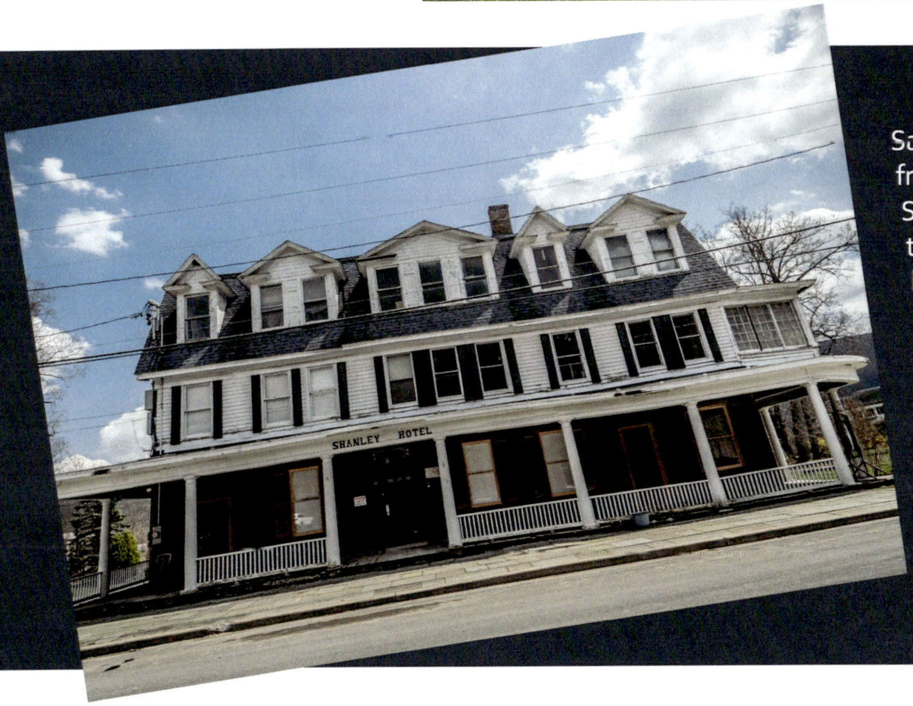

Sal Nicosia owned the hotel from 2005 to 2016, and his son Sal, Jr., has picked up the mantel. Since appearing on shows like *Ghost Lab* and *Ghost Hunters*, the Shanley Hotel has capitalized on the paranormal tourism market, offering special rates for paranormal investigations and marketing itself as a "haunted hotel."

BEECHWOOD STATE PARK

An abandoned Girl Scout camp deep in the woods is something straight from a horror movie, but you can experience these eerie ruins for yourself. Though it feels like trespassing, it's actually part of a public park enjoyed by thousands of visitors a year. Beechwood State Park, along the shore of Lake Ontario, is located about 20 miles east of Rochester, New York, near the small town of Sodus.

In 1929, the Girl Scouts of America purchased 150 acres between Maxwell Bay and Sill Creek for use as a summer camp. A bluff overlooking Lake Ontario, called Sprong Bluff, was an attractive focal point for gatherings. The camp had an in-ground pool, enclosed dining hall, sleeping cabins, and other amenities. Unfortunately, rising tax rates, declining membership, and environmental factors led to the camp's closure and sale in 1996.

New York State bought the land but budget cuts forced it to designate the site as a preserve. The buildings were left to rot. In 2010, a partial solution was found when the Town of Sodus took over management. The park has several miles of trails and is popular with hikers and fishermen, and also the curious who gawk at the camp ruins.

The former camp is remarkably well preserved for having been accessible to the public for over two decades. The presence of other visitors, often heard but not seen, adds to the eeriness. It's worth a detour if you ever find yourself near Rochester.

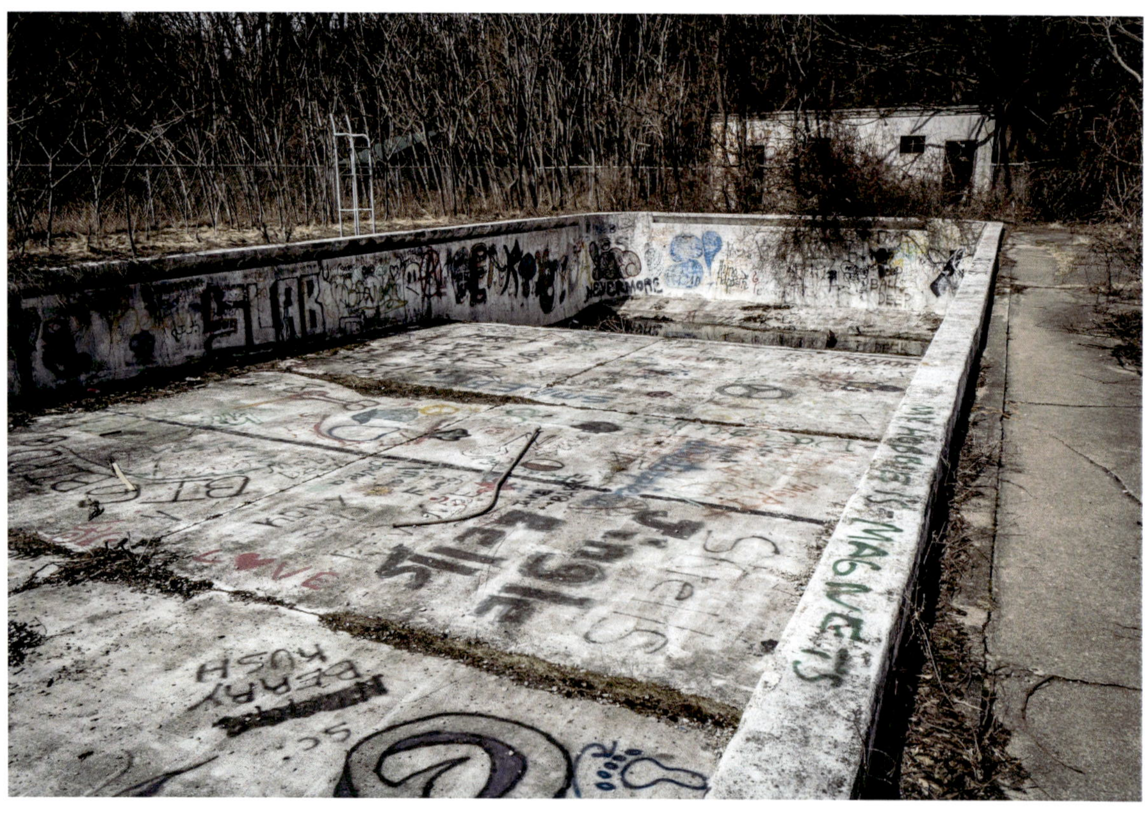

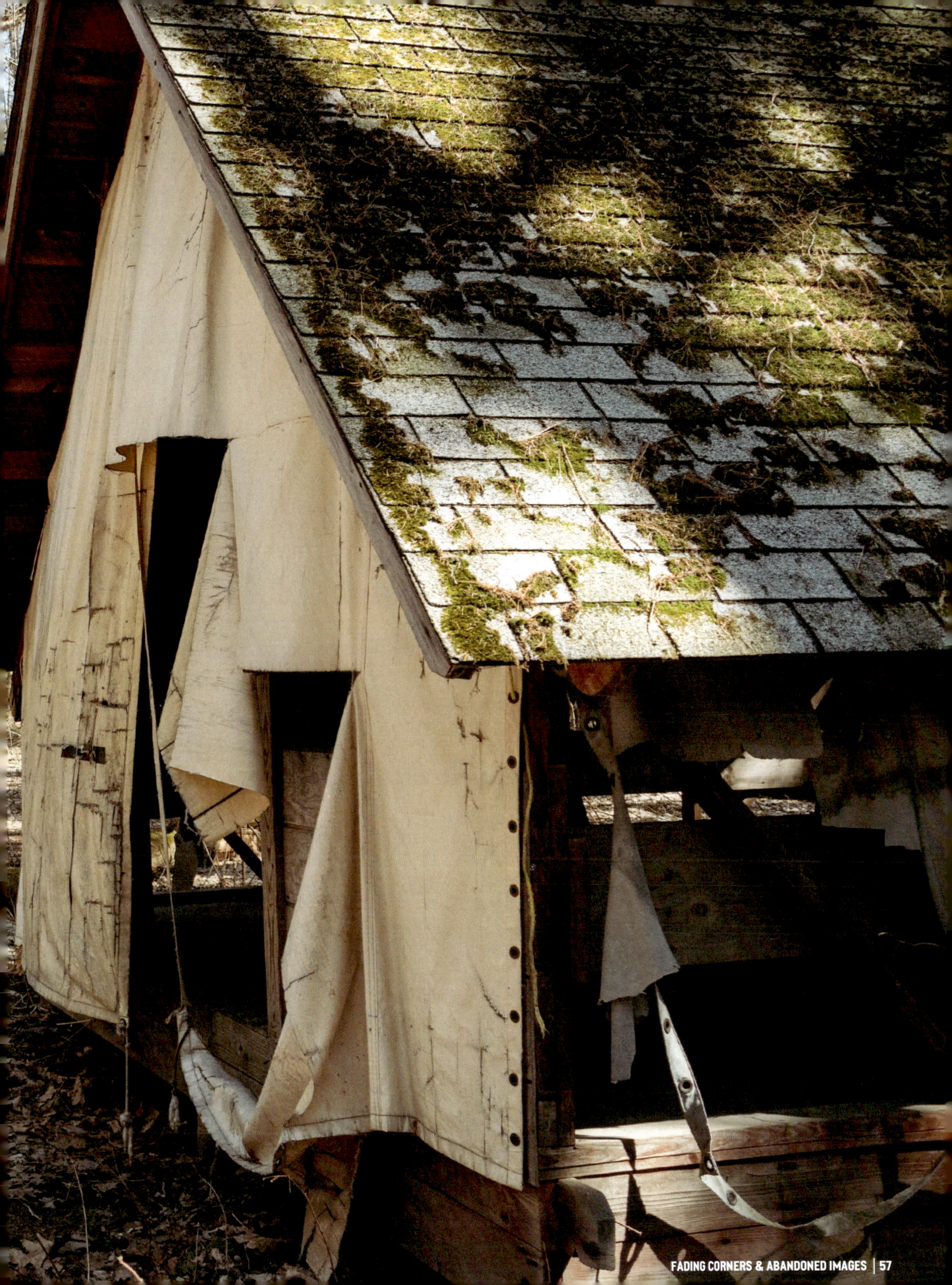

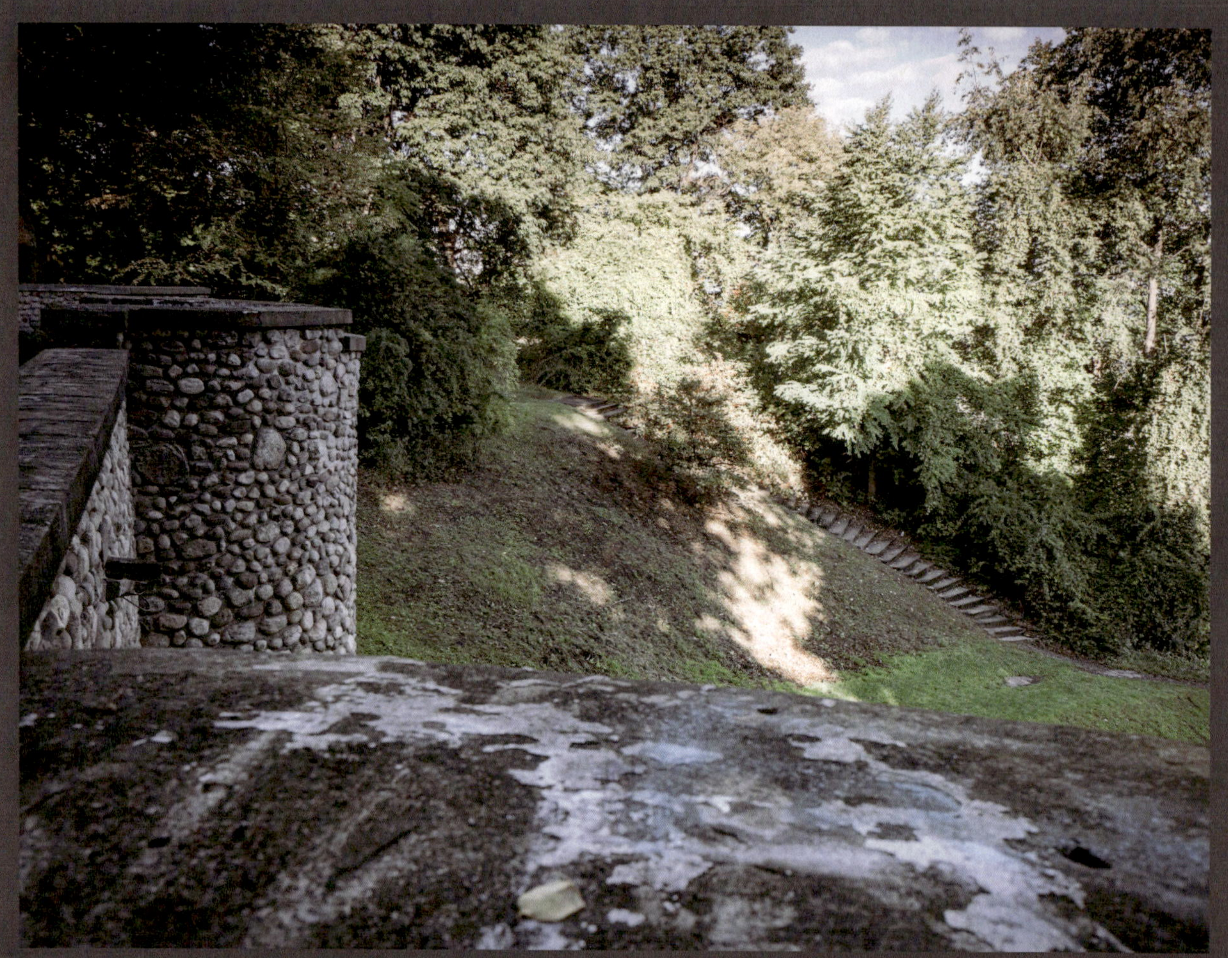

DURAND EASTMAN PARK

Ruins of a majestic mansion and sightings of an ethereal woman dressed in a flowing white gown are ingredients for a classic ghost story, so curious residents of Rochester, New York make furtive nighttime journeys to this park overlooking Lake Ontario, hoping to catch a glimpse of a phantom.

As legend goes, this medieval-looking stone wall was once part of a stately mansion on the hill, occupied by a reclusive woman and her beautiful daughter. The woman forbid her daughter from meeting with male suitors, so when her daughter went for a walk and failed to return home, she feared the worst. She leashed her two hounds and wandered the lake shore, searching for her missing daughter. Eventually, the woman died alone and her house fell into ruin.

She's been called the "Lady in White," "White Lady," or "Lady of the Lake."

The truth is much less romantic. This wall was part of an enclosed picnic shelter or dining room built for park visitors in 1911. The wooden structure burned down and was never rebuilt, leaving this stone wall and winding stone steps.

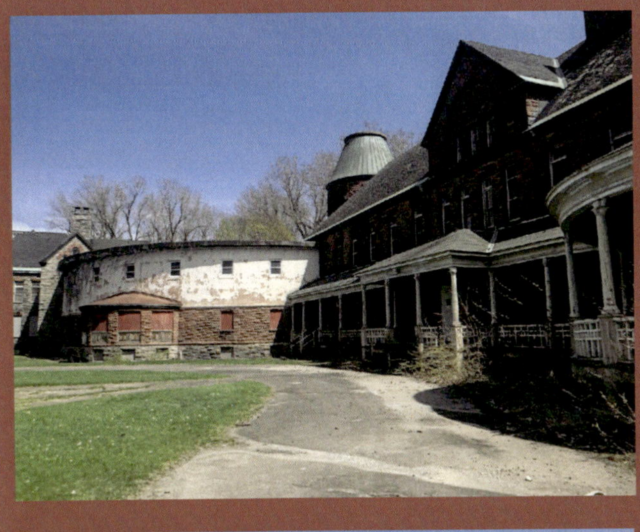

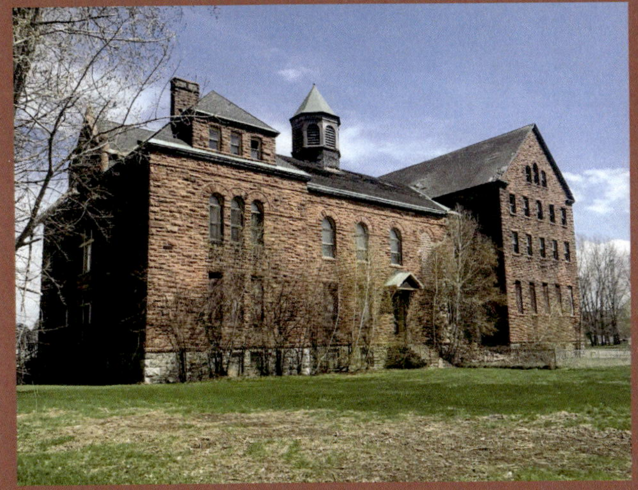

ST. LAWRENCE STATE HOSPITAL (1888-2023)

Closed in 1983, the St. Lawrence State Hospital in Ogdensburg, New York was an integral part of the local community for nearly a century. It treated thousands of mentally ill and disabled patients. Most of the hospital's old buildings were abandoned, but several were sold and opened as private treatment facilities and a NY state prison.

In 1886, a state commission selected Airy Point on the St. Lawrence River in Ogdensburg to build a "State Asylum for the Insane." Architect I.G Perry designed it in modern cottage plan. Construction began in 1888 and it opened two years later.

In 1958, St. Lawrence State Hospital became the second mental hospital in the country to have an "open door policy" when Director Dr. Herman Snow unlocked the wards so patients could freely walk the grounds. Few attempted to escape.

In late summer 2023, Ogdensburg announced it planned to demolish the historic buildings due to deteriorating and unsafe conditions.

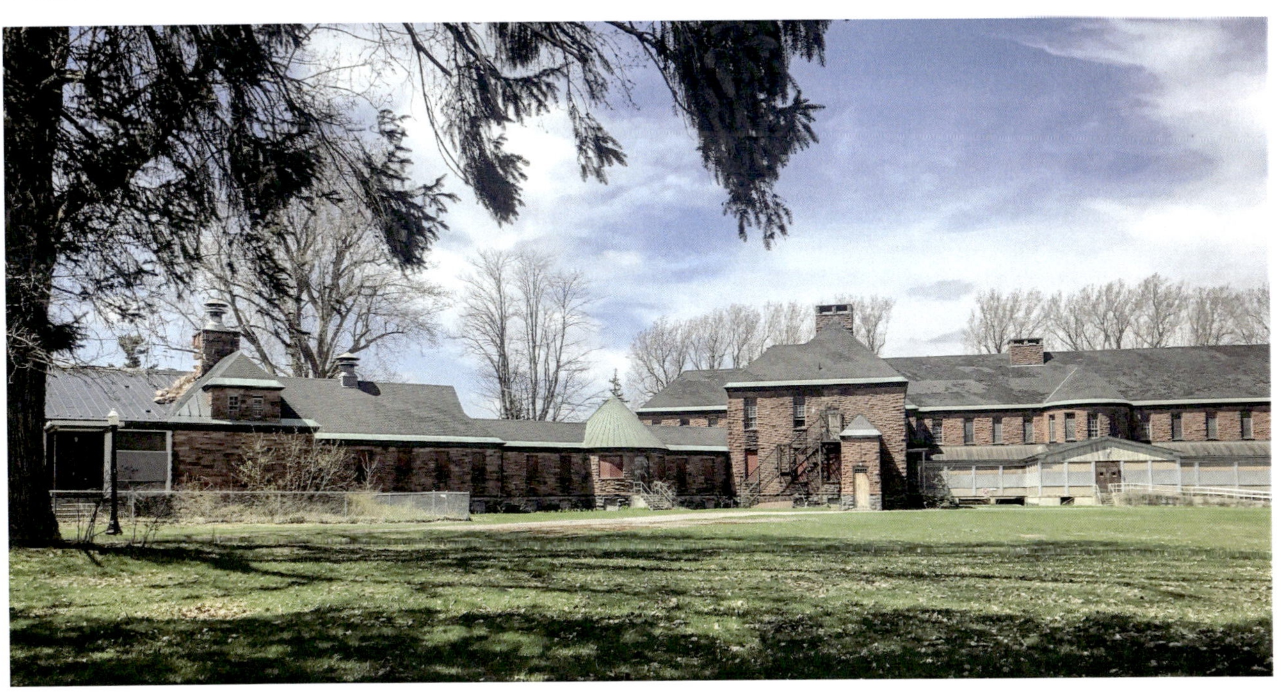

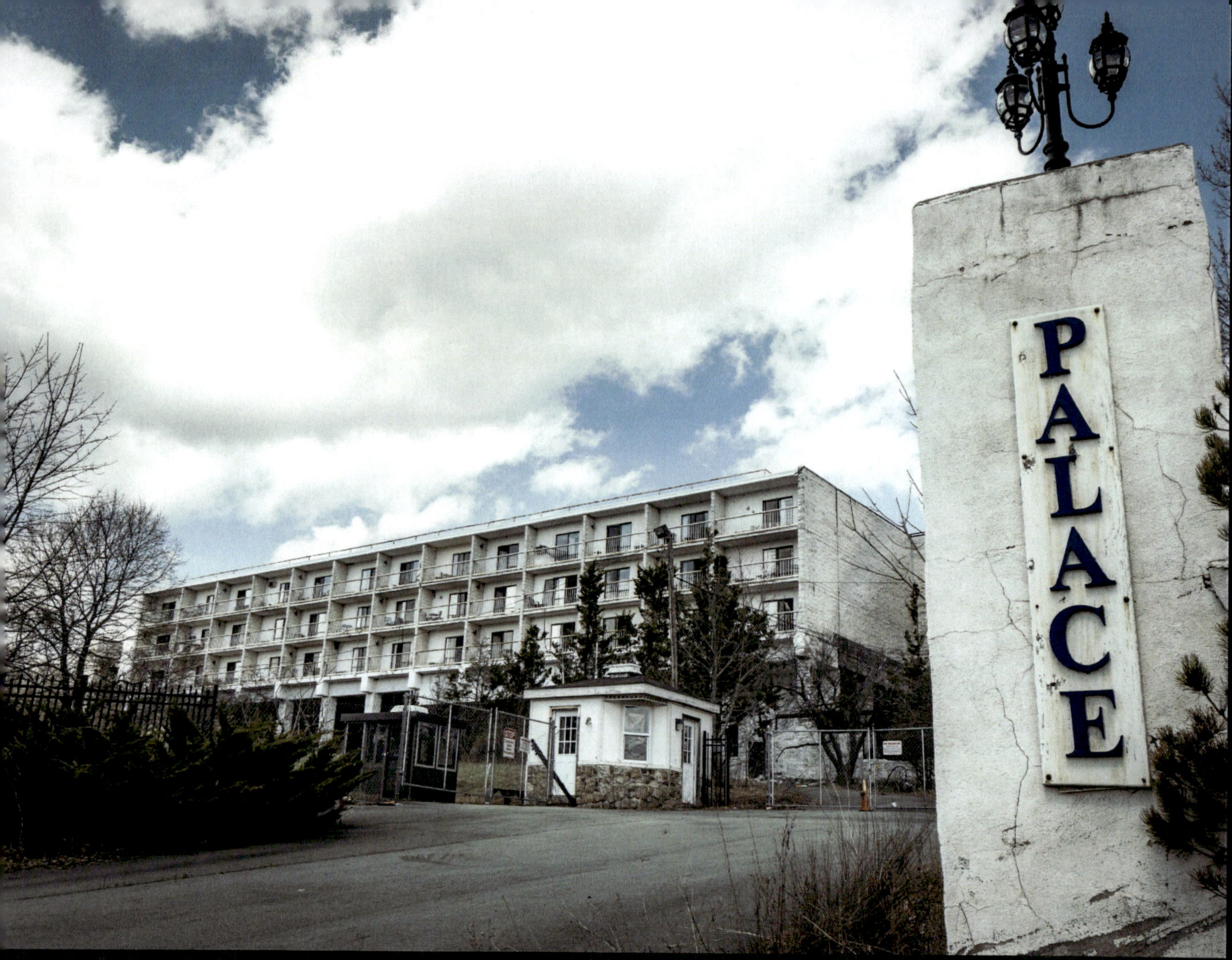

BORSCHT BELT - CATSKILLS

From the 1920s to the 1970s, New York City Jews flocked to Catskill Mountain resorts in the summer months to escape religious discrimination and the stifling heat of the city. There were once over 500 resorts and hotels in the area, known as the "Borscht Belt."

Grossinger's, the Shawanga Lodge, Overlook, and Concord Resort hotels all became legendary. Comedians like Mel Brooks, Rodney Dangerfield, Henny Youngman, and Don Rickles made their careers here. The movie *Dirty Dancing* (1987) was set at a fictional resort in the Catskills.

With increasing religious tolerance and the advent of widespread commercial airliners, many families chose to vacation elsewhere and dozens of these establishments now lay abandoned.

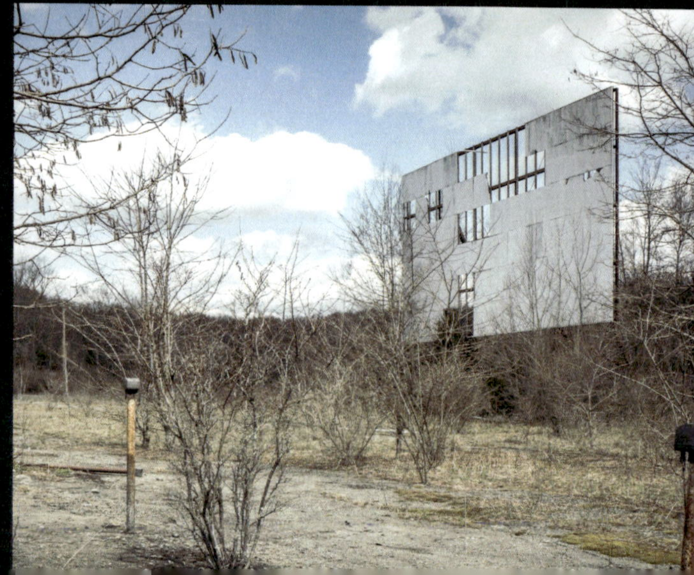

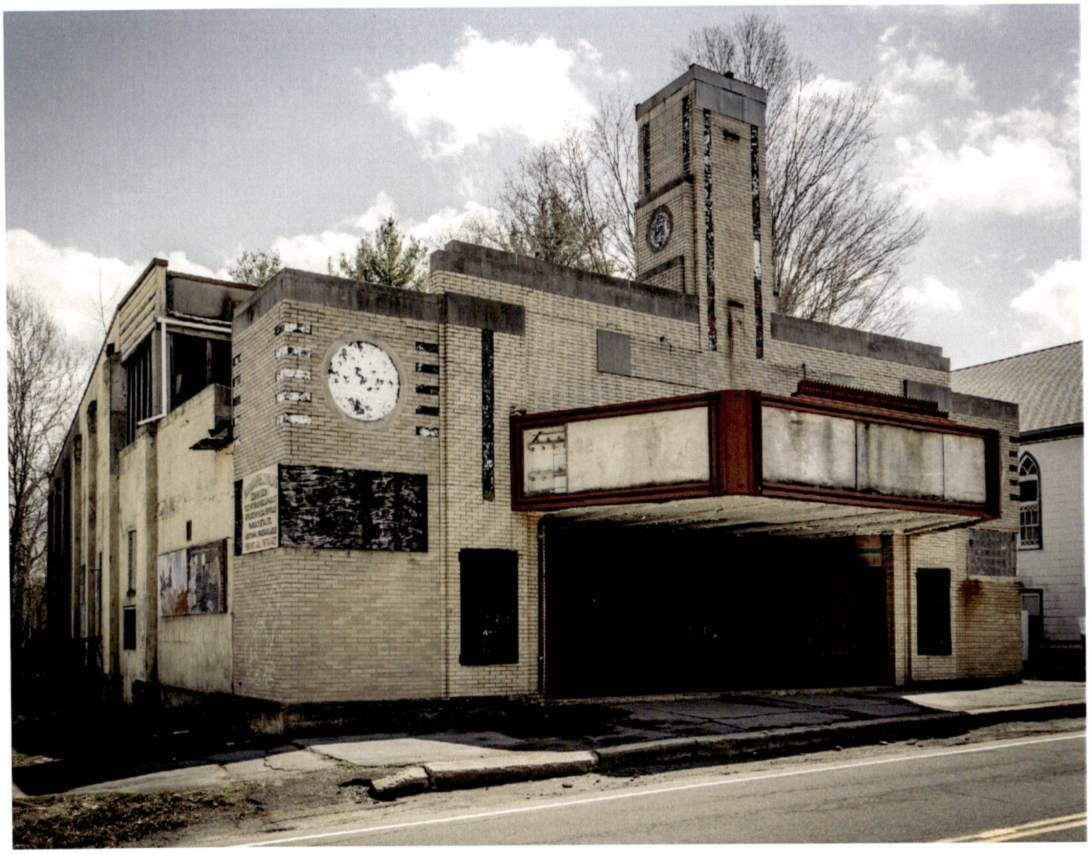

Designed by local architect Abraham H. Okun and built in 1938, this Art Deco theater in Woodbourne was added to the National Register of Historic Places in 2001. Also known as the Center Theatre or Peace Palace, it closed in the 1980s and has sat abandoned ever since.

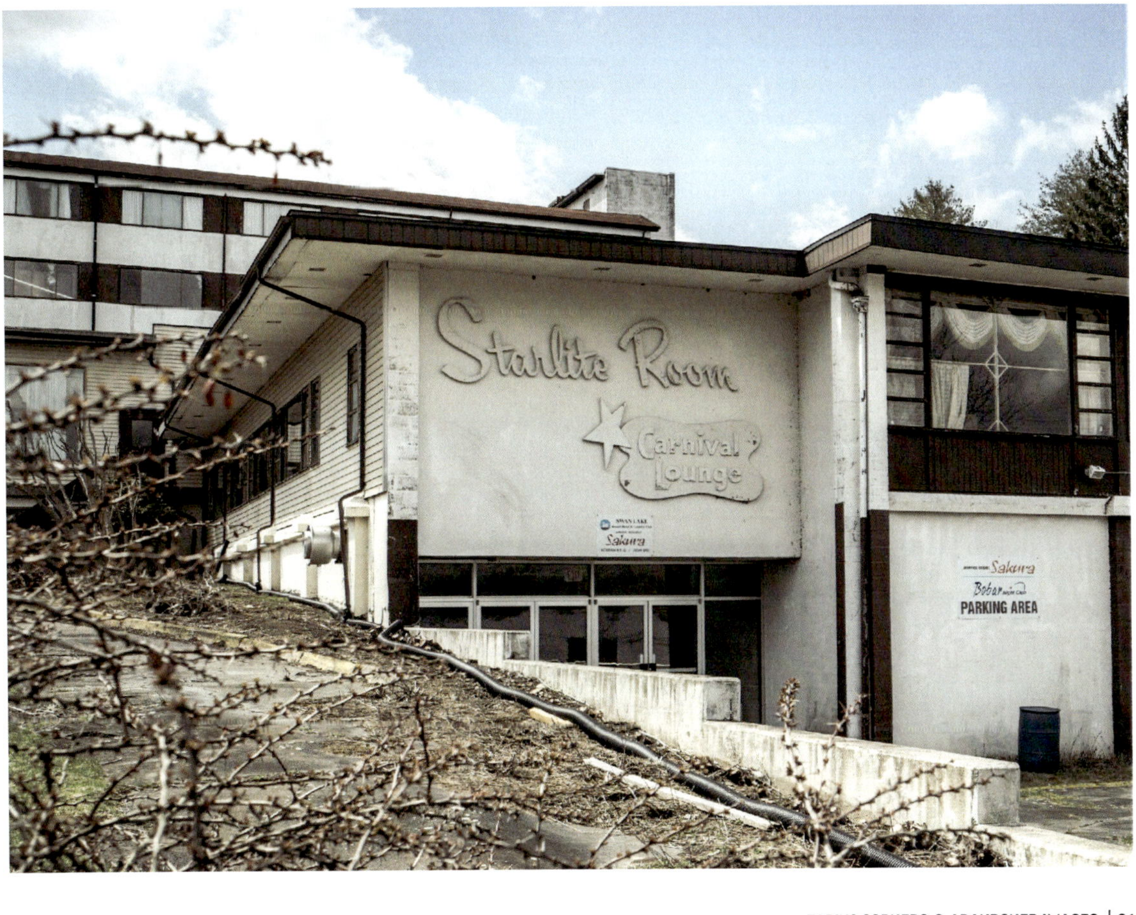

Also known as the Stevensville Hotel, Swan Lake Resort sits at 1626 Briscoe Road in Swan Lake, south of Liberty, New York. An Orthodox Jewish group purchased it in 2015.

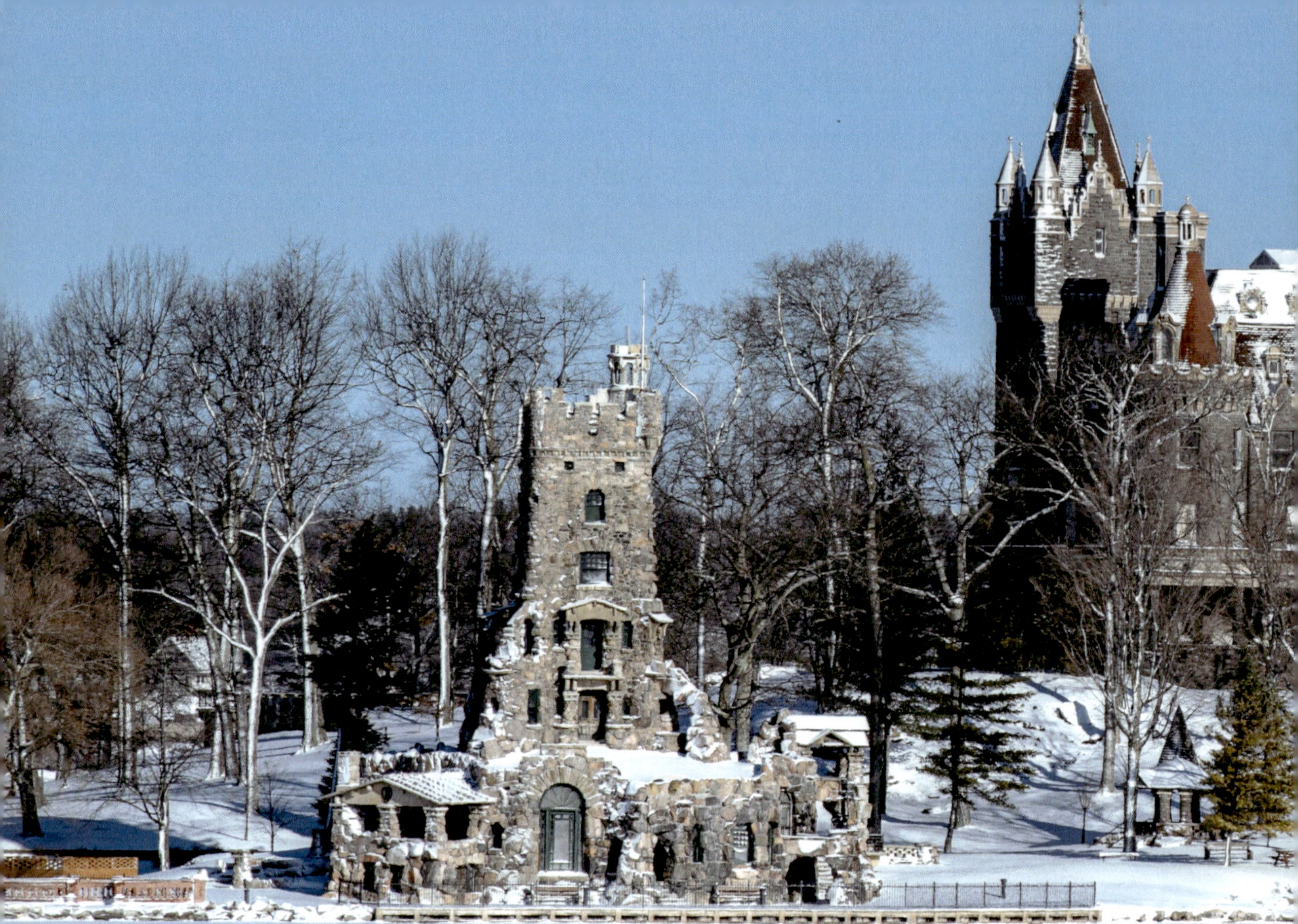

BOLDT CASTLE

The stone walls of a majestic castle rise above the waters of the St. Lawrence River across from Alexandria Bay, NY, creating a romantic visage on tiny Heart Island. Today a major tourist destination, for decades the structure sat abandoned to vandalism and decay.

In 1900, George Boldt, general manager of the Waldorf-Astoria Hotel in New York City and manager of the Bellevue-Stratford Hotel in Philadelphia, began construction on this six story, 120-room castle. It was to be a grand tribute to the love of his life, Louise Kehrer Boldt.

Tragically, Louise Boldt died suddenly in January 1904. Heartbroken, George Boldt sent workers at the castle a telegram telling them to cease construction immediately.

For the next 73 years, the partially-completed castle sat empty and abandoned, left to the mercy of vandals and the elements. Boldt died in 1916. In 1977, the Thousand Islands Bridge Authority bought Heart Island and agreed to commit all proceeds from tours and events toward its restoration.

Today, much of the structural damage has been reversed, and the ground floor is beautifully furnished. The upper floors, however, have been left in a state of disrepair as they would have appeared in the 1970s. Ferries and tour boats bring hundreds of visitors to the island every day.

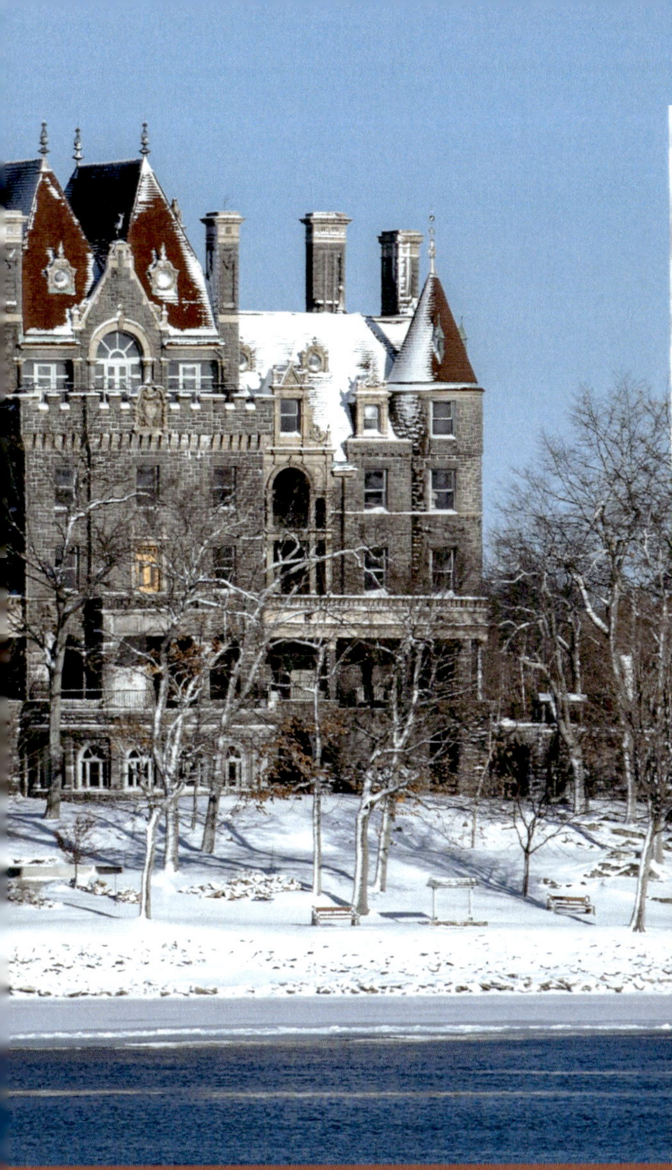

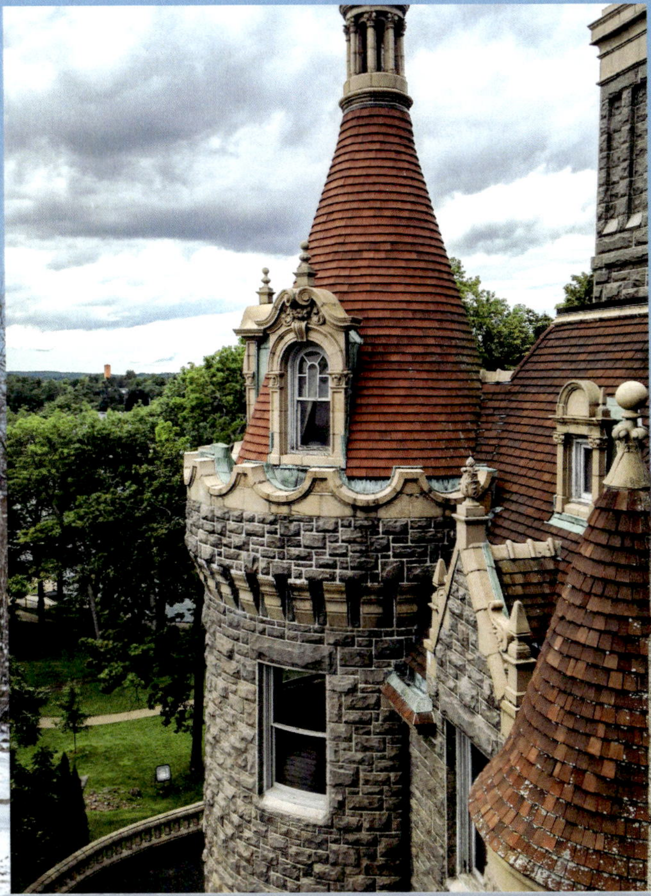

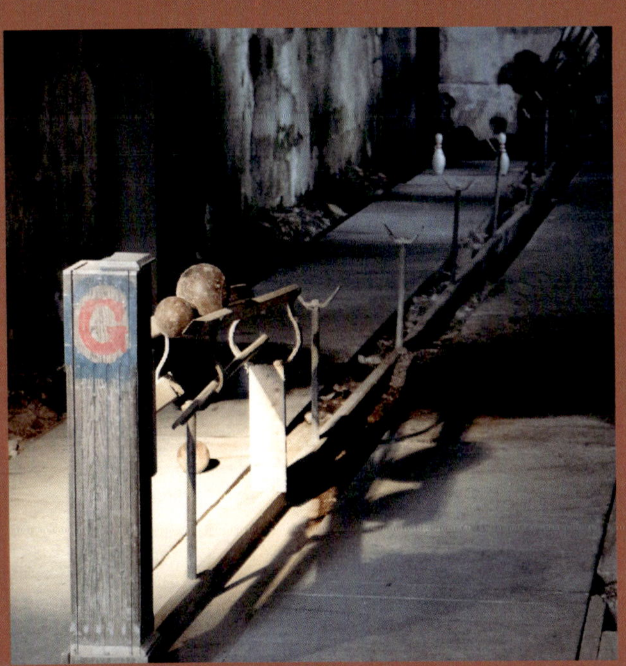

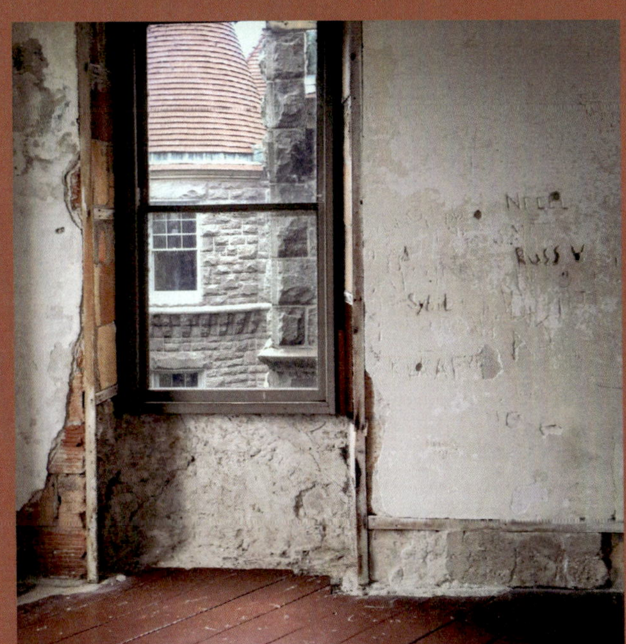

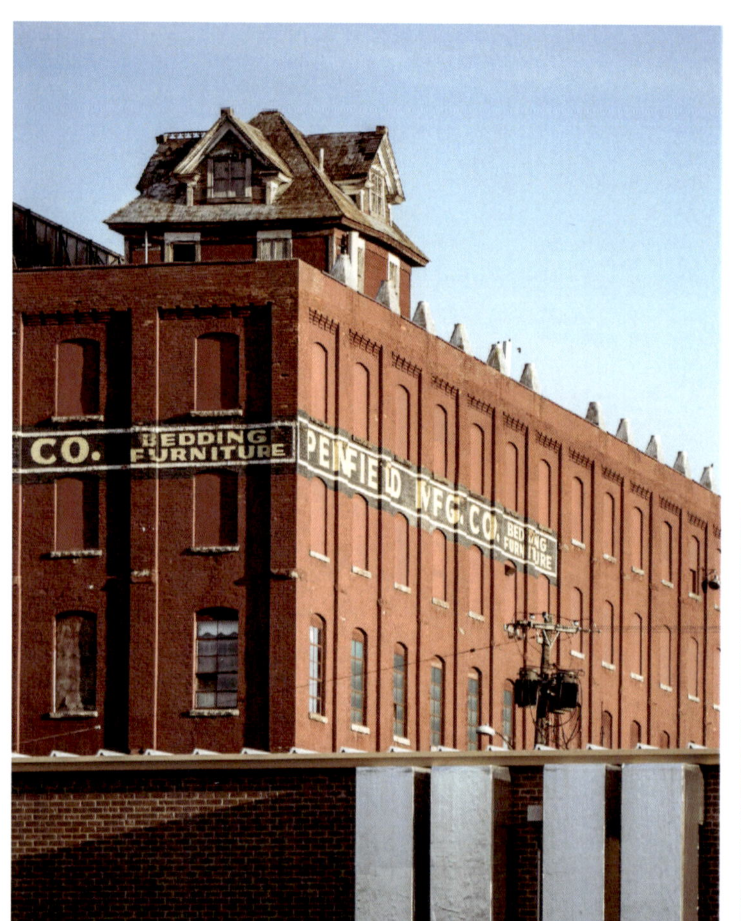

HOUSE IN THE CLOUDS - SYRACUSE

This two-story house atop the former Moyer carriage and car factory, 1710 N Salina Street in Syracuse, New York, was built by Harvey Moyer as a gimmick to attract attention to his business. The weathered facade hides the motor that powers the building's freight elevator. The factory was later owned by the Porter-Cable Machine Company and then the Penfield Manufacturing Company.

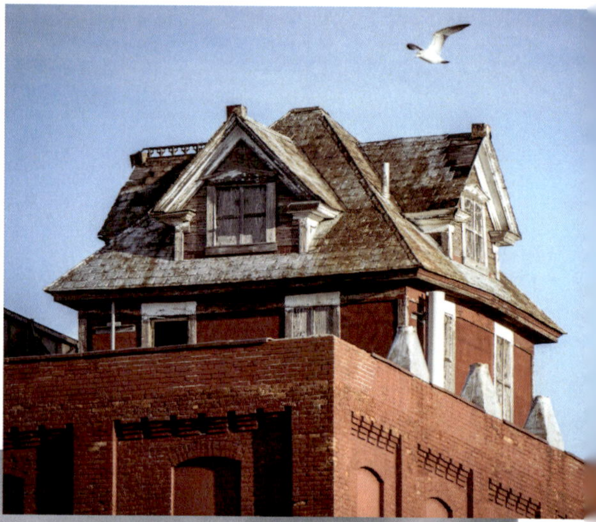

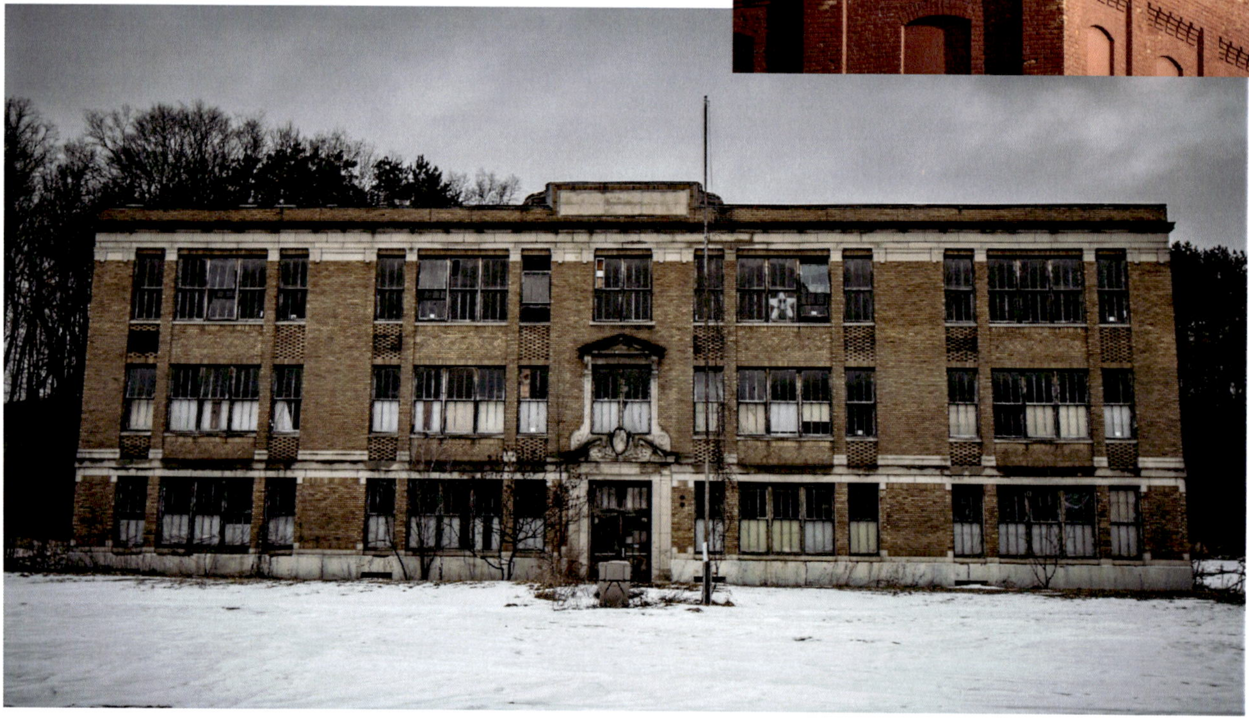

Unknown abandoned school in Newport, Herkimer County, New York. Newport is a small town along NY-28.

ON THE ROAD

Roadside culture has fascinated me ever since I first travelled the open road in my dad's beat-up 1991 Toyota Corolla. Flashing neon lights, a diner that appears like an oasis after a long stretch of dark highway, or even that majestic brick facade of an old home that catches your attention as you pass. It's the idea that some kind of adventure or new discovery lies just beyond the next curve.

The most common expressions of America's love for traversing vast distances are the motor inns, gas stations, convenience stores, restaurants, and diners that sprout up along well-worn avenues. These businesses open their doors to capitalize on a local tourist attraction or vacation destination. But when the fad is over or a faster, more convenient route opens, the lights go out and decay sets in. Only broken glass, cracked cement, a rusted sign, or vine-covered wall remains to remind passersby of what once was.

"Ghost signs", "ghost ads", or "fading ads" are terms for a painted ad on a brick building for a product or business that no longer exists or has moved on from that particular branding. Sometimes neon signs without their glass bulbs or tubes are included in this category. When I bought my first Nikon camera, one of my favorite things to do was drive around looking for these signs. After all, you never know how long they'll remain.

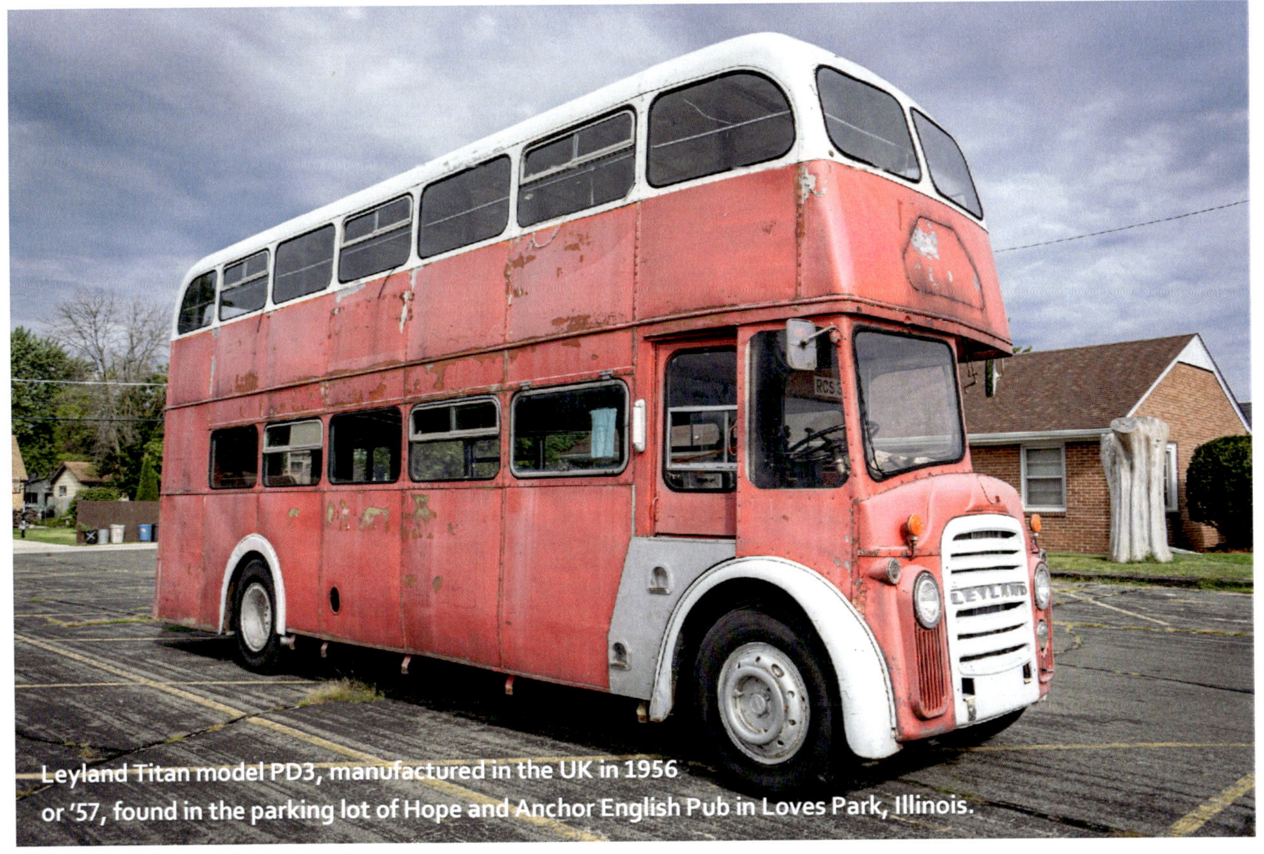

Leyland Titan model PD3, manufactured in the UK in 1956 or '57, found in the parking lot of Hope and Anchor English Pub in Loves Park, Illinois.

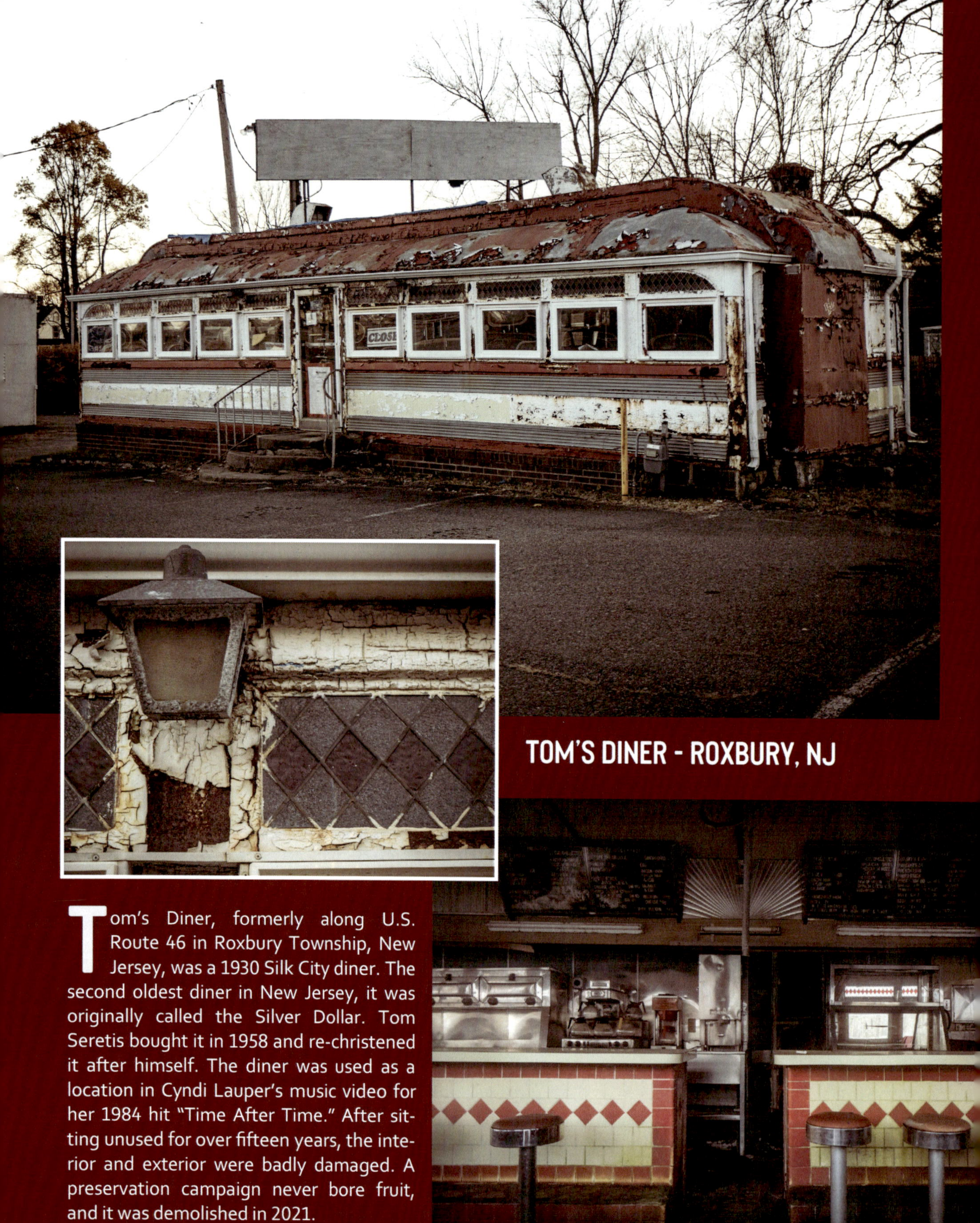

TOM'S DINER - ROXBURY, NJ

Tom's Diner, formerly along U.S. Route 46 in Roxbury Township, New Jersey, was a 1930 Silk City diner. The second oldest diner in New Jersey, it was originally called the Silver Dollar. Tom Seretis bought it in 1958 and re-christened it after himself. The diner was used as a location in Cyndi Lauper's music video for her 1984 hit "Time After Time." After sitting unused for over fifteen years, the interior and exterior were badly damaged. A preservation campaign never bore fruit, and it was demolished in 2021.

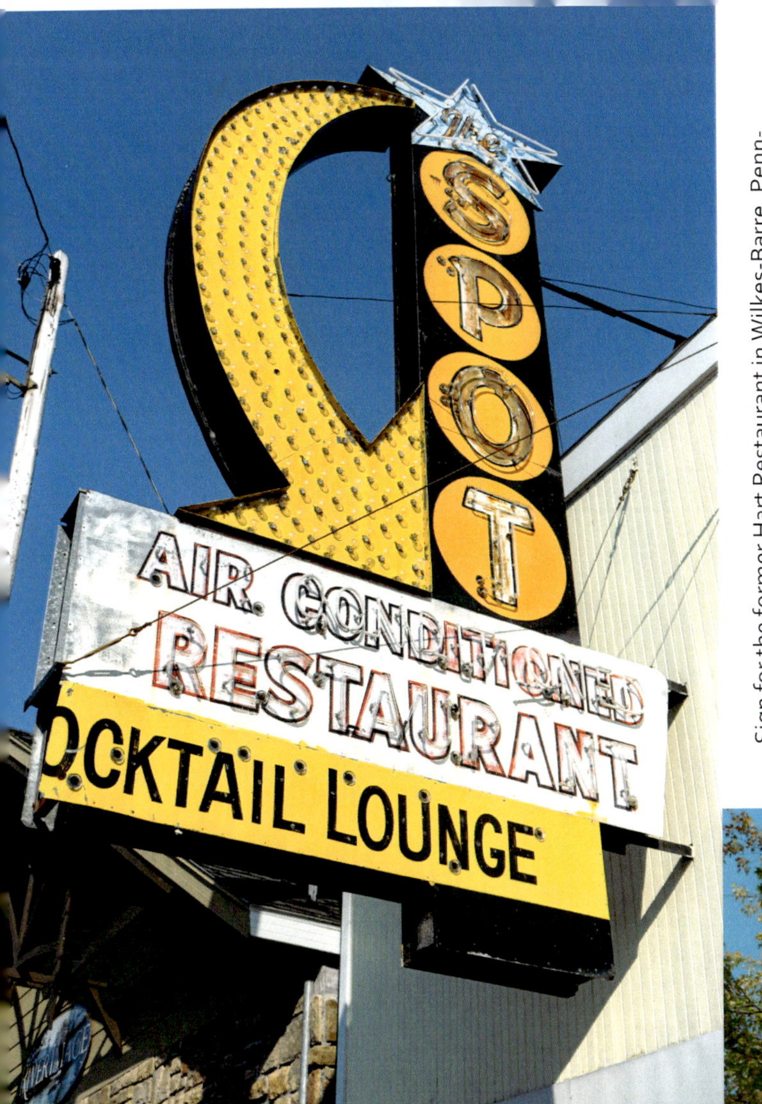

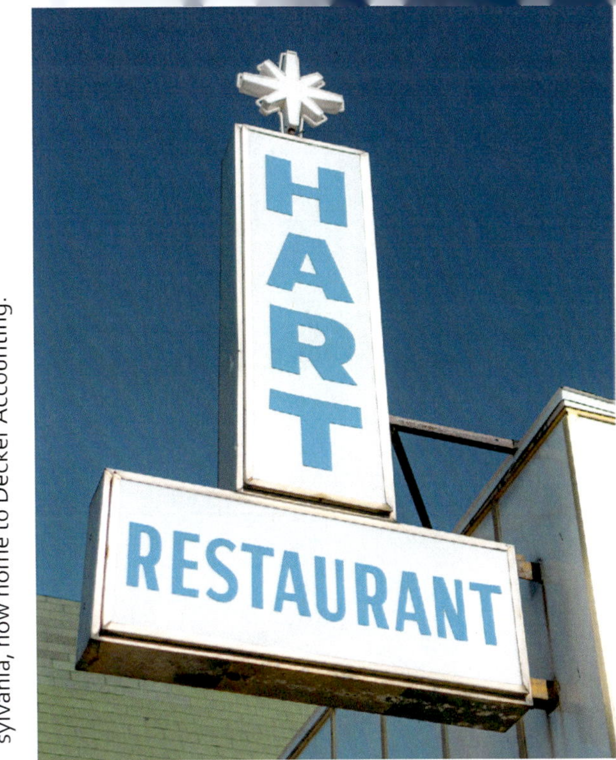

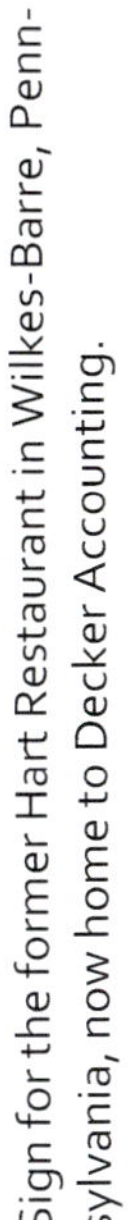
Sign for the former Hart Restaurant in Wilkes-Barre, Pennsylvania, now home to Decker Accounting.

MEALTIME

There is something magical about these old restaurant signs that make people leave them up years, or even decades, after the restaurant itself has closed. They bring to mind a bygone era where people would stroll under neon lights for a night on the town, a more prosperous time when electricity was cheap and attention expensive. Your establishment had to stand out among all those glittering lights, so the more ostentatious the better.

I found these two neon "ghost" signs for The Spot and Homestead Restaurant along James Street in Alexandria Bay, New York, which sits on the St. Lawrence River.

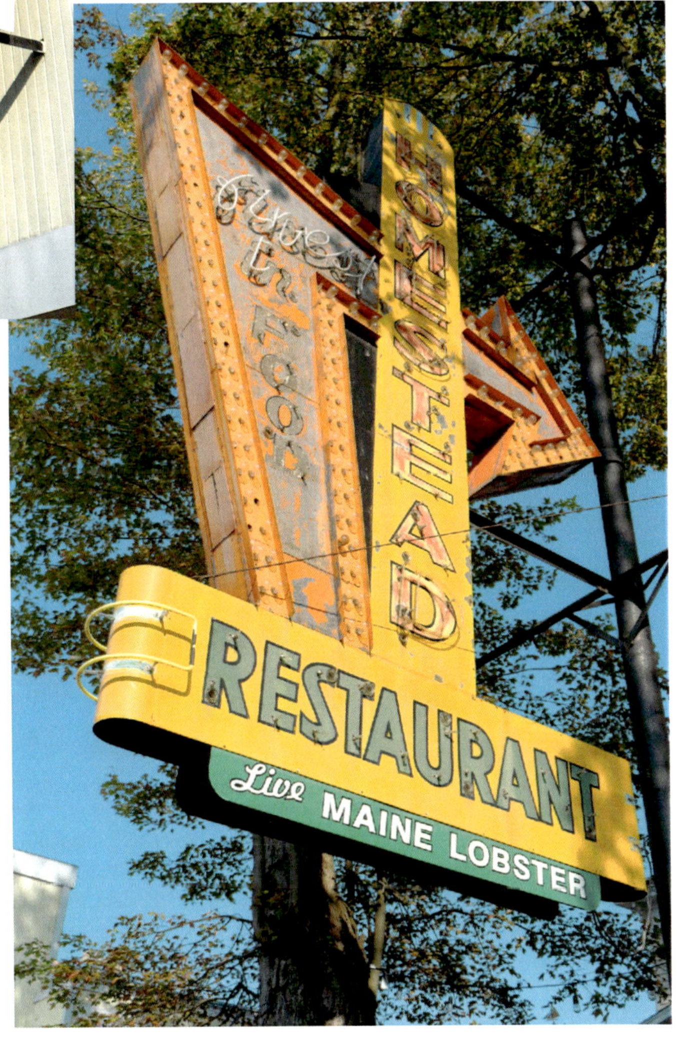

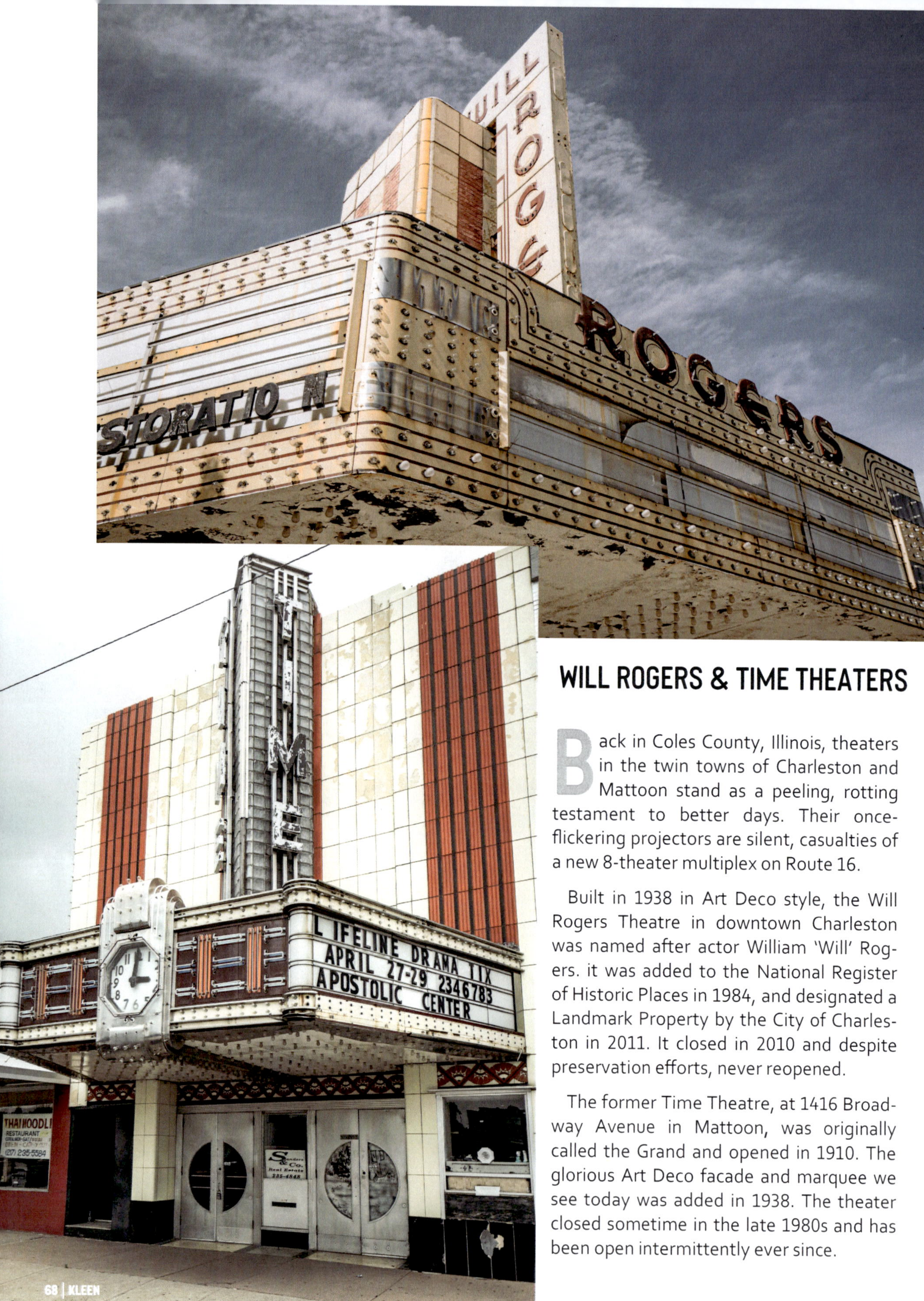

WILL ROGERS & TIME THEATERS

Back in Coles County, Illinois, theaters in the twin towns of Charleston and Mattoon stand as a peeling, rotting testament to better days. Their once-flickering projectors are silent, casualties of a new 8-theater multiplex on Route 16.

Built in 1938 in Art Deco style, the Will Rogers Theatre in downtown Charleston was named after actor William 'Will' Rogers. it was added to the National Register of Historic Places in 1984, and designated a Landmark Property by the City of Charleston in 2011. It closed in 2010 and despite preservation efforts, never reopened.

The former Time Theatre, at 1416 Broadway Avenue in Mattoon, was originally called the Grand and opened in 1910. The glorious Art Deco facade and marquee we see today was added in 1938. The theater closed sometime in the late 1980s and has been open intermittently ever since.

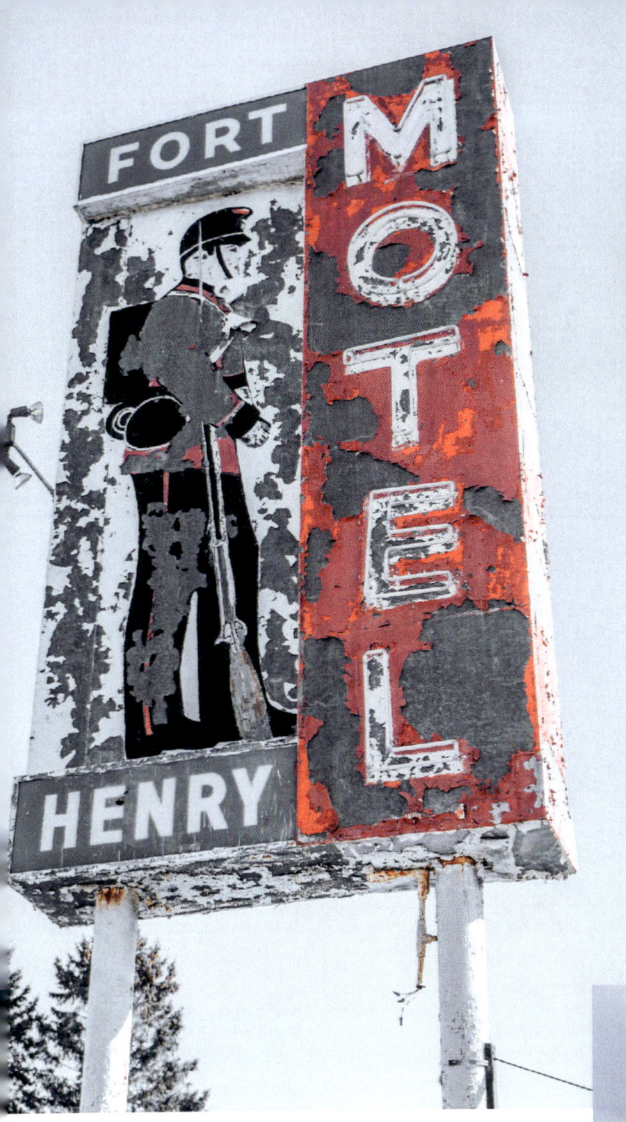

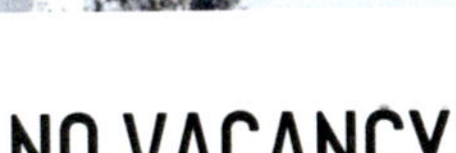

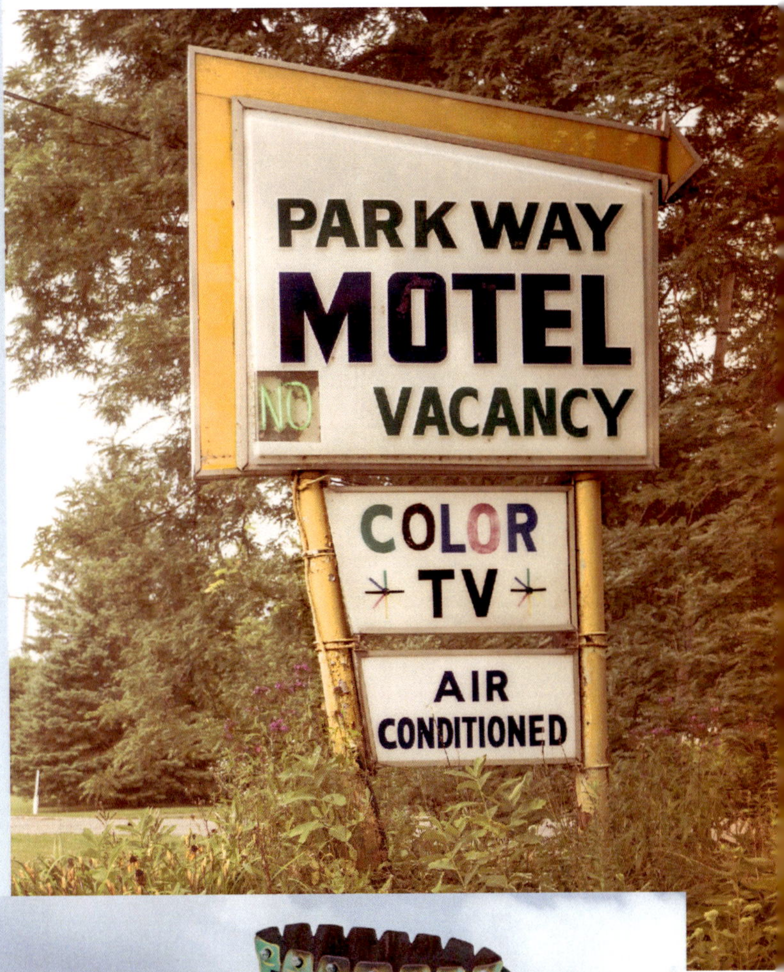

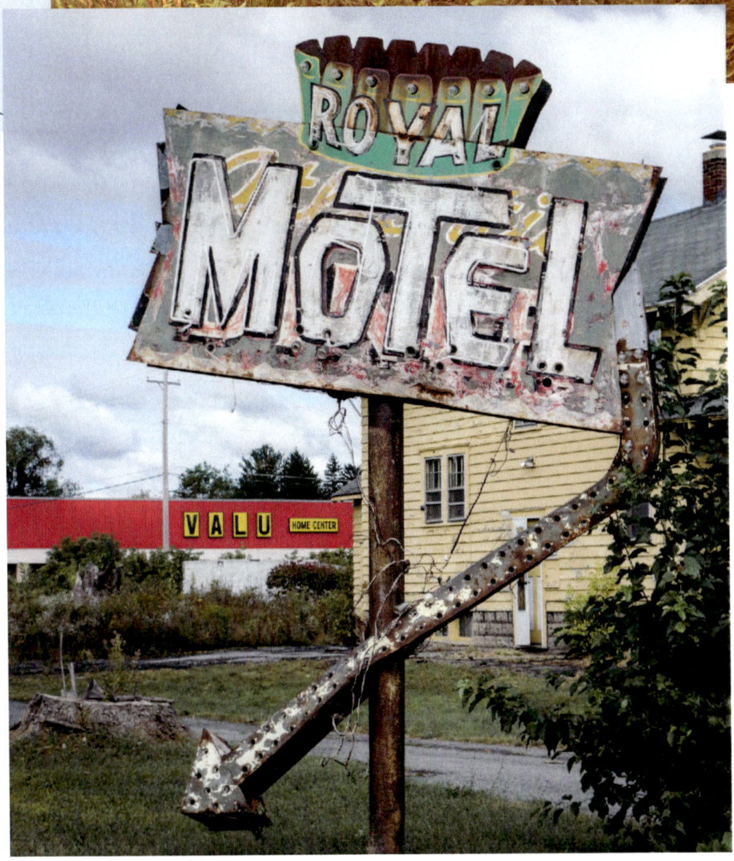

NO VACANCY

Above Left: Weatherbeaten sign for the Fort Henry Motel at 848 Highway 2 East, Kingston, Ontario, Canada, along the St. Lawrence River.

Above Right: Vintage sign for the Park Way Motel on County Rd 2, east of Morrisburg, Ontario, Canada. They have color TV!

Bottom Right: Sign for the defunct Royal Motel along U.S. Route 11 in North Syracuse, New York. I took this photo in 2017 and the sign has since been removed. Looks like this sign was repurposed and it originally read "Atlantic Diner."

NEIGHBORHOOD MARKET

Sometimes when taking an extended family vacation, it's not in the budget to eat fast food or at restaurants for every meal. The old corner store or neighborhood market, like the Market Basket along Blue Mountain Road outside Thurmont, Maryland or Porky's Diner and Groceries in Three Mile Bay, Jefferson County, New York, was there to cater to long-term tourists and campers.

Built in 1985, Porky's included a store, diner, gas station, bait shop, and rooms for rent—everything you would need on a trip up to the North Country.

Unfortunately, when the tourist dollars dry up, many of these places go belly up, unable to sustain themselves on the patronage of "townies" alone. So many fond memories vanish under the bulldozer.

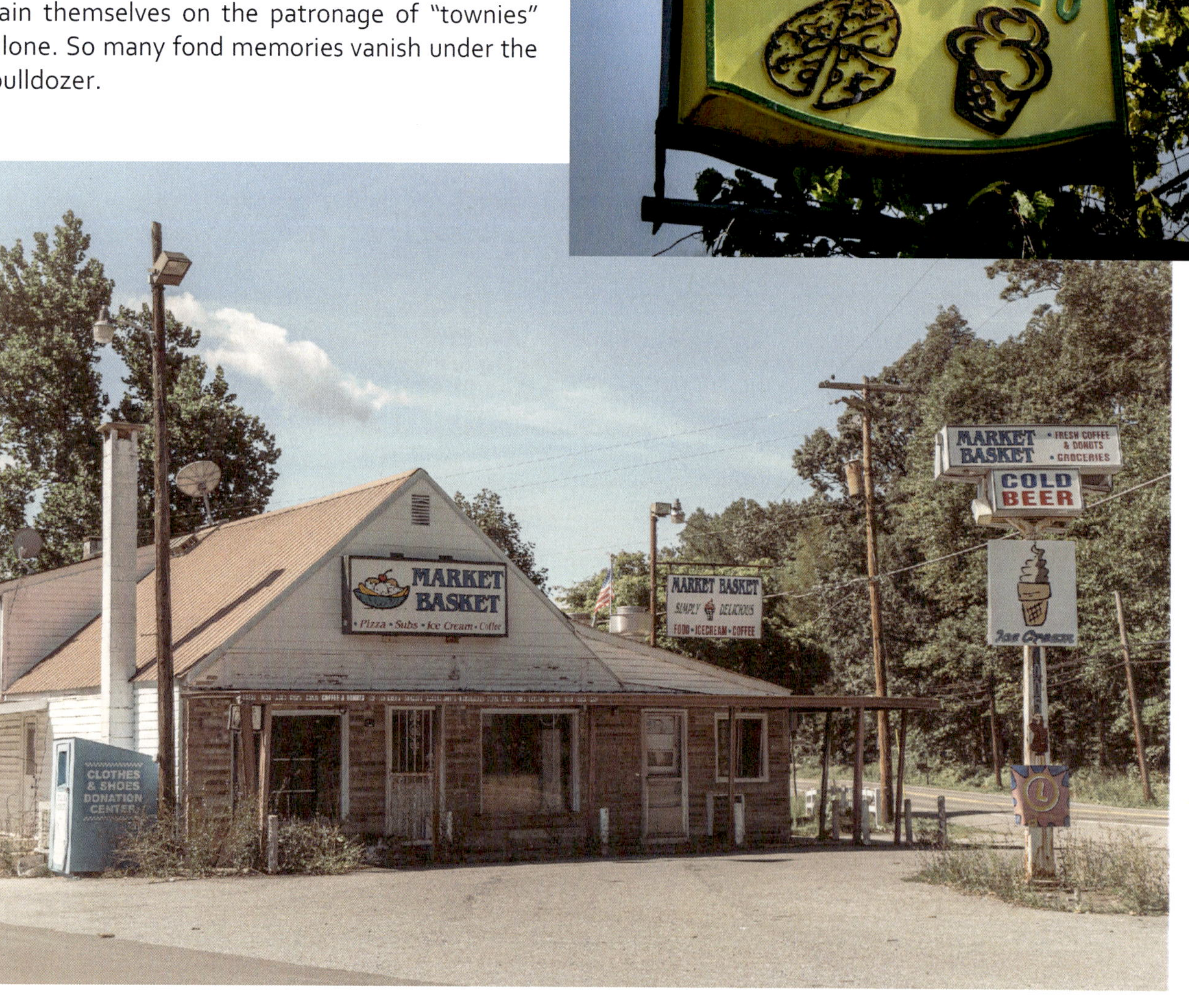

FILL 'ER UP

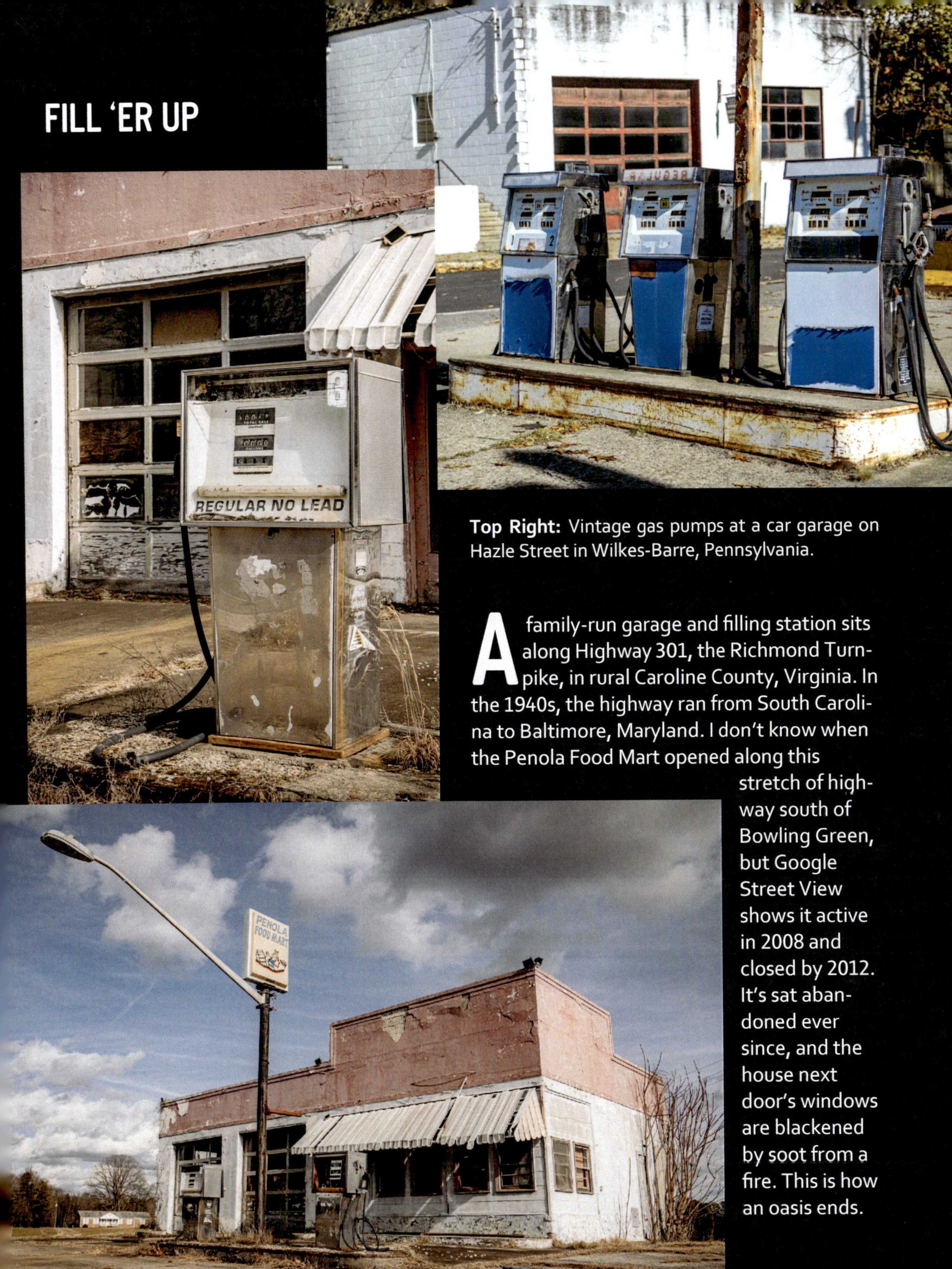

Top Right: Vintage gas pumps at a car garage on Hazle Street in Wilkes-Barre, Pennsylvania.

A family-run garage and filling station sits along Highway 301, the Richmond Turnpike, in rural Caroline County, Virginia. In the 1940s, the highway ran from South Carolina to Baltimore, Maryland. I don't know when the Penola Food Mart opened along this stretch of highway south of Bowling Green, but Google Street View shows it active in 2008 and closed by 2012. It's sat abandoned ever since, and the house next door's windows are blackened by soot from a fire. This is how an oasis ends.

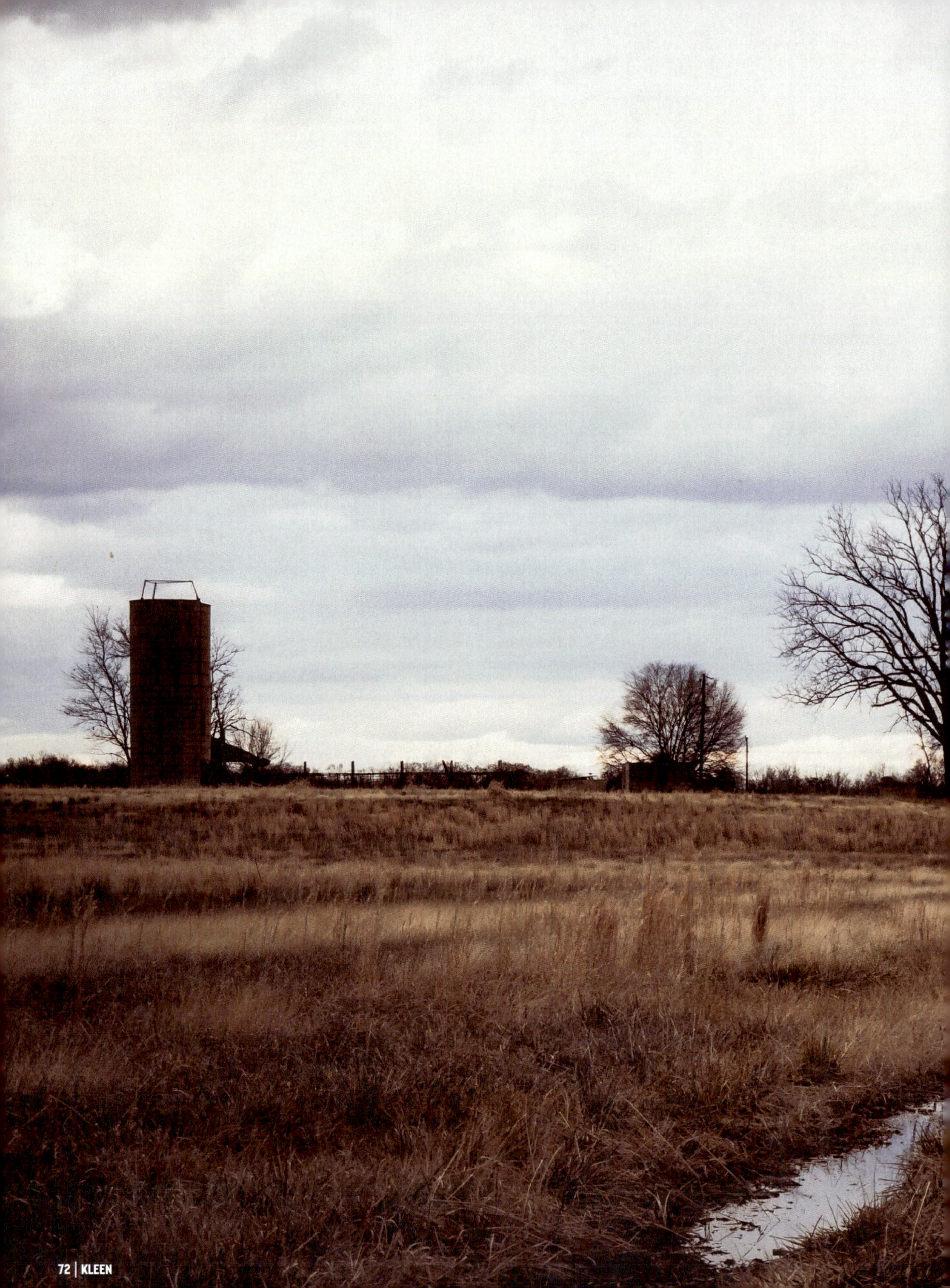

VIRGINIA

Virginia, as one of the thirteen original colonies, is among the oldest states in the country. Jamestown, along the James River in present day James City County, was the first permanent English settlement in the colony. It was established in 1607.

With history stretching back over 400 years, and much longer if you include pre-colonial human inhabitation, one would think the state is teeming with historical sites and ruins. Until after the Civil War, however, Virginia was predominantly rural, with only a handful of towns and cities. Plantation agriculture dominated the coastal region, preventing the kind of growth and development you see in Northern states. Many of these stately plantation homes still stand to this day and are private residences or museums. A few, like Rosewell in Gloucester County, lay in ruins and have been preserved as historic sites.

The American Civil War raged across Virginia. Over the course of four years of bloody conflict, farms burned, forests vanished, and buildings were destroyed. In some places, like the Shenandoah Valley, this destruction was quite deliberate and thorough. A large portion of the state's antebellum infrastructure was simply erased. More recently, in northern Virginia, rapid suburbanization has completely altered the landscape. So if you go looking for historic structures today—abandoned or not—they are surprisingly few and far between.

Most abandonment in Virginia is of a more recent variety. Failed attractions are among the state's most well-known abandoned sites, including a collection of large presidential busts, a slavery museum, a Biblical theme park, roadside monster museum, and even a Renaissance Faire.

The same pattern of deinstitutionalization that left large mental hospitals moldering in plain sight across the country played out in the Old Dominion as well. Like the old Lorton Reformatory / Occoquan Workhouse, some of these places have been repurposed and restored as arts centers, museums, hotels, or even apartment complexes.

Then there is the tragic story of Accomack County on Virginia's Eastern Shore, where decades of steady economic decline resulted in hundreds of abandoned structures. For five months between 2012 and 2013, a series of mysterious fires broke out. By the time a former volunteer firefighter and his accomplice were caught, the pair had set over 68 fires in vacant homes, garages, motels, and even a church. It was like The Burning of '64 all over again.

I moved to Virginia in 2019 and found a state wrestling with how to go forward. Should the old relics of yesteryear be preserved, or should they be allowed to just fade away to be replaced by strip malls and data centers? Would Virginia be like my home state of Illinois, and simply bulldoze unsightly reminders of the past? Only time will tell.

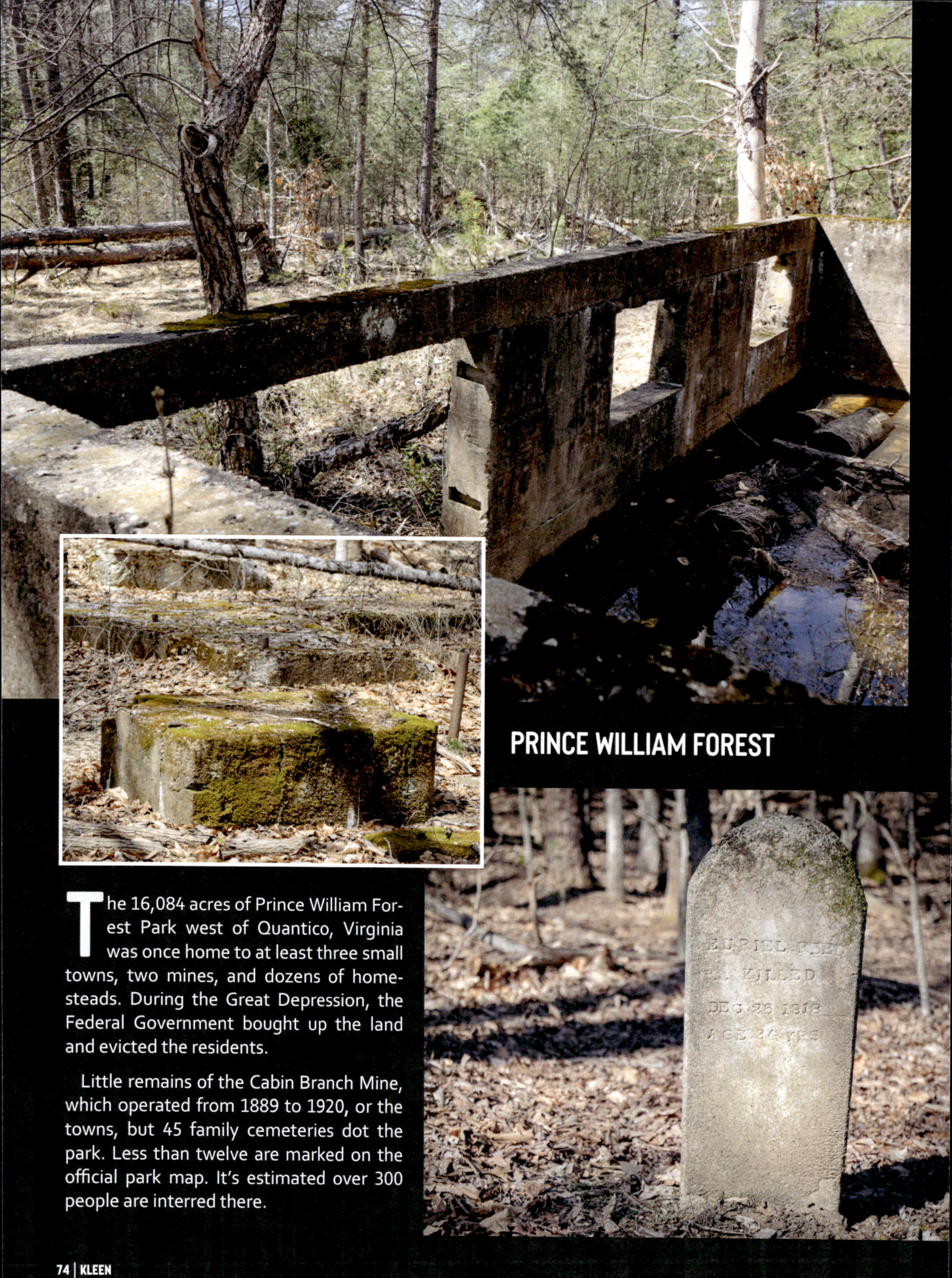

PRINCE WILLIAM FOREST

The 16,084 acres of Prince William Forest Park west of Quantico, Virginia was once home to at least three small towns, two mines, and dozens of homesteads. During the Great Depression, the Federal Government bought up the land and evicted the residents.

Little remains of the Cabin Branch Mine, which operated from 1889 to 1920, or the towns, but 45 family cemeteries dot the park. Less than twelve are marked on the official park map. It's estimated over 300 people are interred there.

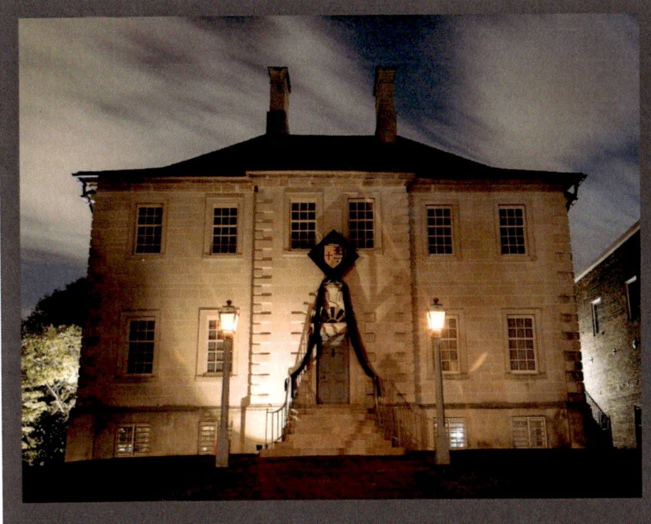

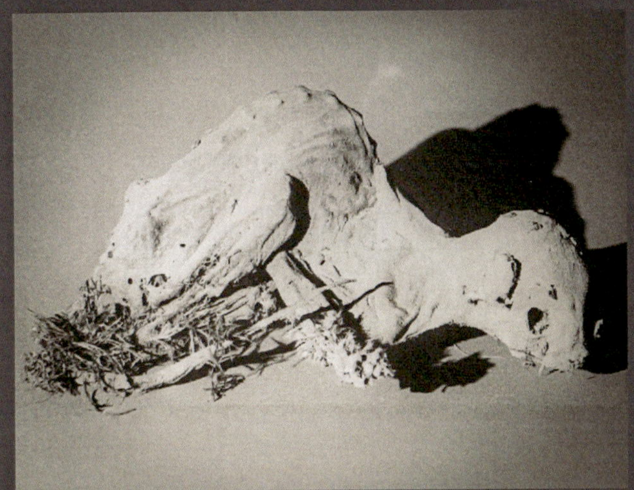

CARLYLE HOUSE - ALEXANDRIA

Built by Scottish merchant John Carlyle on premier lots along the Potomac River from 1751 to 1753, this mid-Georgian stone manor is older than our country. History was made in its parlor. Yet, it became a Colonial Era ruin hidden for decades behind an antebellum hotel.

During the American Civil War, occupying Union forces turned the adjacent Mansion House Hotel into a hospital, which was later depicted in PBS's miniseries *Mercy Street*. After the war, the hotel became an apartment building, and Carlyle House deteriorated to the point where it was at risk of collapse. It was added to the National Register of Historic Places in 1969, and in 1970, NOVA Parks acquired the property and began a six-year effort to restore the house to its former glory.

During restoration, workers discovered the mummified body of a cat sealed inside the foundation, an old British custom thought to bring good luck.

Carlyle House Historic Park, at 121 N. Fairfax Street, is now open for tours.

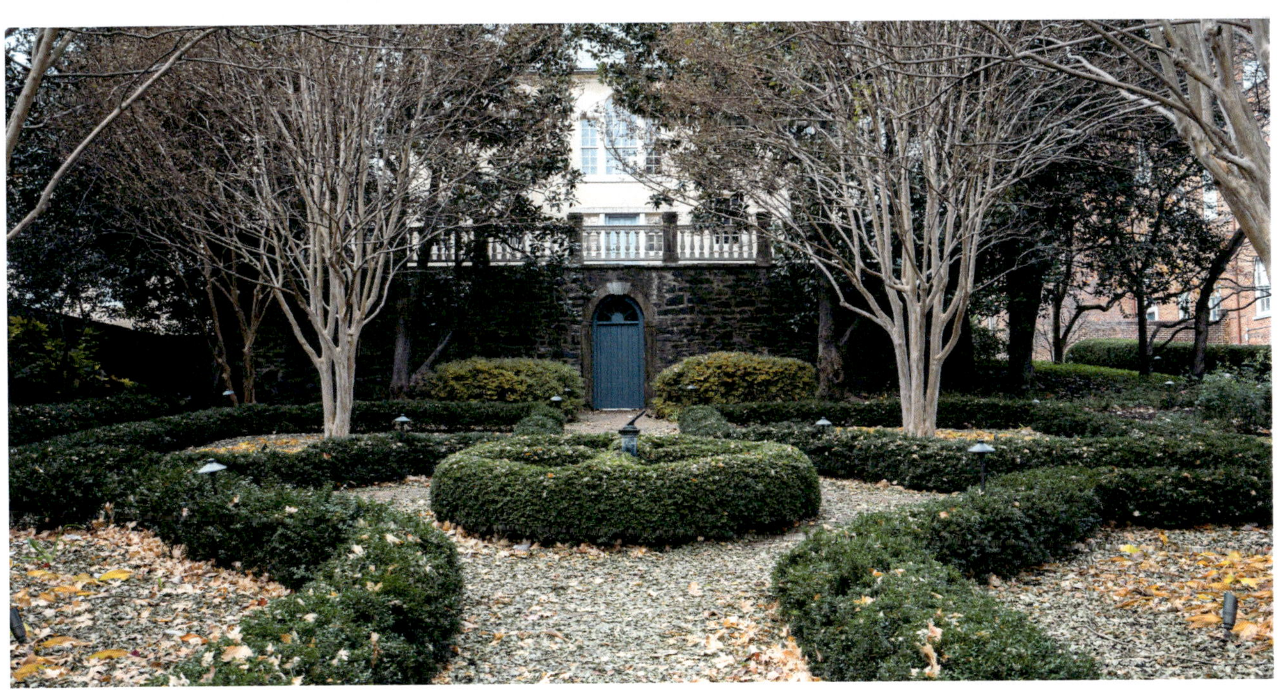

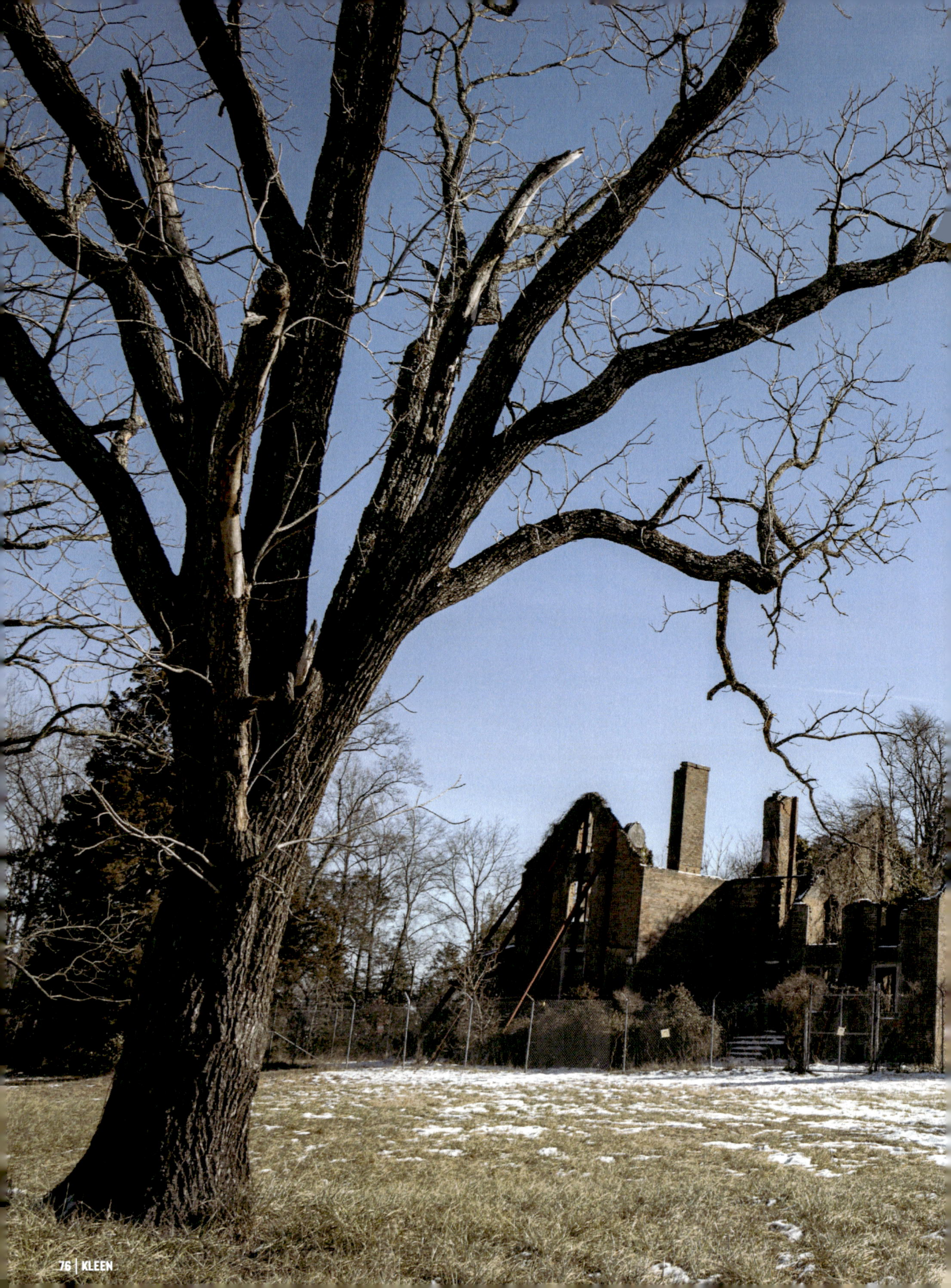

IDLEWIND RUINS

In the 1850s, a planter named William Yates Downman purchased over 200 acres of land south of Fredericksburg known for being a tangled wilderness. He called it "Idlewild" and built a Gothic Revival -style mansion with all the outbuildings common to plantations at that time.

The mansion was finished shortly before the American Civil War, and was on the periphery of several major battles. General Robert E. Lee used it as his headquarters immediately following the Battle of Chancellorsville in 1863. Idlewild survived the war, but William Yates Downman didn't.

Downman's last surviving heir died in the 1940s and the mansion continued to serve as a private residence for several decades, until becoming vacant in the 1990s. Preservationists battled developers, curiosity-seekers, and vandals over the historic home's future. Disagreement among the property owners and the extensive cost of renovations prevented anything from being done with it.

Finally, in April 2003, a devastating fire consumed most of the interior, leaving an empty shell. The external buildings, including a kitchen and storehouse, remain intact. A chain link fence was erected to keep out trespassers.

It is unfortunate that the ruins of Idlewild can't be opened to the public, like Gloucester County's Rosewell, to help educate future generations about this important period of American history.

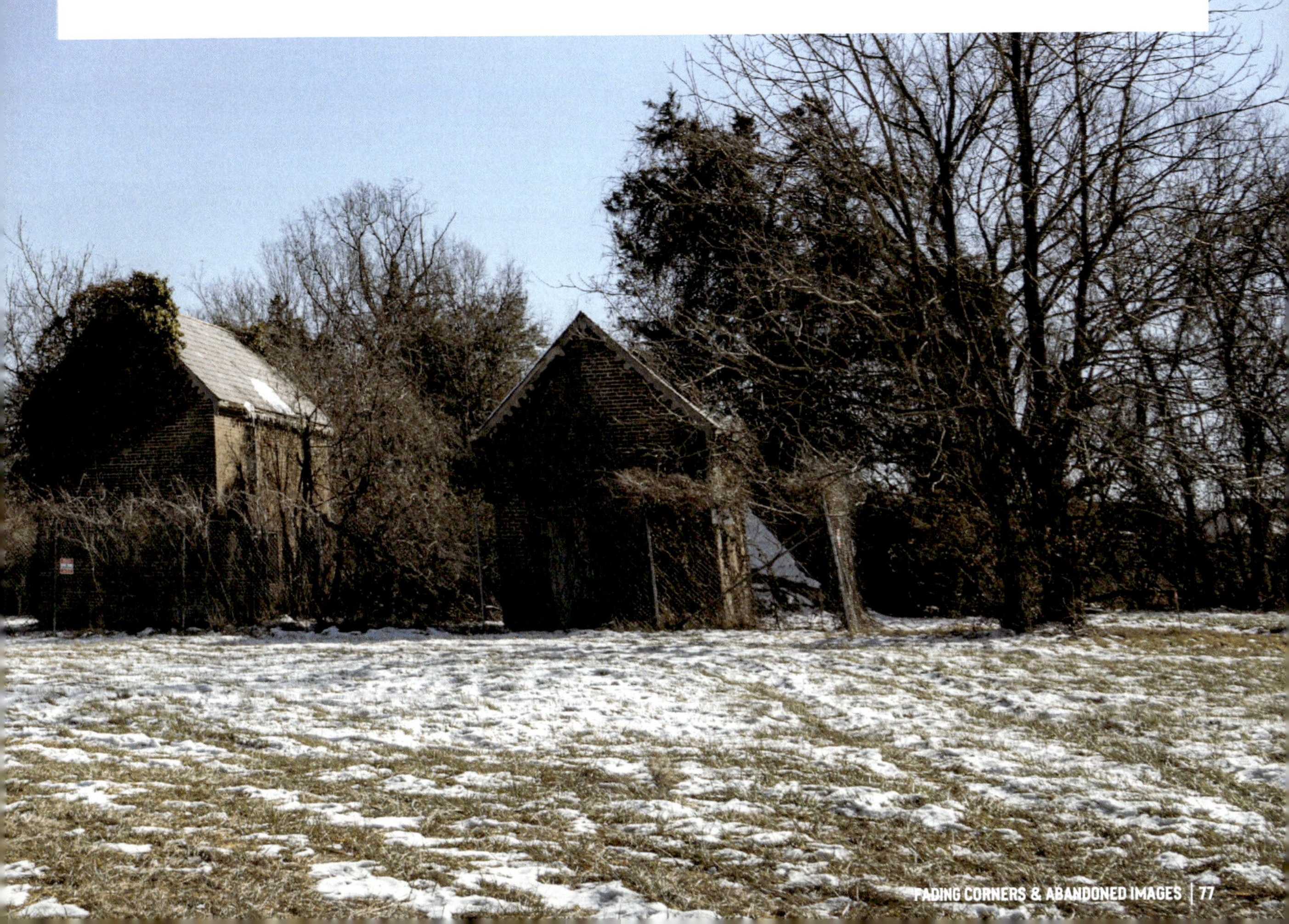

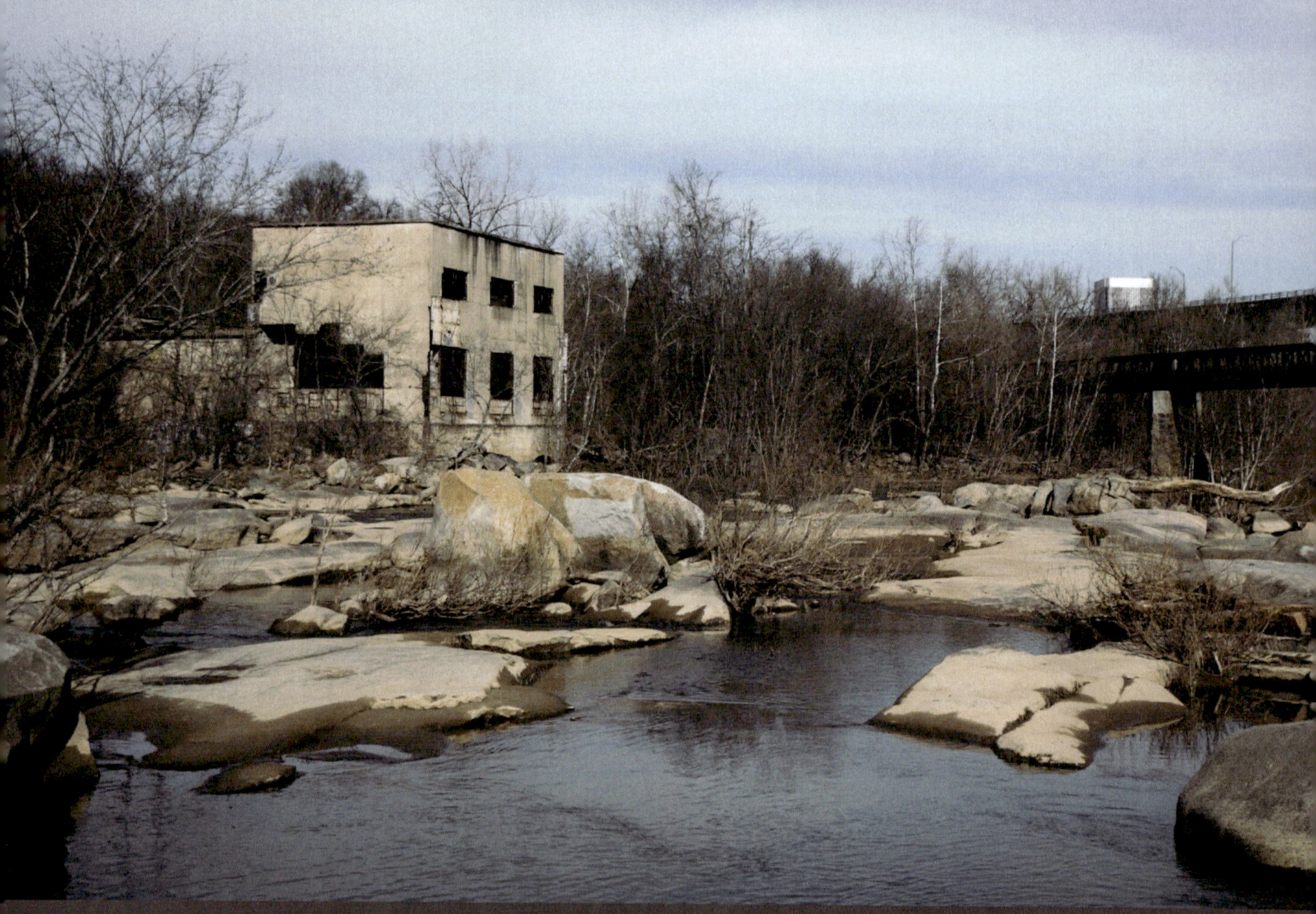

BELLE ISLE - RICHMOND

Traces of human activity on Richmond's Belle Isle date back hundreds of years, starting with American Indians who found the island in the James River ideal for fishing. Captain John Smith explored it in 1607. Industry soon followed with an iron and nail factory in 1814 and a granite quarry. By the 1860s, this industry had attracted a small community, but their idyllic life was interrupted by war. When Virginia seceded in 1861, the Confederate government found Belle Isle an ideal place for a prisoner of war camp.

The Confederacy could barely care for men in its own armies, let alone its numerous prison camps. Disease, starvation, and exposure took a toll, and as many as 1,000 prisoners died on the island.

In the twentieth century, the Virginia Electric Power Company operated a hydroelectric power plant on Belle Isle. The ruins of the power plant and the nail factory can still be seen to this day. Filmmakers deemed the empty cement structure sufficiently creepy to form a backdrop for one scene in the movie *Hannibal* (2001).

The City of Richmond opened Belle Isle as a public park in 1973, building hiking trails, bicycle paths, and placing interpretive signs explaining the history of the island. It was added to the National Register of Historic Places in 1995.

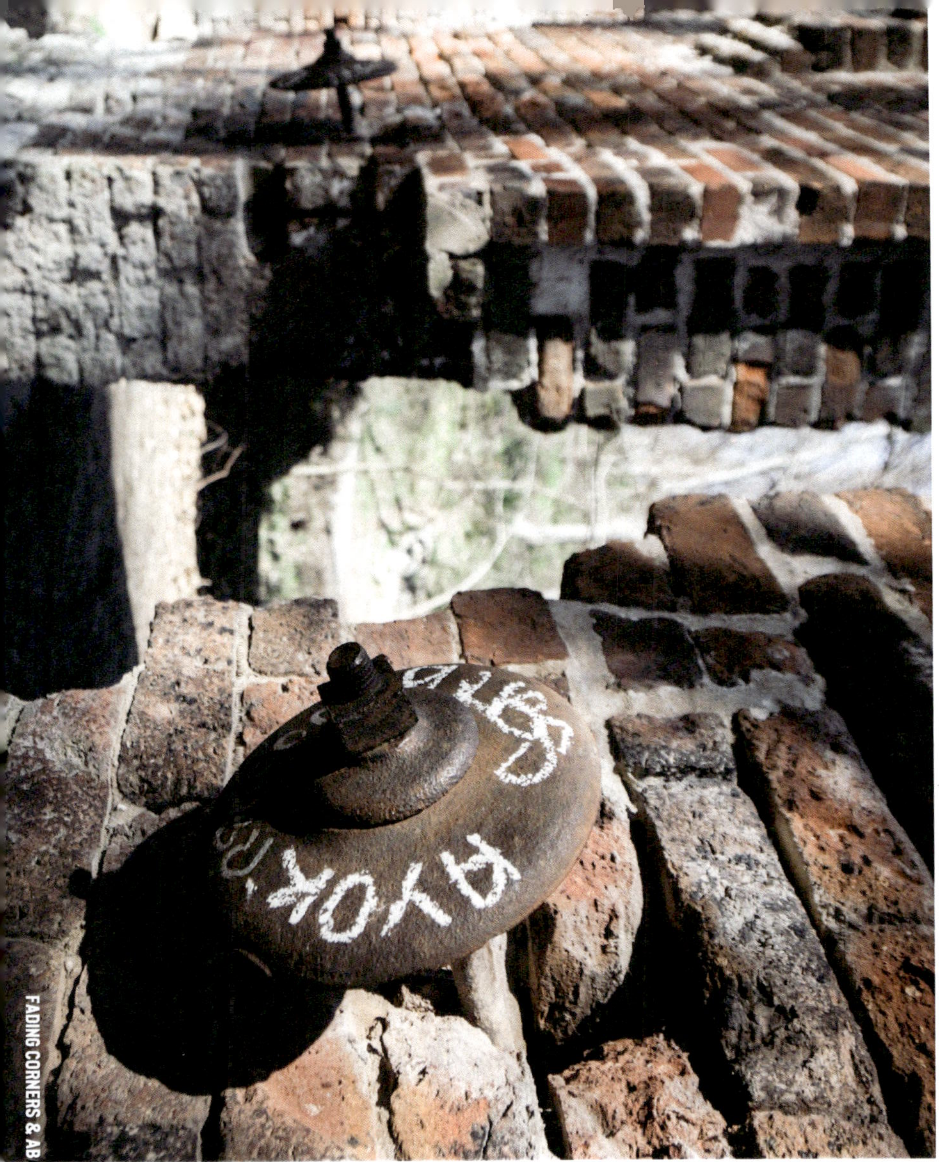

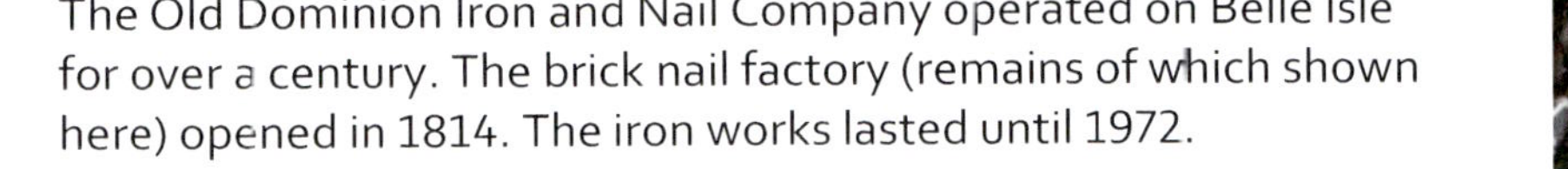

The Old Dominion Iron and Nail Company operated on Belle Isle for over a century. The brick nail factory (remains of which shown here) opened in 1814. The iron works lasted until 1972.

The Virginia Electric Power Company operated a hydroelectric power plant on Belle Isle from 1904 to 1967. Remains of other industries, like a granite quarry, can be found all over the island.

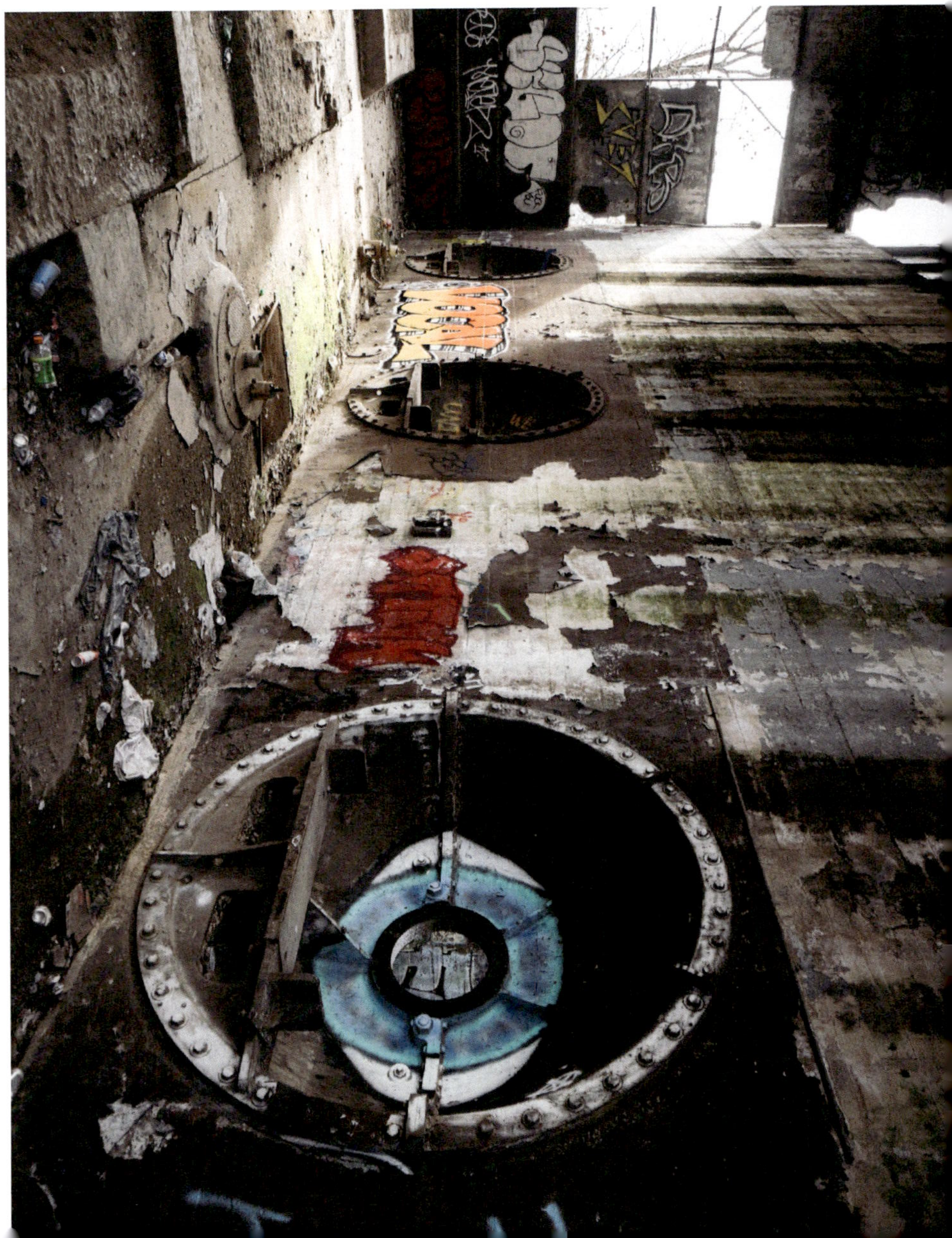

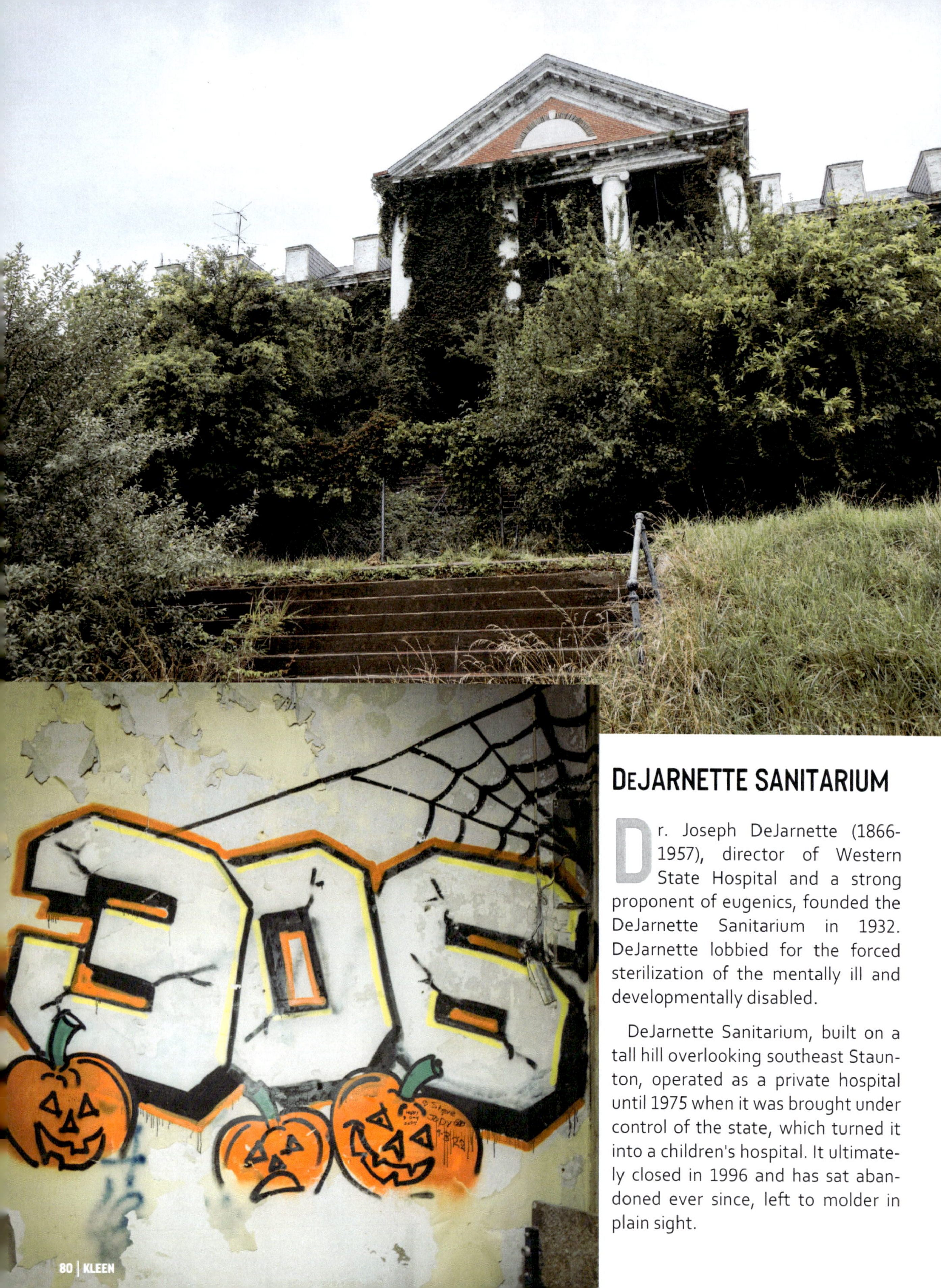

DEJARNETTE SANITARIUM

Dr. Joseph DeJarnette (1866-1957), director of Western State Hospital and a strong proponent of eugenics, founded the DeJarnette Sanitarium in 1932. DeJarnette lobbied for the forced sterilization of the mentally ill and developmentally disabled.

DeJarnette Sanitarium, built on a tall hill overlooking southeast Staunton, operated as a private hospital until 1975 when it was brought under control of the state, which turned it into a children's hospital. It ultimately closed in 1996 and has sat abandoned ever since, left to molder in plain sight.

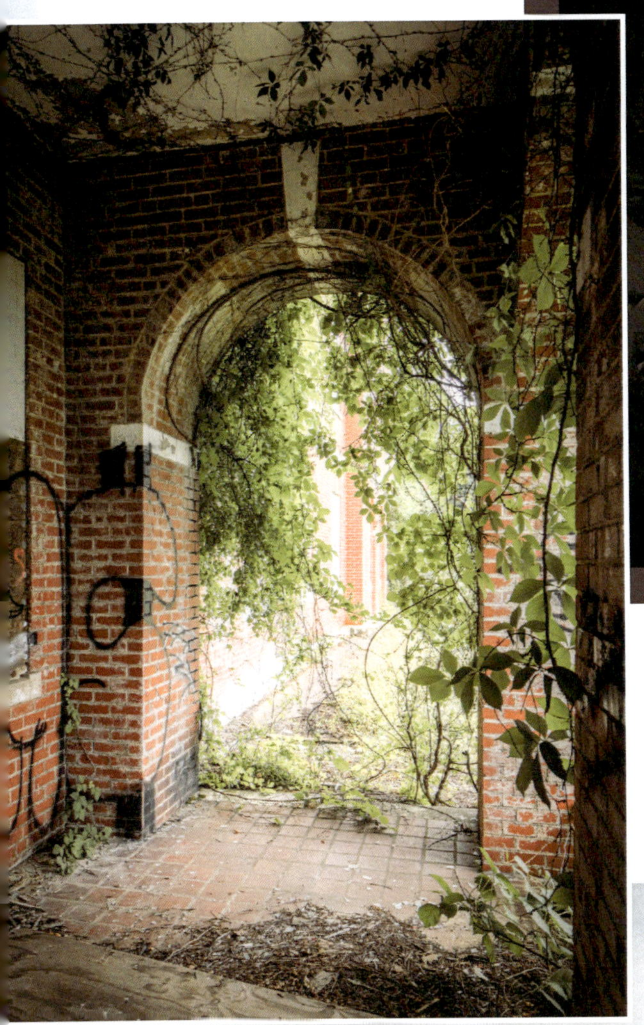

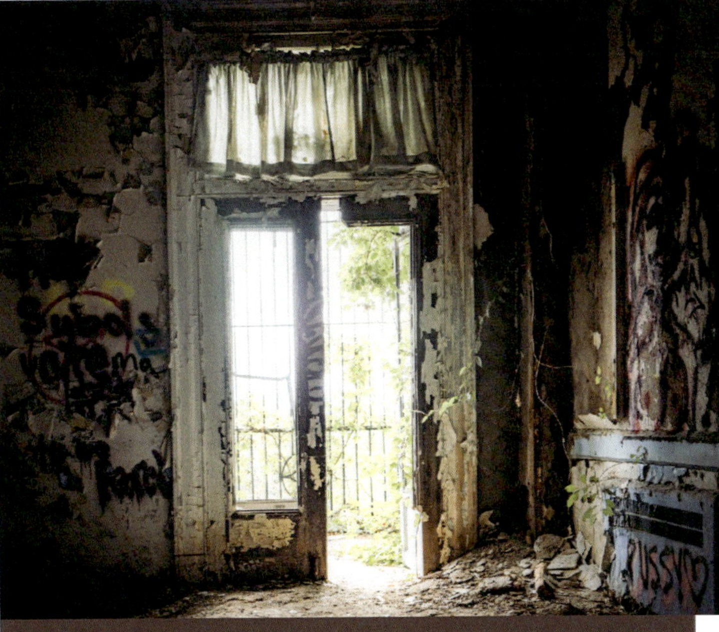

Dr. DeJarnette oversaw his sanitarium from the day it opened until 1947. Though autocratic in leadership style, he did implement reforms designed to make life at the asylum easier for its inmates. As public opinion turned against the practice of involuntary sterilization, however, DeJarnette's reputation and legacy were irrevocably tarnished.

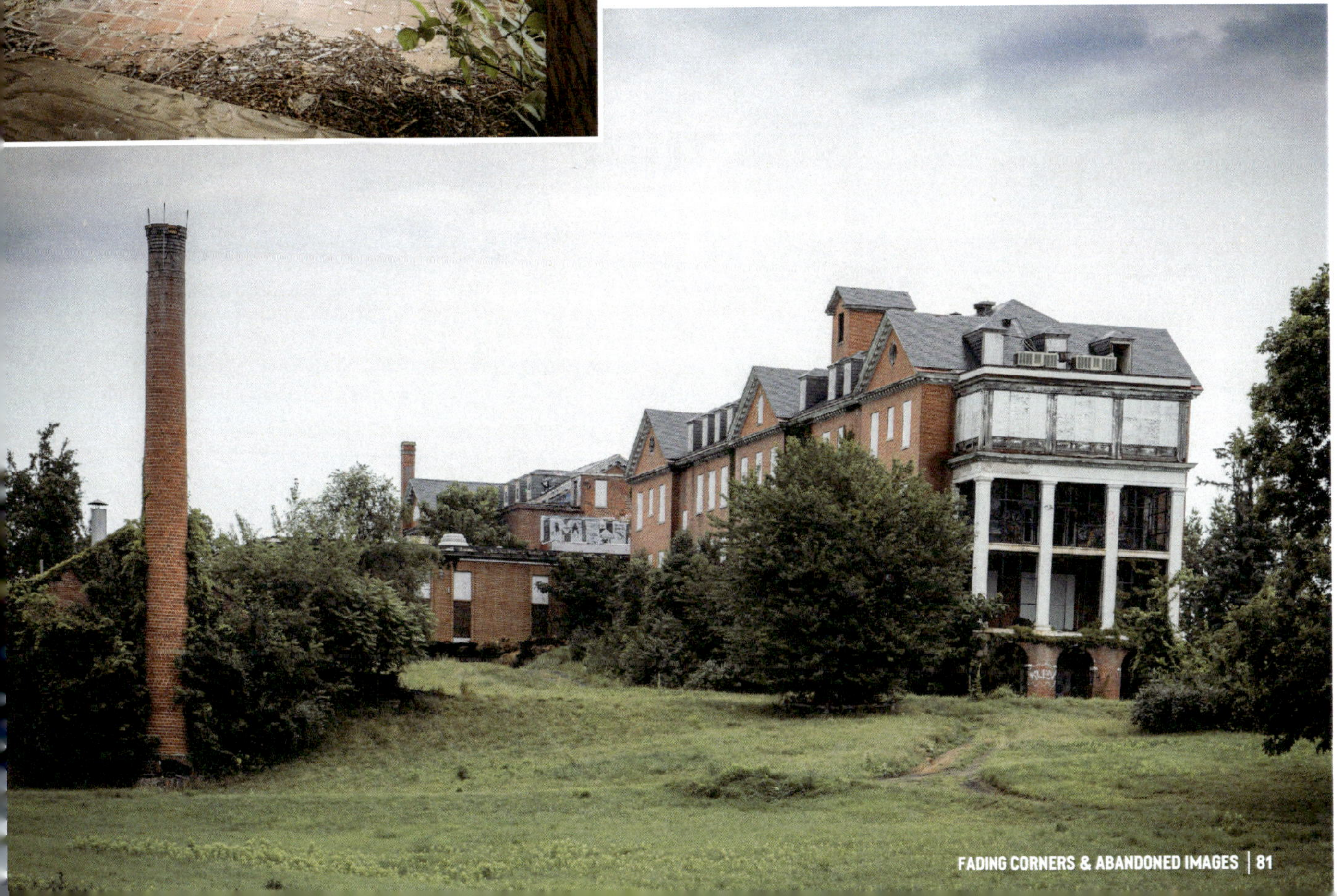

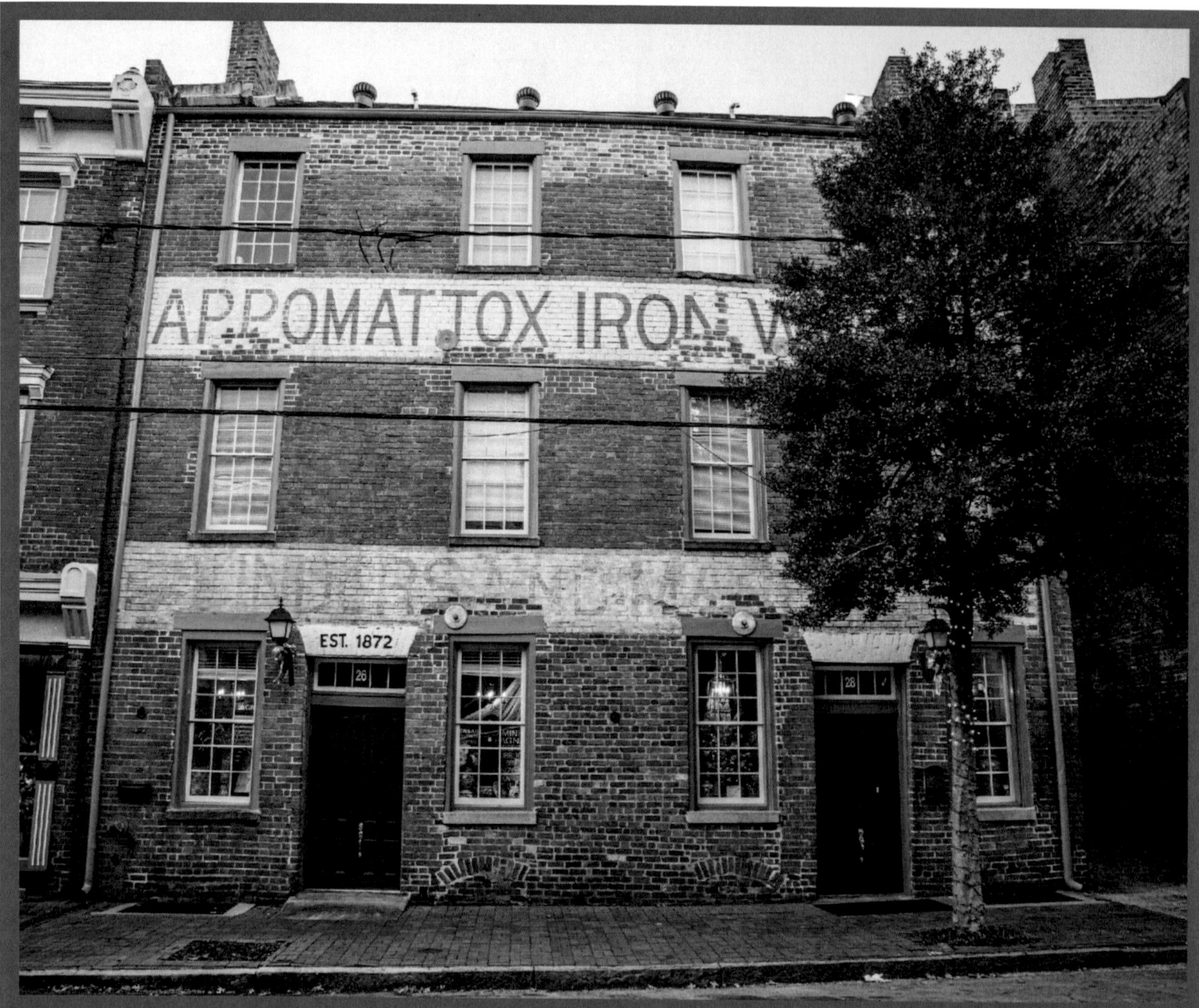

APPOMATTOX IRON WORKS

Esek Steere (1831-1908), a New Yorker by birth, founded the Appomattox Iron Works & Supply Co. in Petersburg, Virginia in 1872. The business stayed in the family for several generations. In 1899, the company moved into a complex of brick Federal-style buildings on Old Street. The oldest (pictured above) predates 1815.

The complex included a foundry, machine shop, mill, and hardware store. It manufactured saw mills and other machine parts. By the mid-twentieth century, the business began to close, first with the foundry in 1946, machine shop in 1952, and hardware store twenty years later. Pictures taken for the Historic American Engineering Record in the late 1960s show it overgrown with weeds and covered in dirt and dust.

The site fell into disrepair and it was turned into a museum. A tornado damaged it in 1993. Finally, in the early 2000s, it was rehabilitated again as apartments. Today, many of the old lathes and machinery are on display in the courtyard, alongside the old workshop and boiler.

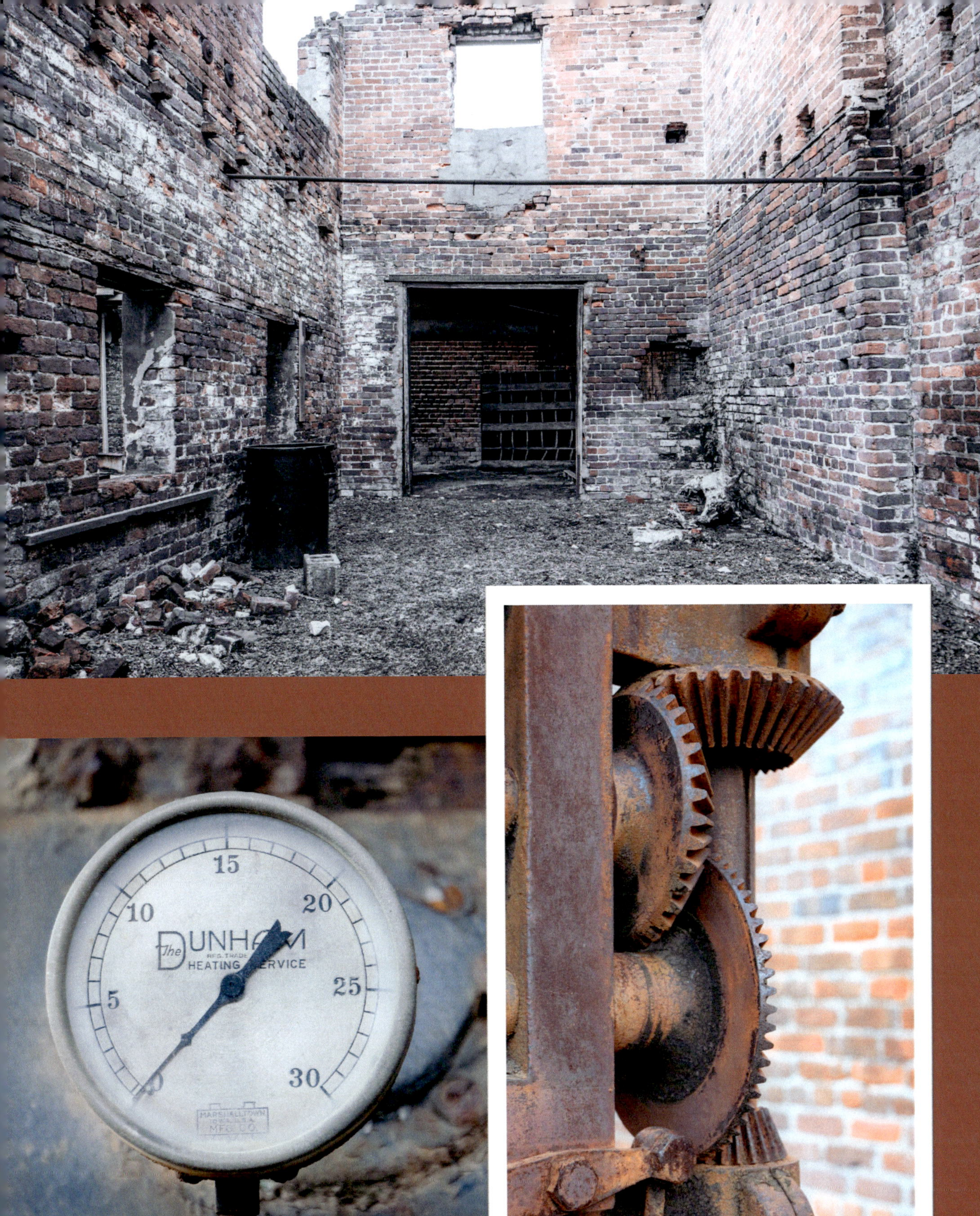
15
10
20
The
HEATING
5
25
30

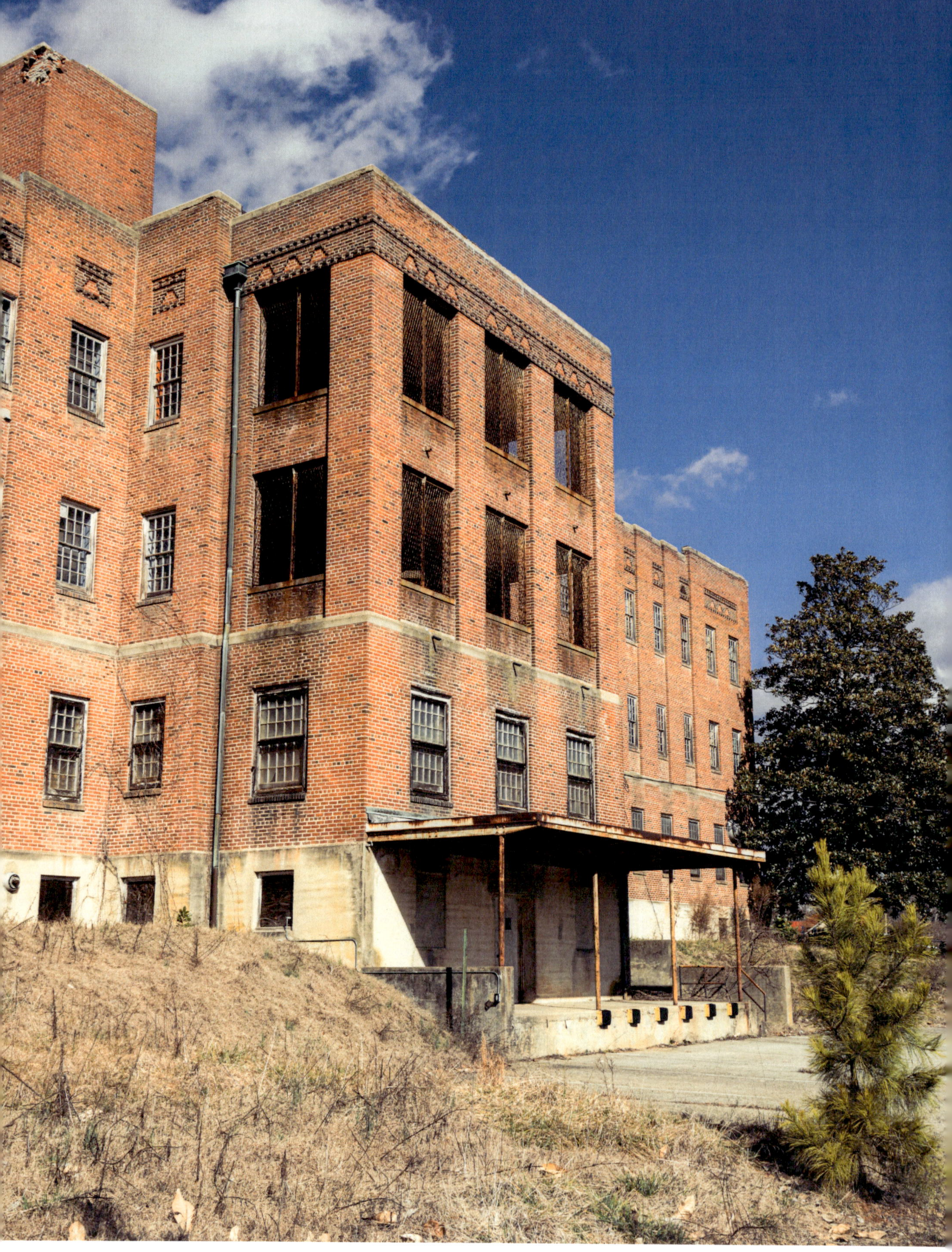

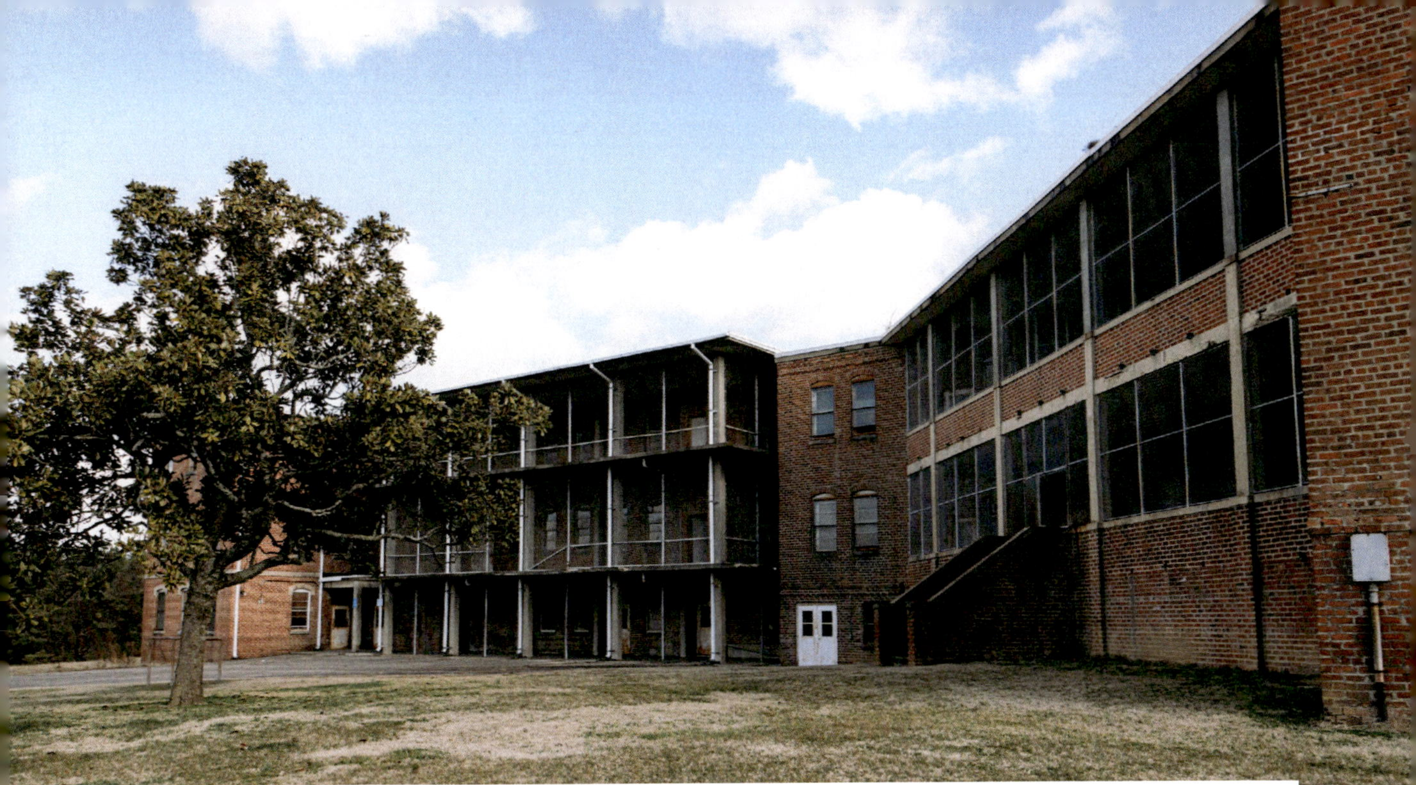

CENTRAL STATE HOSPITAL

Central State Hospital west of Petersburg, Virginia opened its doors in 1870 and gradually expanded to encompass over 500 acres. At various times, it included a Maximum Security Forensic Unit, Training School, Geriatric Center, home for delinquent girls, and a chapel.

The asylum's original Kirkbride building, standing at the turn of the last century, has long since been demolished. Other buildings are in various stages of abandonment, although some are still in use.

The Female Psychopathic Building (pictured above) was built in 1904. Prior to 1972, people with developmental disabilities were housed here alongside the mentally ill. Between 1924 and 1973, thousands of patients were involuntarily sterilized.

In 1997, the U.S. Department of Justice investigated Central State and found a high level of "injuries and dangerous situations that place patients at risk of harm." Today, the institution's future is uncertain.

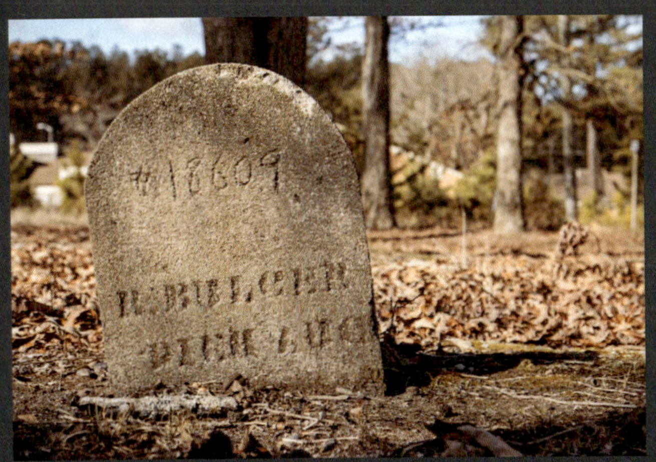

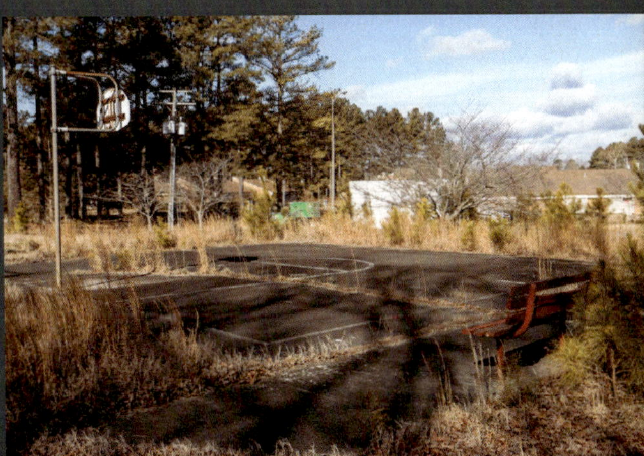

UNION LEVEL GHOST TOWN

Union Level is a former railroad town in Mecklenburg County, Virginia. Established in 1836, the town didn't take off until the Atlantic & Danville Railway (aka Norfolk, Franklin, and Danville Railroad) opened in 1890. All signs pointed to a thriving community, as general stores, barbers, a pharmacy, bank, dance hall, and even a motorcycle dealership opened along the main drag.

The Great Depression hit Union Level hard, and sadly, like many railroad towns, it began to die as highways became the main mode of transportation. Its post office closed in 1990. Though a few residents live nearby, its visitors today mainly consist of the curious, come to gawk at the ruins.

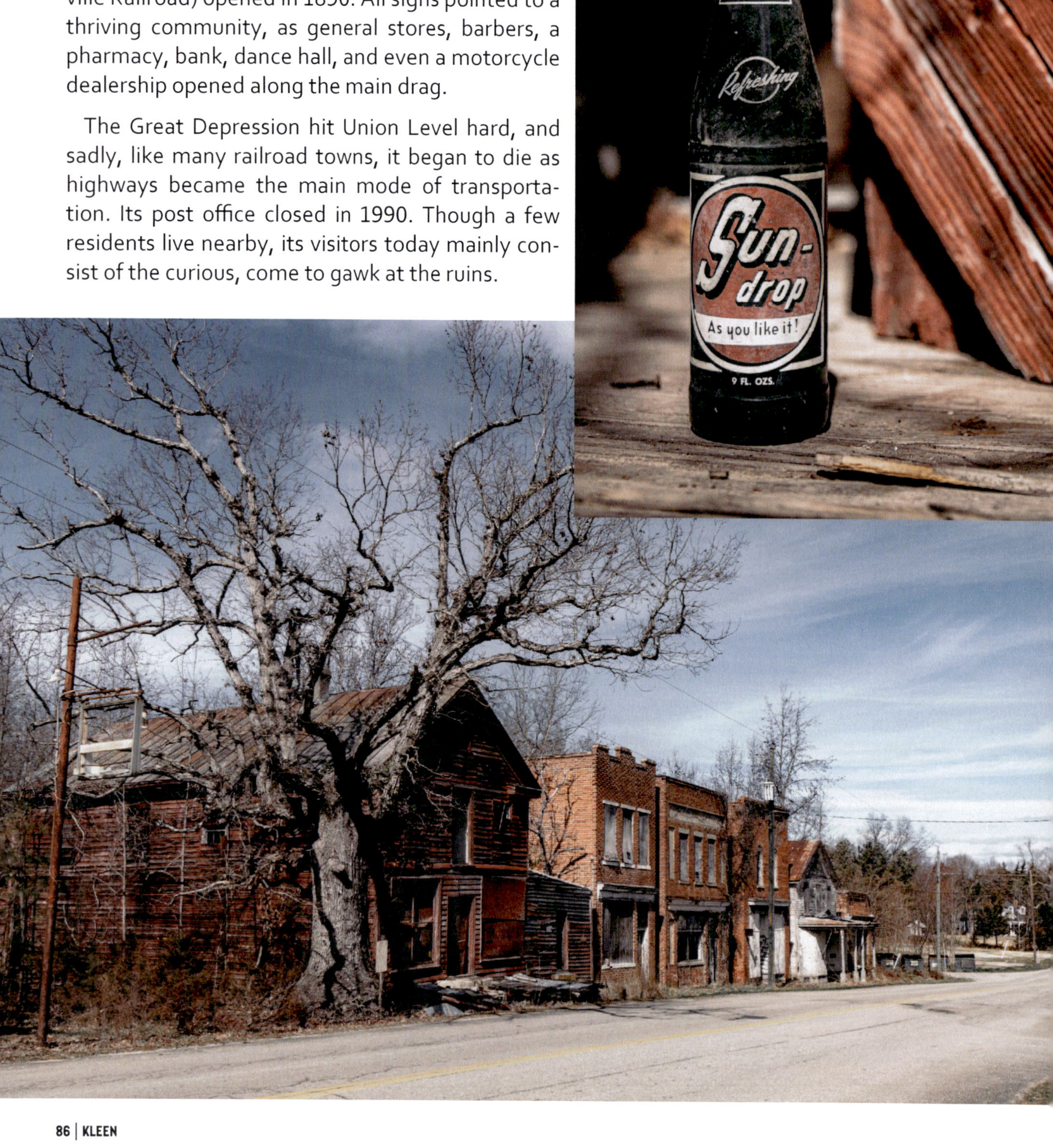

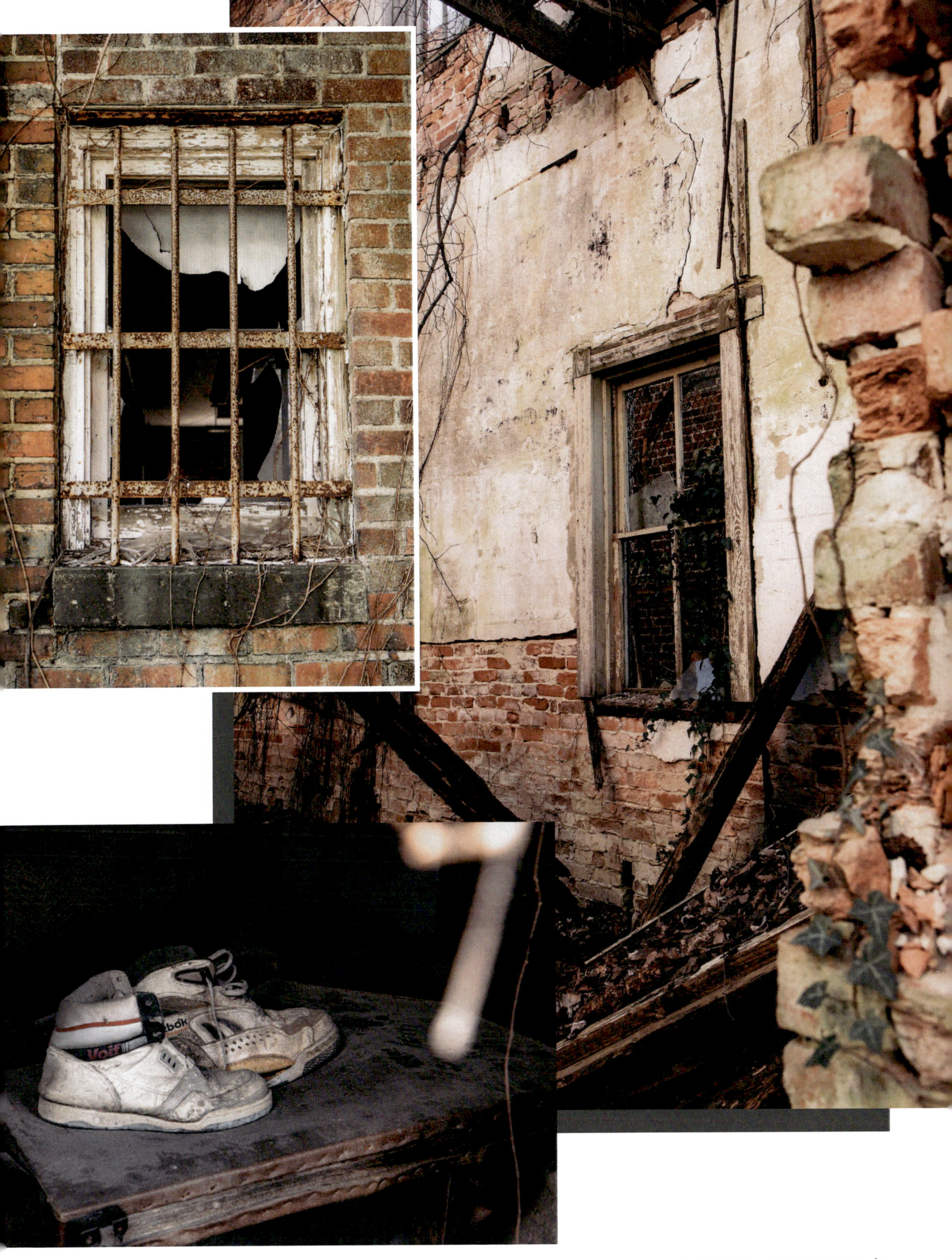
Voit

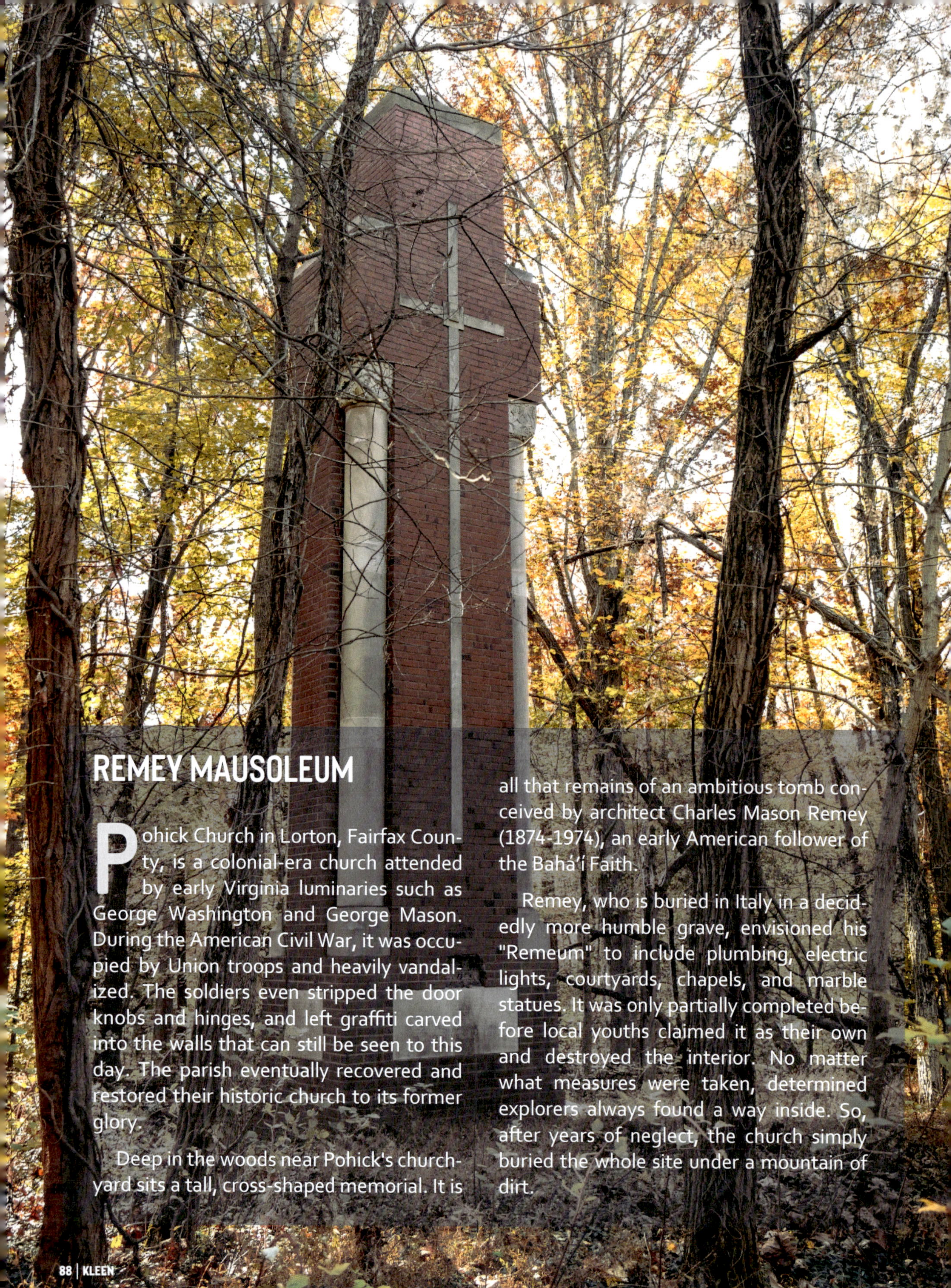

REMEY MAUSOLEUM

Pohick Church in Lorton, Fairfax County, is a colonial-era church attended by early Virginia luminaries such as George Washington and George Mason. During the American Civil War, it was occupied by Union troops and heavily vandalized. The soldiers even stripped the door knobs and hinges, and left graffiti carved into the walls that can still be seen to this day. The parish eventually recovered and restored their historic church to its former glory.

Deep in the woods near Pohick's churchyard sits a tall, cross-shaped memorial. It is all that remains of an ambitious tomb conceived by architect Charles Mason Remey (1874-1974), an early American follower of the Bahá'í Faith.

Remey, who is buried in Italy in a decidedly more humble grave, envisioned his "Remeum" to include plumbing, electric lights, courtyards, chapels, and marble statues. It was only partially completed before local youths claimed it as their own and destroyed the interior. No matter what measures were taken, determined explorers always found a way inside. So, after years of neglect, the church simply buried the whole site under a mountain of dirt.

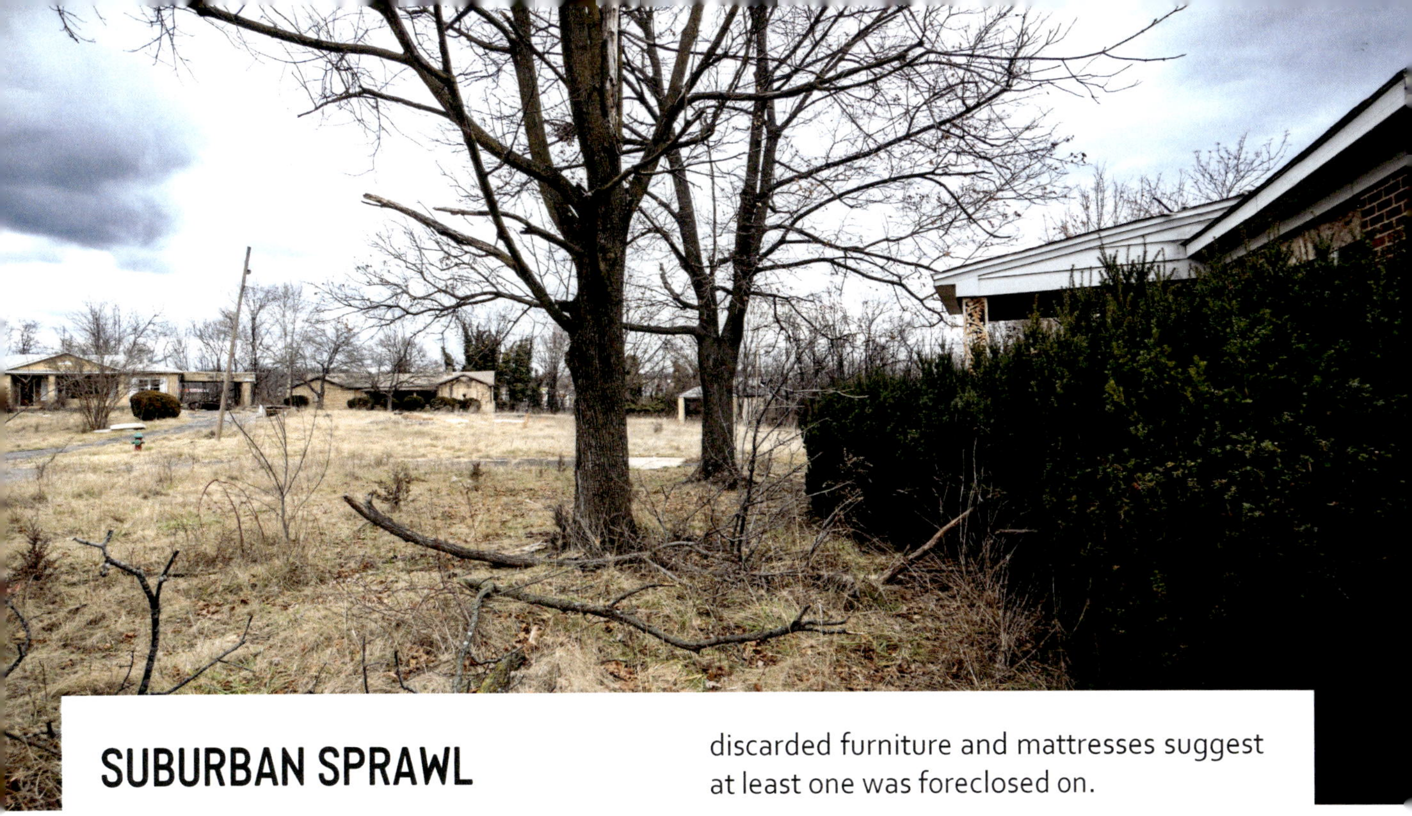

SUBURBAN SPRAWL

A quartet of brick, mid-century modern homes sit around a cul-de-sac outside the City of Winchester, Virginia. It's a fairly typical suburban scene, until you look closer. Each house sits abandoned, windows and doors busted out, articles of furniture littering the lawn. When did this happen, and why?

According to popular realty websites, these single-family homes were constructed in the 1940s and '50s. The discarded furniture and mattresses suggest at least one was foreclosed on.

For many decades, the 220 Seafood Restaurant stood nearby. It closed in 2008 and was torn down sometime later. A Maryland developer bought this entire parcel in 2020 for $4 million, promising to build over one hundred townhomes. Four years later, and the neighborhood remains frozen in time.

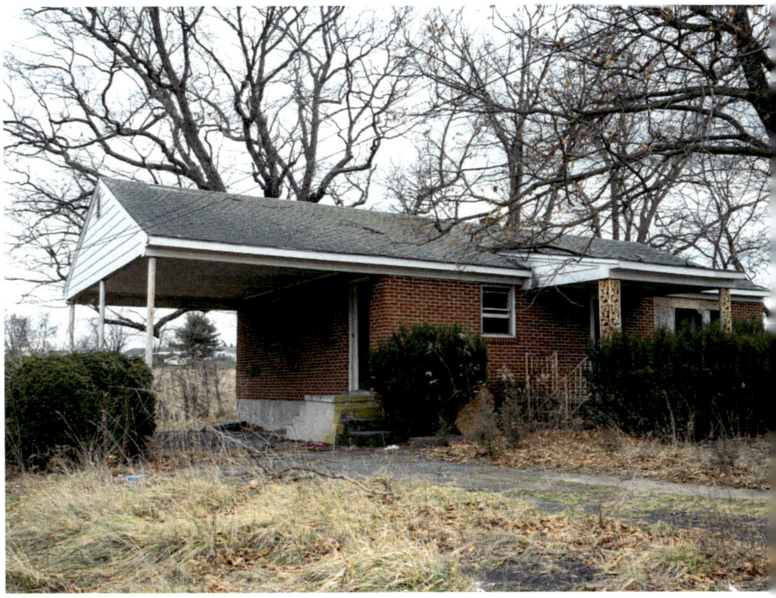

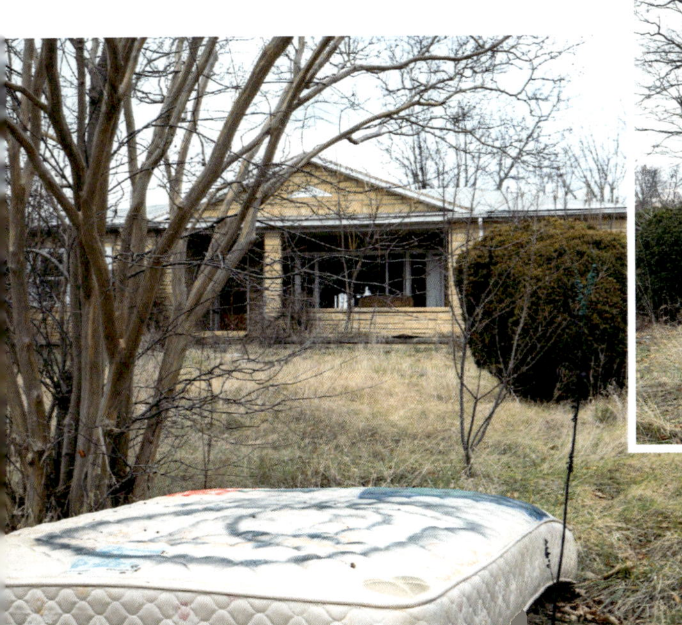

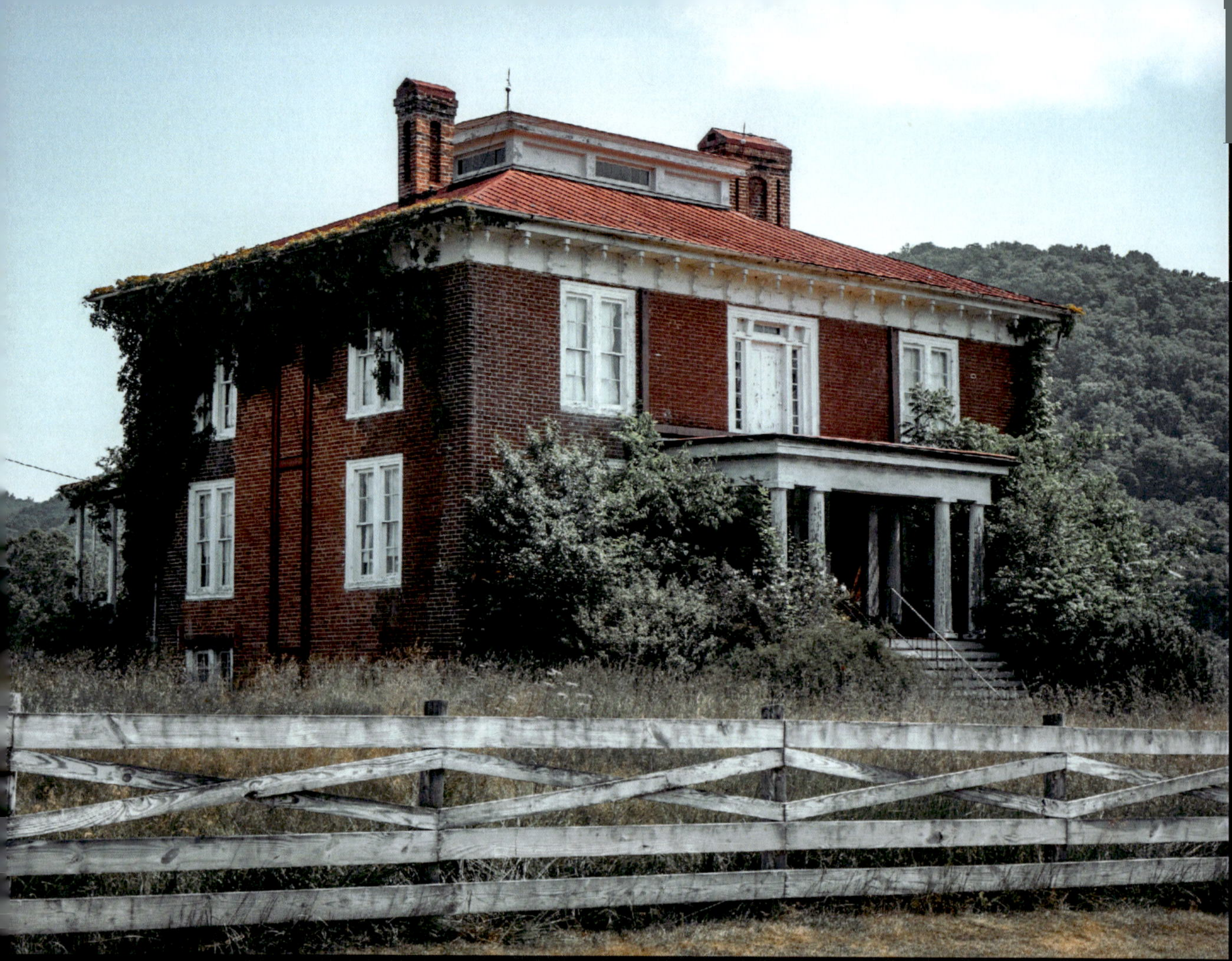

Above: The Greek Revival-style Felix Hull House in McDowell, Virginia, was built circa 1855. During the Civil War, it was used as a headquarters by Union Brig. Generals Robert Milroy and Robert C. Schenck and Confederate Maj. Gen. Thomas J. "Stonewall" Jackson before and after the Battle of McDowell, May 8, 1862. The house has been abandoned for several years, but remains majestic.

Bottom Right: Built in 1759, Beverley Mill (aka Chapman Mill) near Broad Run, Virginia, was a stone grist mill in operation through World War 2. Jonathan and Nathaniel Chapman constructed the mill and owned it during the Civil War. It was added to the National Register of Historic Places in 1972, but vandals burnt the historic mill 26 years later.

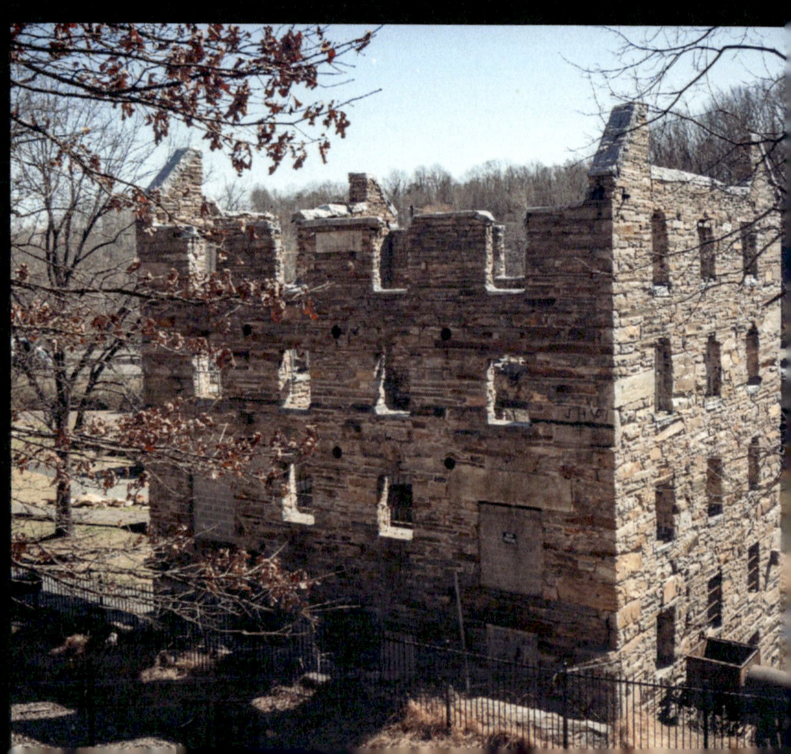

AFTERWORD

We live as though everything is permanent, but time is inexorable. The cycle of birth, life, decay, and death applies to things as well as people. There is a glorious moment when most everyone moves on and nature begins to slowly reclaim what we once tamed with brick, steel, and concrete. That's the moment when the urban explorer, photographer, and graffiti artist converge to appreciate what remains before it vanishes forever. And how long does it last? For a portion of Pennsylvania State Route 61, it was a few decades before what became known as "Graffiti Highway" vanished under tons of dirt.

The choice is always the same: Do we preserve what's left in the name of education, tourism, or recreation? Or do we erase it from existence as an unsightly embarrassment, a relic from a time best forgotten? I will always choose preservation, even if all I can do is take a photograph.

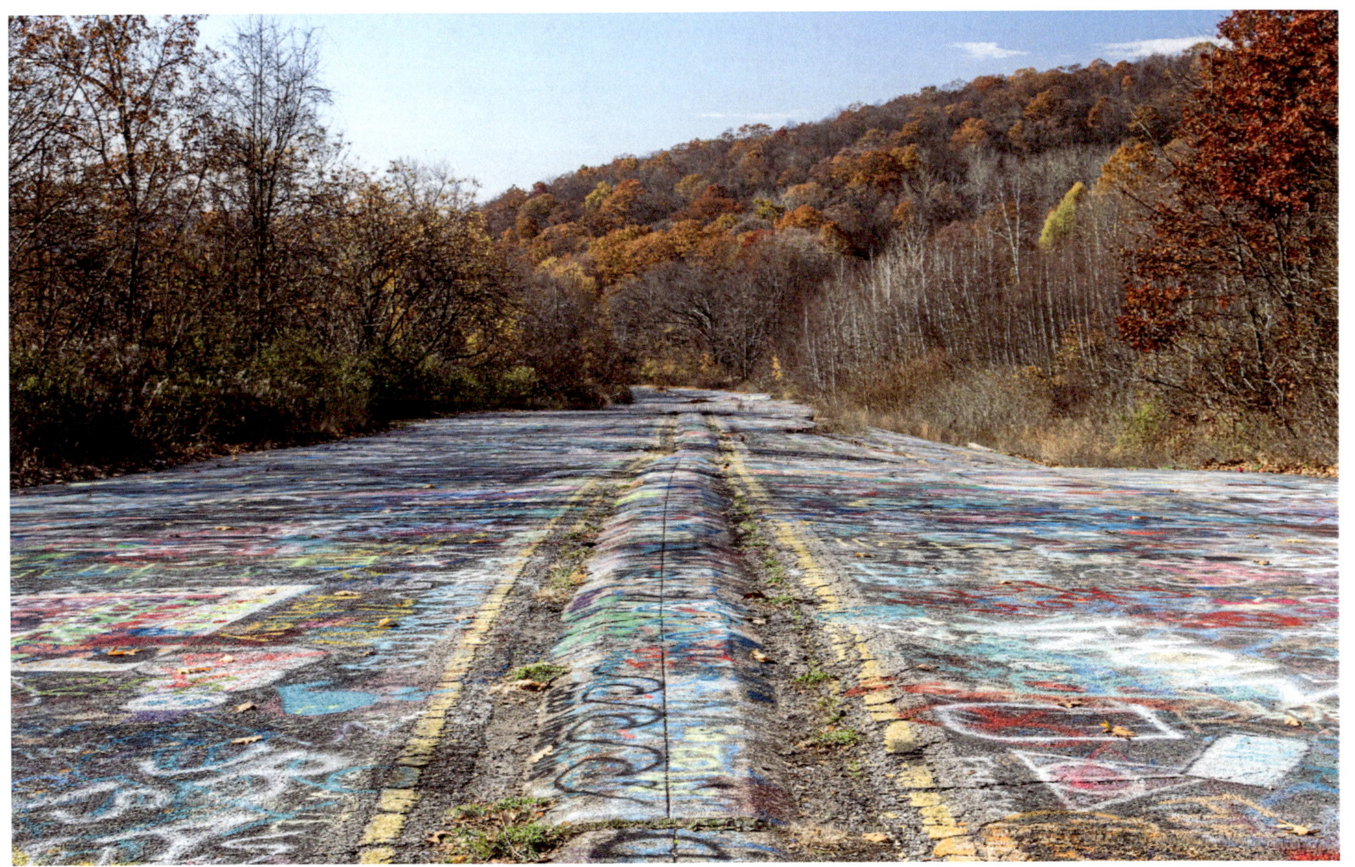

Centralia, Pennsylvania was evacuated following a coal mine fire, which has been burning beneath the town since 1962. In 1992, Pennsylvania condemned the town and claimed it under eminent domain. A section of State Route 61 was abandoned after it began to buckle and crumble from the underground fire. This has become known as "Graffiti Highway." A few years ago, the state completely covered it with dirt.

CATOCTIN IRON FURNACE

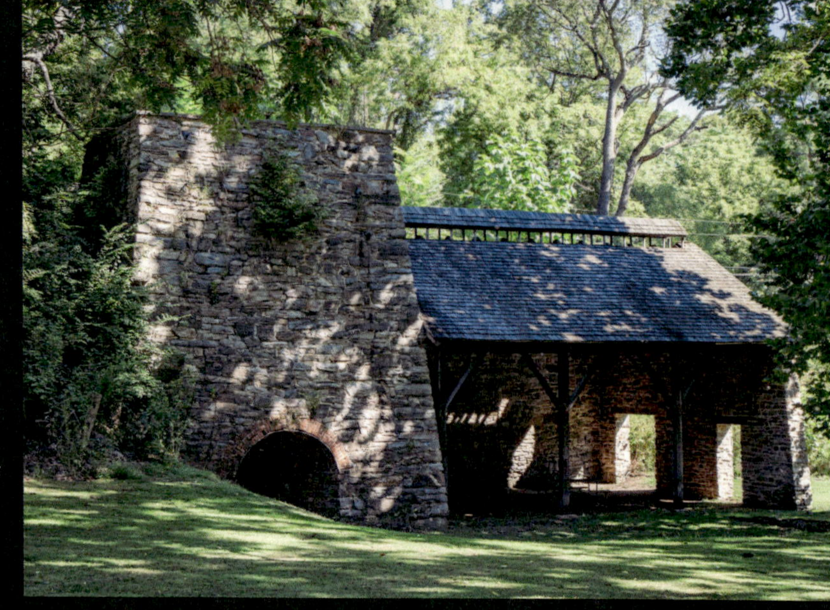

Catoctin Iron Furnace is a historic iron forge along U.S. Route 15 from Frederick to Thurmont in Frederick County, Maryland. Though forges were present when the ironworks were operational, there is currently no forge at the site. But you can still tour the grounds and the ruins of the "Isabella forge" casting shed and the owner's mansion.

For over a century, the furnace smelted iron, its forges spewing smoke and burning red hot. In the eighteenth and nineteenth centuries, it fueled the machines of war. Much of this backbreaking work was done by slaves.

The whole complex closed in 1903, and the remains of the ovens and their environs are found in Cunningham Falls State Park.

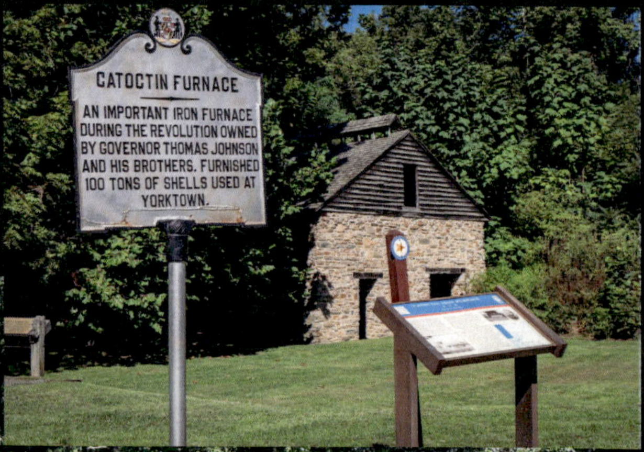

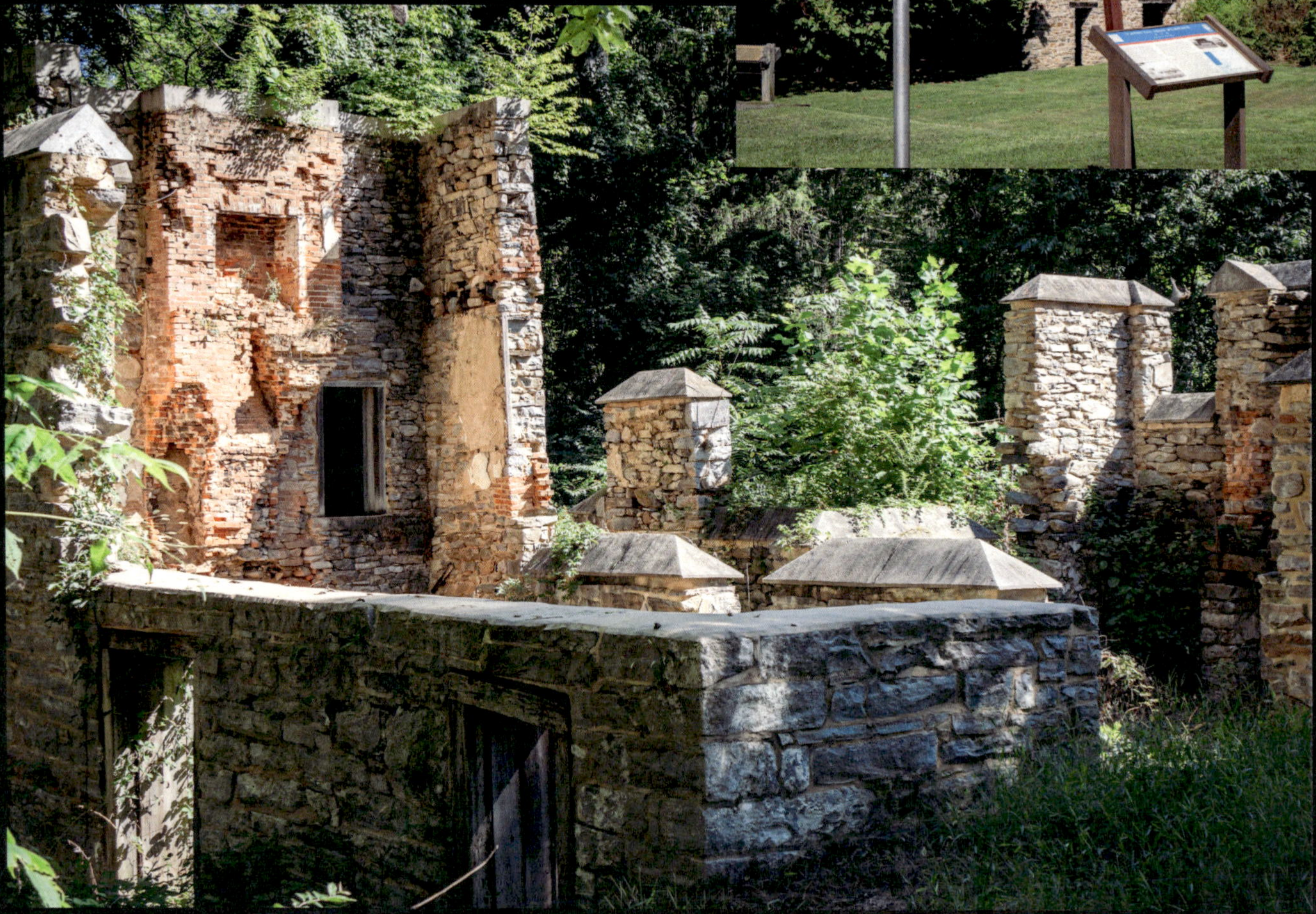

SOURCES

Adams, Joey. *The Borscht Belt*. Indianapolis: Bobbs-Merrill Company, 1959.

Beard, Lisa. *Abandoned Illinois: Secrets Behind The Spaces*. Charleston: America Through Time, 2019.

____________. *Abandoned Illinois: Forgotten Places and Lost Histories*. Charleston: America Through Time, 2019.

Benjamin, Susan S. *Historic and Architectural Assessment: Charles A. Lindbergh School*. Chicago: Historic Certification Consultants, 1998.

Bentley, Dave. *Abandoned Virginia: Forgotten in Time*. Charleston: America Through Time, 2021.

Cassada, Linda G. *Abandoned Eastern Virginia: Forsaken Fragments of the First Colony*. Charleston: America Through Time, 2019.

Chasen, Donna. "Idlewild: In ruins, but still proud." *The Free Lance-Star* (Fredericksburg, VA) 17 April 2004.

Committee on State Charitable Institutions. *Brief History of the Charitable Institutions of the State of Illinois*. Chicago: John Morris, 1893.

Darbey, Nancy K. *The Ohio State Reformatory*. Charleston: Arcadia Publishing, 2016.

Debies-Carl, Jeffrey S. *If You Should Go at Midnight: Legends and Legend Tripping in America*. Jackson: University Press of Mississippi, 2023.

Dolan, Francis X. *Eastern State Penitentiary*. Charleston: Arcadia Publishing, 2007.

Foley, Malcolm and John Lennon. *Dark Tourism: The Attraction of Death and Disaster*. Cengage Learning EMEA, 2000.

Finkler, Lauren. "Bartonville: A Broken Home Where the Haunted Roam." *Western Illinois Magazine* 1 (Spring 2010): 6-9.

Handwerk, Joel. *Abandoned Virginia: The Forgotten Commonwealth*. Charleston: America Through Time, 2021.

Hawley, Joshua. *Tombstone's Most Haunted*. Tombstone: Tombstone Paranormal, 2009.

Heatwole, Thelma. *Ghost Towns and Historical Haunts in Arizona*. Phoenix: Golden West, 1991.

Hinckley, Jim and Kerrick James. *Ghost Towns of the Southwest: Your Guide to the Historic Mining Camps and Ghost Towns of Arizona and New Mexico*. Minneapolis: Voyageur Press, 2010.

Janney, Josh. "Developer eyes town homes, retailers for former 220 Seafood Restaurant site." *The Winchester Star* (Winchester, VA) 25 February 2020.

Jenkins, T.C. *Ohio State Reformatory, Mansfield, Ohio 1896-1934*. Privately Printed, 1934.

Kahan, Paul. *Eastern State Penitentiary: A History*. Charleston: The History Press, 2008.

Kanfer, Stefan. *A Summer World: The Attempt to Build a Jewish Eden in the Catskills, from the Days of the Ghetto to the Rise and Decline of the Borscht Belt*. New York: Farrar, Straus and Giroux, 1989.

Kelley, Jeffrey G. "Making it work: Appomattox Iron Works dodged demolition, survived tornado and is reborn, again." *Richmond Times-Dispatch* (Richmond, VA) 22 February 2004.

Kinney, Pamela. *Virginia's Haunted Historic Triangle*. Atglen: Schiffer Publishing, 2019.

Kleen, Michael. *Paranormal Illinois*. Atglen: Schiffer Publishing, 2010.

Lawless, Seph. *Abandoned: Hauntingly Beautiful Deserted Theme Parks*. New York: Skyhorse Publishing, 2017.

Lazzaro, John. *A Vanishing New York: Ruins Across the Empire State*. Atglen: Schiffer Publishing, 2022.

Lee, Anne Carter. "Appomattox Iron Works", [Petersburg, Virginia]. SAH Archipedia, eds. Gabrielle Esperdy and Karen Kingsley. Charlottesville: UVaP, 2012—, http://sah-archipedia.org/buildings/VA-02-DW19.

Lewis, Chad and Terry Fisk. *The Illinois Road Guide to Haunted Locations*. Eau Claire: Unexplained Research Publishing, 2007.

Lisman, Gary. *Bittersweet Memories: a History of the Peoria State Hospital*. Victoria: Trafford Publishing, 2005.

"Manteno Madness," *Time*, 23 October 1939.

Micheau, Kelly. "Virginia Ghost Town Abandoned by the Railroad." *Forgotten South*, February 11, 2019. https://theforgottensouth.com/union-level-virginia-ghost-town-history/

Powell, Jack. *Haunting Sunshine: Ghostly Tales from Florida's Shadows*. Sarasota: Pineapple Press, 2001.

Ritter, Geoffrey. "'Haunted Haven' is No More." *Carbondale Times* (Carbondale, IL) 8 November 2013.

Roll, Liz. *Abandoned Southern Virginia: The South Begins Here*. Charleston: America Through Time, 2021.

Rose, James. *Trans-Allegheny Lunatic Asylum: A Short History*. By the Author, 2015.

Rosenthal, Odeda. *Hedwig Michel: The patron saint of the Koreshan State Historic Site*. Koreshan Unity Books, 1992.

Sheppard, Nancy E. *Abandoned Tidewater: Forgotten Relics of Southeastern Virginia*. Charleston: America Through Time, 2020.

Sherman, James E. and Barbara H. Sherman. *Ghost Towns of Arizona*. Norman: University of Oklahoma Press, 1969.

Shults, Sylvia. *Fractured Spirits: Hauntings at the Peoria State Hospital*. Hertford: Macabre Ink, 2012, 2023.

Sonnenberg, Mike. *Lost In Ohio: Discovering Strange and Historic Places in the Buckeye State*. Saginaw: Etaoin Publishing, 2022.

Tassin, Susan Hutchison. *New York Ghost Towns: Uncovering the Hidden Past*. Mechanicsburg: Stackpole Books, 2013.

____________. *Pennsylvania Ghost Towns: Uncovering the Hidden Past*. Mechanicsburg: Stackpole Books, 2007.

Taylor, Troy. *Weird Illinois: Your Travel Guide to Illinois' Local Legends and Best Kept Secrets*. New York: Sterling Publishing, 2005.

Toler, Sean. *Forgotten Virginia: Abandoned Places and Things in the Old Dominion*. Charleston: America Through Time, 2020.

Vasko, Cindy. *Abandoned Northern Virginia: Desolate Beauty*. Charleston: America Through Time, 2022.

____________. *Abandoned Southern Virginia: Reckless Surrender*. Charleston: America Through Time, 2021.

Wilson, Amie Marie and Mandi Dale Johnson. *Historic Bonaventure Cemetery*. Charleston: Arcadia Publishing, 1998.

Zeller, George Anthony. *Befriending the Bereft*. Peoria State Hospital: by the author, 1938.

INDEX

www.ingramcontent.com/pod-product-compliance
Lightning Source LLC
LaVergne TN
LVRC090924100826
845154LV00013B/157

* 9 7 8 1 6 1 8 7 6 0 2 6 5 *